TOONS IN TOYLAND

Merchandise based on famous cartoon characters frequently would alter their established personalities. Bugs Bunny's primary creator, Tex Avery, once explained how wrong it was to show Bugs running in terror from anyone. "If he runs, it's because he has a trick in mind," Avery said.

TOONS IN TOYLAND

The Story of Cartoon Character Merchandise

TIM HOLLIS

UNIVERSITY PRESS OF MISSISSIPPI • JACKSON

www.upress.state.ms.us

Designed by Peter D. Halverson

The University Press of Mississippi is a member of the Association of American
University Presses.

First printing 2015

∞

Library of Congress Cataloging-in-Publication Data

Hollis, Tim.
Toons in toyland : the story of cartoon character merchandise / Tim Hollis.
pages cm
Includes bibliographical references and index.
ISBN 978-1-62846-199-2 (cloth : alk. paper) — ISBN 978-1-62674-500-1 (ebook)
1. Comic strip character toys—United States—Marketing. 2. Cartoon characters—
Social aspects—United States. 3. Licensed products—United States. I. Title.
NK9509.95.C65H65 2015
688.7—dc23   2014024119

British Library Cataloging-in-Publication Data available

CONTENTS

Introduction 3

1. License to Toon 7

2. Funny Business 49

3. Read More about It 71

4. Toying Around with Your Friends 101

5. Windows into Another World 135

6. For the Record 149

7. Happy Holidays 191

8. Eat, Drink, and Be Funny 209

9. Car Toons 239

10. To Infinity and Beyond 277

Bibliography 287

Index 293

TOONS IN TOYLAND

You can see that my life has been
connected with cartoon character
merchandise practically from the
beginning: the party supplies
for my first birthday featured
Huckleberry Hound and Yogi Bear.

Now it's my fifth birthday, and you
can tell I am less than thrilled with all
the guests doing their best to break
as many of my toys as possible. The
two girls in the foreground are busy
destroying Hasbro's Talking Snow
White Telephone.

INTRODUCTION

When those who are familiar with my previous books (this is my twenty-fifth) have asked what I was working on next, they often expressed puzzlement as to why I would choose to devote so much time and space and so many words to this particular topic. Well, it had to happen sooner or later, but its beginning had absolutely nothing to do with books.

As an only child born at the very end of the post–World War II baby boom, I always had lots of toys. Now, I knew other kids who had even more than I did, but I was also aware that many others had far fewer. (The ones who had fewer toys tended to show up at my birthday parties and break stuff, bringing me closer to their own totals.) Since I was an animated cartoon nut since before my memory bank even kicked in, most of what I had was cartoon-related in one form or another. . . . Even the tablecloth, plates, cups, and napkins from my first birthday party featured Yogi Bear and Huckleberry Hound, so that's going back a long way.

Typically, as the years went by, many of my toys disappeared. Occasionally my parents would gather up a bunch they felt had outlived their purpose and give them to some needy family (all of my Little Golden Books and Whitman books met this fate). Others were thrown away or simply lost in the yard. Fragments of them, and sometimes entire toys, continued to show up decades later, proving how nondegradable plastic really can be. But my parents and I saved quite a number of them as well, not as collectibles (that term was not being thrown about in those days) but simply as childhood mementoes.

Then came a fateful day in either the spring or summer of 1981. I was in college by then and was spending a not-so-fun morning in the waiting room at the dentist's office. I was reading a magazine that may or may not have been anywhere near current—comedians love to joke about the magazines in waiting rooms discussing Lindbergh's flight and so on—but it had an article about some fellow who collected cartoon character toys. I have no idea who he was or where he lived or whether he's still around, but there was a terrific color photo of him sitting in front of a display wall with an eye-popping array of jigsaw puzzles, board games, Soaky bubble bath toys, and so on.

On that morning, the thought occurred to me that 95 percent of the items I saw in that photo were

Perhaps as revenge for the many toys that were lost or broken over the years, I eventually decided to try to buy them all back as collectibles. As you can see from these shots of the resulting museum, that project eventually got a little out of control.

things I used to have or still had, boxed up in closets and cabinets throughout the house. I decided that a most interesting goal would be to gather all of it together and then, as time and finances permitted, try to fill in the gaps by locating things I used to have. The process of organizing what I already had was under way by September 1981, but it was just short of a year later before I went to my first antique show at a local mall and actually bought anything. Just to show how it works, that first collectible I ever bought was not even something I used to have as a kid. So as I tell people now, the whole idea was shot before it got started.

After about twenty-five years of following this pattern, I needed to build a museum to hold all of these toys, and that is just what I did. (The toys take up most of the top floor, while the bottom floor would be familiar to anyone who knows anything about my other books. It contains tourism memorabilia, a section devoted to each major holiday, and re-creations of the rooms in the house as they were when I was growing up, using the original furniture.)

Since I had turned so many of these other collections into books, this one had to happen eventually.

Now that you understand how it began (which, I realize, is far from understanding the mania for collecting cartoon merchandise), let me explain a bit about what this book is and is not. With the major exception of Disney, most previous books that have dealt with licensed toys and other items have done so either as a footnote to their primary focus on the various animation studios or because they were price guides intended to help dealers and collectors agree on how much a given item might be worth. (Plenty of examples of both types can be found in the bibliography.) As I said, Disney merchandising is the exception, to the point that many dealers in collectibles consider "Disneyana" a separate classification. To date, there seem to be no comparable categories for "Hanna-Barberana" or "Looney Tunesana," for example.

While this may be the most comprehensive study on the subject of cartoon character licensing published to date, it is not *totally* comprehensive. To

My first camera was the one my parents ordered from this Bugs Bunny/Kool-Aid offer in September 1967. Yes, I still have it, and it's in the museum. (Donnie Pitchford collection)

truly cover every possible type of toy, book, and knick-knack ever produced bearing the image of a popular character would require a set of encyclopedias. This book is meant as an overview, and if your particular favorite character or type of toy seems to get unnecessarily brief mention, just try to keep that in mind. And the vast amount of international merchandise is a completely different story that would have bloated this volume to unmanageable proportions. Someone else could write a version of this book and use totally different examples than I have to illustrate the point—and if they do, I will be more than happy to buy it.

Also, a brief word is in order to explain the years that are the book's primary focus. Even though cartoon licensing goes back to the 1890s, the explosion of Disney merchandise was a product of the Great Depression, and it appears there will never be an end to the concept of connecting toys and other such items to favorite characters, the core of this book is the baby boomer era. The first baby boomers were born in 1946, and the last of them were growing out of childhood in 1980–81, so that is the target time frame for our story here. However, don't begin yelling and pointing fingers when certain parts of it stray on either side of those boundaries; it's my book, after all, and I can do what I want with it. So there, nyahhh.

(Now are you beginning to understand why those kids were so intent on wrecking my toys when they would come to visit?)

Chapter One

LICENSE TO TOON

As strange as it may seem, the development of merchandise based on well-known cartoon and comic strip characters was not some sort of gradual evolution. No, indeed; cartoon merchandise has existed as long as there have been cartoon characters, and that came about in 1895.

Of course, the tradition of caricature and political cartooning goes as far back as the American Revolution. However, none of these efforts had produced what we would consider today to be a true cartoon character. That had to wait until an artist named Richard F. Outcault, working for the *New York World*, instituted a pictorial feature he called *Hogan's Alley*. This was not a comic strip but a series of full-page drawings depicting the chaotic goings-on in the titular low-rent-district alley. Almost hidden in the crowd of figures in the first drawing was a bald-headed kid in a dirty nightshirt; no, it was not Charlie Brown, but a personality who came to be known as the Yellow Kid.

Although the Yellow Kid did have vaguely Asian facial features, his ethnicity was not the source of his name. Instead, that appellation came about because the editor of the *World*, Joseph Pulitzer (no

prize for guessing what makes his name live on today), was keen on improving the quality of color printing in the newspaper. For one reason or another, yellow had always been a particularly difficult hue to replicate on the early color printing presses, and when one of Pulitzer's staff developed what he hoped would be a suitable yellow ink, he randomly chose the nightshirt of the then-anonymous chrome-domed brat in one of Outcault's drawings as the test area. Overnight, the peculiar tyke became the Yellow Kid—but that was not all.

Outcault was a pioneer not only of American newspaper comics but also in realizing the commercial value of their characters. Within a year, the Yellow Kid was appearing on games, puzzles, dolls, toys, and books reprinting the cartoons—all of which would become the standard for future cartoon stars, right down to the first half of the twenty-first century.

The success of Outcault and his Yellow Kid prompted Pulitzer's fiercest rival, William Randolph Hearst, to hire Outcault away to draw the feature for his own paper, the *New York Journal*. Pulitzer retaliated by hiring George Luks to continue the Yellow

The Katzenjammer Kids is the oldest comic strip still in publication. Merchandise based on the characters was introduced in the late 1890s and was still available when this coloring book was issued in the 1970s.

Kid cartoons in the *World*, and for a while, the feature continued in two different newspapers under the two different artists. (This sort of cutthroat competition in the newsprint business gave rise to the term "yellow journalism.") For the next several years, it was not uncommon for the same strip to be drawn by varying artists for separate newspapers until the sticky legal morass of who owned the rights to what could be sorted out.

Another huge step for big-footed cartoon characters came in 1897, when Rudolph Dirks began *The Katzenjammer Kids*, which would eventually become the first comic strip to reach the hundred-year mark. As a matter of fact, the adventures of the rambunctious Katzenjammer family became the first true comic strip of all, using a series of panels and speech balloons to tell its stories. In a situation quite similar to what happened with the two Yellow Kids, an ownership dispute eventually resulted in two long-running strips with the exact same cast of characters, the original Katzenjammers and their other manifestation, *The Captain and the Kids*. The two versions coexisted well into the 1970s, although the Katzenjammers proved to be the surviving feature. In 2014, artist Hy Eisman was still producing new Katzenjammer Sunday strips.

While plenty of Katzenjammer toys were in stores, Outcault led the charge when it came to licensed merchandise. The 1904 World's Fair in St. Louis was remarkable for being the birthplace of several later pop culture icons, not the least of which was the ice cream cone. Besides exhibiting the world's largest cast-iron statue and providing the inspiration for the later classic movie *Meet Me in St. Louis*, the fair was also where Richard Outcault proved once and for all that when he set his mind to license his cartoon creations, he was serious about it.

By that time, Outcault had given up on the Yellow Kid and had come up with a much more versatile comic star, Buster Brown. Buster dressed like Little Lord Fauntleroy but had a mean streak that more closely resembled Dennis the Menace; his grinning, toothy dog, Tige, was usually alongside to mumble sarcastic comments on the action, not unlike a later comic strip hound named Snoopy. At the World's Fair, Outcault set up a booth for the express purpose of licensing Buster Brown merchandise to anyone who had the ready cash to pay for the rights. Many manufacturers took Outcault up on his offer, and stores soon were overrun with Buster Brown toys, books, games, dolls, and all the other usual suspects. However, the two that proved to have the most sticking power were the Brown Shoe Company (which, remarkably, already bore that name before securing the right to make Buster Brown Shoes) and the Buster Brown Textile Company. Both survived long enough to become standard memories for post–World War II baby boomers: Buster Brown Shoes in particular became a childhood icon with their signage of Buster and toothsome Tige and the accompanying slogan: "I'm Buster Brown! I live in a shoe! That's my dog Tige! He lives in there too!" These advertising images and their related merchandise lasted for decades after their foundational comic strip had ended.

During the rest of the 1910s and early 1920s, comic strips remained the biggest source of characters for licensed merchandise. Such titles as *Happy Hooligan*, *The Toonerville Trolley*, *Moon Mullins*, *Smitty*, and *Bringing Up Father*

Buster Brown Shoes kept Outcault's creation before the public long after the comic strip—and Outcault himself—had been forgotten. These wacky cardboard children's spectacles were only one of the hundreds of different promotional items issued over the years.

At the 1904 World's Fair, cartoonist Richard Outcault set up a booth to sell licensing rights to his popular comic strip character, Buster Brown. The most famous company to sign one of those deals was Buster Brown Shoes.

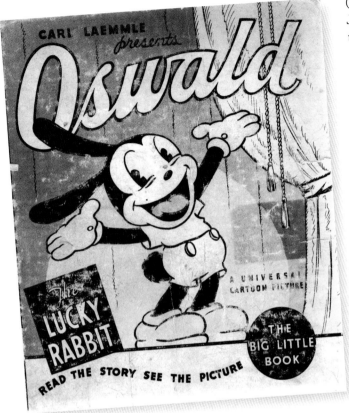

Oswald the Rabbit was created by Walt Disney but legally owned by Universal Pictures. In 1928, control of Oswald was wrested from Disney and eventually passed to Walter Lantz.

(with that original dysfunctional married couple, Maggie and Jiggs) may now be familiar only to cartoon historians, but in their time they all produced shelves full of toys that youngsters of that era craved for Christmas, birthdays, or no special occasion at all.

There was a very good reason more toys were based on newspaper characters than on animated cartoons, and it was that most of the early animated cartoons were adaptations of newspaper strips. Only occasionally was the print-to-screen cycle broken, with such early animated originals as Walter Lantz's *Dinky Doodle*, Pat Sullivan's *Felix the Cat*, and Paul Terry's *Farmer Al Falfa*. In the mid-1920s, a young filmmaker from Kansas City journeyed west to try to make a name for himself in the still-primitive cartoon industry. He was Walt Disney, and his cartoon creation would become an early success in licensed merchandise based on an animated character. No, it was not the character you are likely thinking about: it was Oswald the Lucky Rabbit.

Disney produced only twenty-six cartoons featuring Oswald for release by Universal Pictures, but during that relatively short span, the happy hare became popular enough to inspire a few toys and other tie-in items. Disney knew when he had a good thing, and in 1928 he made a trip to New York to ask for more money to produce each Oswald cartoon. Instead, he was informed that he did not own any rights to Oswald and that Universal would be assigning the character to another producer. On the long train ride back to California, Walt did some serious thinking about a character to replace the departed Oswald, and he came up with Mortimer Mouse. Once back in Hollywood, Walt's wife wisely persuaded him that Mickey sounded friendlier, and Walt set about to make sure moviegoers knew exactly who Mickey Mouse was and who was responsible for his films. Never again would Walt or any of his successors at the company he founded lose control of any of their characters or films, and that control extended into merchandising.

(Incidentally, you may wonder whatever became of Oswald after he was so unceremoniously yanked out from under Disney. Never fear; we will run into him more often than you might think in the chapters that follow.)

Walt Disney had little time to grieve over the loss of Oswald because he was determined to plow every cent he got for each Mickey Mouse short back into the studio, constantly pushing his staff to improve the animation and gags with every film. This also meant that money was usually a bit scarce, and while on another New York visit in the autumn of 1929, Walt made an unplanned deal that was to have far-reaching implications. A man approached Walt in a hotel lobby and offered him three hundred dollars for the right to put Mickey's picture on the front of a school writing tablet. Since Walt could really use three hundred dollars at the moment, he closed the deal, and the school tablet became the first-ever piece of Disney merchandise. As if you needed to be told, it would hardly be the last one.

This lobby encounter must have reminded Walt of the success he had viewed from afar when Universal was promoting Oswald merchandise, because in December 1929, he and brother/business partner Roy set up an official character licensing and merchandising department as a part of their still-new studio. As Disney historians Robert Heide and John Gilman write, "Disney realized that the future of the studio could become secure only if enough revenue was generated by the character merchandising division." This would prove to be true for virtually every animation studio in the future, well into the television era and beyond.

During 1930 and 1931, some of the earliest (and now most valuable) Mickey Mouse merchandise made its way into stores, but the true genius of that division of the Walt Disney Studios was Kay Kamen, who came to work there in 1932. Kamen was no stranger to licensing, having previously handled the *Our Gang* kids who appeared in Hal Roach's comedy shorts. Kamen's salesmanship soon pushed the already-spinning Disney merchandising machine into hyperaction, just as the Great Depression was tightening its grasp on the public's collective throat (not to mention its wallet). Most Disney histories give at least a nod to the success of the merchandise of this period, and two companies in particular—Lionel electric trains and the Ingersoll-Waterbury Clock Company—attribute their comeback from impending bankruptcy to the introduction of their Mickey Mouse products. Lionel made a toy handcar for use with its train sets that depicted Mickey and Minnie pumping furiously, while Ingersoll came up with the now-iconic Mickey Mouse watch.

Kamen established a New York licensing office, and there was also a branch on Disney's home turf in California. According to Heide and Gilman,

Thanks to promotional genius Kay Kamen, licensed Mickey Mouse and other Disney character merchandise became a major economic force during the Great Depression years. (Hake's Americana and Collectibles collection)

The release of *Snow White and the Seven Dwarfs* in late 1937 set a new precedent for Disney merchandise. Books, toys, and other related items would be on store shelves well in advance of a movie's premiere, helping build anticipation and familiarity with the characters.

After Donald Duck made his screen debut in 1934, he joined the already-crowded field of characters featured on Disney merchandise.

Design and artwork was supplied free of charge to licensees to ensure that the images of Mickey Mouse and his friends were consistent with the cartoon film characters, who might change, sometimes imperceptibly, from film to film. Disney and Kamen both agreed that licenses were not to be granted for products deemed undesirable for children; products like cigarettes, laxatives and liquor were turned down. Kamen insisted not only on top quality merchandise but that it be made available at Depression prices, the philosophy being that every kid who went to a dime store should be able to buy a Mickey Mouse product.

We shall now continue without pausing to wonder what sort of potential licensee thought the idea of Mickey Mouse laxatives was a good one. Naturally, the more characters the studio created, the more opportunities there were for merchandise. Mickey and Minnie were followed in rapid succession by Pluto, Clarabelle Cow, Horace Horsecollar, Goofy (originally known as Dippy Dawg), and in 1934 the cantankerous Donald Duck, who soon threatened to overshadow Mickey's film stardom.

Even Donald had to take a temporary backseat, though, with the advent of Disney's first feature-length cartoon, *Snow White and the Seven Dwarfs*, which had its Hollywood premiere in December 1937 and general release in February 1938. Kamen's plan for blanketing the country with a blizzard of Snow White set an important precedent for all future Disney animated features: merchandise promoting the film and its characters would be in stores well in advance of the feature's arrival in theaters, so that by the time viewers got to see it, they would already be familiar with its elements. Heide and Gilman point out that this strategy also served the important purpose of helping Disney secure the copyright on all the characters before the film's actual debut, something that was no doubt deemed vital after the Oswald fiasco.

At Sears...the Walt Disney-inspired collection of
SNOW WHITE and the 7 DWARFS

For *Snow White*'s thirtieth anniversary in 1967, Sears promoted an entire line of exclusive merchandise. Neither Snow nor the dwarfs appears to have aged a bit.

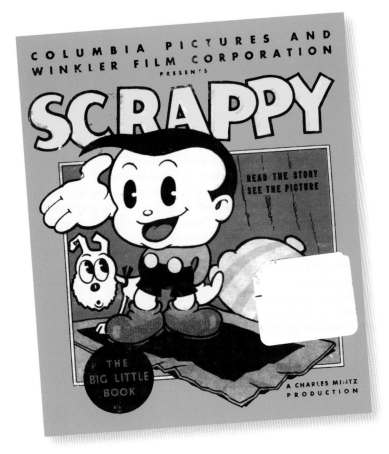

Columbia Pictures' Scrappy may be the most famous animated character no one has ever heard of. Although he inspired dozens of licensed items during his brief screen career, only animation history buffs and toy collectors seem to remember the cheerful little guy.

This Porky Pig coloring book from 1938 is one of the earliest items based on any of the familiar Looney Tunes characters.

Throughout the 1940s, Kay Kamen continued his work of promoting each and every Disney character and feature film. In 1949, he was busy preparing the public for *Cinderella*, who would be losing her glass slipper in theaters worldwide early in 1950. On October 28, 1949, however, Kamen and his wife were killed in an Air France plane crash over the Azores, and things would never be quite the same. Oh, not that Disney merchandise suffered—it would just not be the same as when the charismatic Kamen was in charge.

Before continuing the saga of Disney merchandise in the post-Kamen era, we now need to see how the other animation studios perceived his success. From 1929 until 1932, Disney's cartoons were released through Columbia, so that studio no doubt was aware of the early success of the Mickey merchandise. Therefore, when Columbia's own animation division came up with a new character named Scrappy in 1931, it should have been no surprise to anyone that Columbia set sail on a voyage to make Scrappy a new force to be reckoned with in Toyland. By 1935, the industry publication *Toys and Novelties* was reporting that Scrappy's "list of licensees ranks among the longest in the field." The same article stated,

> One national magazine group invites children to write letters on "Why I Like Scrappy," and gives prizes in the form of merchandise featuring the smiling little cartoon character. A nationally known chocolate maker recently began to market chocolate cakes under Scrappy's name, and has begun to distribute a million Scrappy magazines featuring merchandise wearing Scrappy's license.

All of this adds up to no doubt make Scrappy the most famous cartoon star no one has ever heard of today. Although his films were popular at the time—at least to hear Columbia tell it—Scrappy apparently did not have what it took to become a lasting star of the magnitude of the Disney gang or the crowd of Looney Tunes loonies.

And that brings us to the next topic. Although cartoon fans and even the general public know them as "Warner Bros. cartoons," from 1931 until 1944, the rights to all of the related characters were actually owned by producer Leon Schlesinger, with Warner Bros. merely the releasing company for the films. Early Looney Tunes/Merrie Melodies characters such as Bosko and Buddy received little attention from merchandisers, probably because the cartoons in which they appeared were hardly causing laugh riots in movie theaters. Schlesinger's first breakout star, Porky Pig, made his stuttering debut in 1935 and soon thereafter began what turned into several decades of Looney Tunes merchandise (and it has not stopped yet). In fact, research has

Warner Bros. character items have been available continuously since the late 1930s. This intriguing array of loud, fluorescent items was available through Sears in 1971.

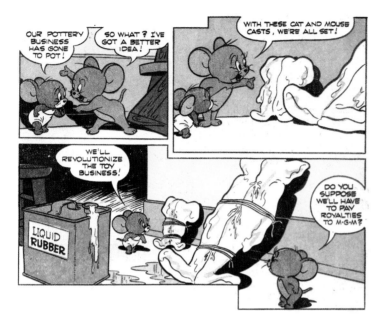

In these amusing panels from a 1955 Tom and Jerry comic book, Jerry and his pal, Tuffy, give a shout-out to their own copyright owner.

In the mid-1940s, Walter Lantz was still promoting Oswald the Rabbit along with his more famous creations, Andy Panda and Woody Woodpecker.

shown that some of the most legendary members of the cast, including Bugs Bunny and Elmer Fudd, received their names in licensed merchandise *before* being so designated on-screen.

In 1944, Schlesinger sold his animation studio outright to Warner Bros., and at that point the copyright on the merchandise switched from "Leon Schlesinger Productions" to "Warner Bros. Cartoons." According to historian Jerry Beck, Schlesinger continued to oversee the licensing end of the business until his death in 1949, but merchandise of all types featuring Bugs Bunny and his many friends and enemies continued without abatement even afterward.

The most prestigious of all movie studios, Metro-Goldwyn-Mayer (MGM), had its own cartoon division beginning in the early 1930s but took a bit longer to hit upon characters popular enough to be merchandised. Barney Bear came out of hibernation to find some minor success in 1939, but not until early the following year did MGM's true stars, Tom and Jerry, make their screen debut. Their creators, William Hanna and Joseph Barbera, would have a bigger influence on licensing about twenty years later, but throughout the 1940s and 1950s, the artwork for Tom and Jerry merchandise would be some of the most attractive licensed by any animation studio. A series of well-made ceramic figures marketed during the 1940s were certainly of higher quality than the dime-store doodads that were the mainstay of most character licensing divisions.

Meanwhile, Walter Lantz had spent most of the 1930s trying to keep Oswald the Rabbit (with whom Lantz had ended up after Disney's ouster) fresh, no small task when Oswald had only the barest personality traits. By the end of the decade, Lantz was ready to try something more creative, and the initial result was 1939's Andy Panda. Like MGM, Lantz did not hit true cartoon pay dirt until 1940, when Woody Woodpecker was introduced. All the Lantz characters received much merchandising, although, as we shall see in a later chapter, more than any other cartoon cast, their offscreen antics were largely dictated by a single licensee, Western Printing and Lithographing. Lantz's cartoons continued to be released by Universal (except for a short period in the late 1940s and early 1950s when a temporary dispute sent him to United Artists).

If Disney, Warner Bros., MGM, and Universal were considered the "quality" names of the theatrical cartoon world, the shorts released by 20th Century Fox existed somewhere at the other end of that spectrum. Paul Terry had been in the business since the late 1910s, but the only continuing character he had managed to introduce who had enough screen appeal to last was Farmer Al Falfa. That changed in the early 1940s, when Terrytoons (a catchy name for his output, at least) introduced Mighty Mouse. Actually, the superpowered rodent was originally named Super Mouse, but since there was already a comic book character by that name, the catchier moniker was chosen after only a year or so. Terry's second-biggest stars, the wiseacre magpies Heckle and Jeckle, first appeared in 1946. While a smattering of licensed Terrytoons products appeared during the 1940s and early 1950s, Terry's sale of his entire studio and characters to CBS in 1955 really made the difference. Even the earlier characters such as Farmer Al Falfa, Gandy Goose, and Sourpuss the Cat found new lives in the 1950s and 1960s Terrytoons merchandise, alongside Mighty Mouse, Heckle and Jeckle, and the created-for-TV Tom Terrific and Deputy Dawg.

Then there was the case of Paramount. This entertainment giant had the good fortune of aligning with the Max Fleischer animation studio during the 1920s, and after a long run of silent *Out of the Inkwell* cartoons starring Koko the Clown, Fleischer hit on a new star in 1930, Betty Boop. (Actually, the plots of a number of Betty's cartoons involved other characters hitting on her, but in a different way.) Betty was certainly the sexiest cartoon star of her day—and many other days to come—but she also had enough appeal to kids that toys and other merchandise were licensed before too many years had passed.

On this 1950s jigsaw puzzle, happy Terrytoons characters gather to celebrate the birthday of their hero, Mighty Mouse.

An early 1930s press kit illustrates such items as a Betty Boop candy bar, a toy racing car, soap with Betty's picture printed on each bar, handkerchiefs, playing cards, and other assorted dime-store toys. The licensing was handled by the Fleischer Studio rather than Paramount, but this would be one of the few times Max and his partner, brother Dave, would drink from the sweet fountain of merchandising success.

A 1933 Betty Boop cartoon served as the animated debut of a character who had been gaining steadily in popularity since his 1929 newspaper comic strip introduction: Popeye the Sailor, the creation of Elzie Segar. The Fleischers' adaptation of Popeye from strip to screen was a tremendous success, and while Popeye merchandise already existed, its numbers increased wildly after the animated series began. And thereby comes one of the greatest ironies in licensing history; even though Popeye was the most successful cartoon series the Fleischers would ever produce, they saw absolutely no revenue from any of the Popeye products that saturated the toy market. Popeye and his cast of characters were legally the property of King Features Syndicate; in fact, Paramount's right to release Popeye cartoons was, in and of itself, a licensing deal.

(A misunderstanding stemming from this arrangement would eventually come to have a major effect on Popeye merchandise. The Fleischers had chosen Bluto out of a crowd of various villains who had appeared in Segar's newspaper strip; although the bearded bully had been a part of only a single story line, he was, of course, King Features' property. Someone had forgotten that fact by the late 1950s, and even King Features was under the erroneous impression that Bluto was a Fleischer/Paramount creation. Therefore, for quite a few years, when the physical image of Bluto was used in merchandise, he either went unnamed or was designated by such labels as "Mean Man." Finally, King Features renamed him Brutus, and to this day, merchandise can be found with the same character designated both Bluto and Brutus.)

The Fleischers' other experience with merchandising came when Paramount allowed them to make an animated feature, *Gulliver's Travels* (1939). Since Disney's *Snow White* had already established the precedent of how to market such a film, licensees signed up to produce Gulliver merchandise in time to have it in stores before the actual release date. The

Popeye was an unusual case in that his merchandise could be based on his appearance in his newspaper comic strip, his comic book stories, or his hundreds of animated cartoons. Dirty work afoot by Bluto is a good indication that this Jaymar jigsaw puzzle was meant to remind people of the cartoon shorts.

Fleischers' second animated feature, *Mr. Bug Goes to Town* (1941), was not nearly so fortunate, and its financial failure prompted Paramount to physically remove Max and Dave Fleischer from their own studio and install some of their former personnel as the leaders instead. Before that happened, though, the Fleischers and Paramount had one final hurrah with a magnificent series of *Superman* cartoons. The situation was exactly the same as that with Popeye; no matter how much Superman merchandise was inspired by the films, the Man of Steel was owned by National Periodical Publications (aka DC Comics), and neither Paramount nor the Fleischers saw any income from related products.

After the Fleischers were jilted, the studio that had formerly carried their name was reorganized as Famous Studios. One of its early successes was with a series based on Marjorie Buell's *Little Lulu* panel cartoons from the *Saturday Evening Post*; again, Paramount found itself with a merchandisable character for which it owned no merchandising rights. The studio was apparently getting tired of seeing this happen again and again, so beginning in the mid-1940s, Paramount seems to have deliberately attempted to create original characters that it could fully own and exploit to its heart's content.

One of the first was Casper the Friendly Ghost. Then along came Little Audrey, the replacement for Little Lulu. Herman and Katnip were a mouse-and-cat team that managed to outdo even Tom and Jerry for levels of violence, and Baby Huey was an overgrown duckling with an undergrown brain. Buzzy the Crow was a smart-aleck wisecracker with a voice based on Jack Benny's sidekick, Rochester, and Moe Hare really seemed to have no reason for existing except to give Famous Studios a character who looked and sounded almost exactly like Bugs Bunny. Tommy Tortoise went one step further: he didn't seem to have any reason at all for existing. In our next chapter, we will see how these characters made their biggest impression on merchandising when Harvey Comics licensed them for comic book appearances—and it only got bigger from there.

Even while Famous Studios was working hard on its original properties, Popeye was still its most valuable property, and the number of King Features' licensed products continued to grow as if it had been eating spinach. A unique aspect of the Popeye merchandising story is that no other cartoon

Harvey Comics was as enthusiastic about merchandising as any other company, but rarely did any cartoon company promote it as bombastically as Harvey did in this 1974 ad. (At the risk of contradicting Wendy's aunt, the good little witch was never as major a merchandising success as her ghostly friend, Casper.)

The licensing of Hanna-Barbera's many TV characters was handled through Ed Justin's New York Screen Gems office. This remarkable 1963 photo shows just a fraction of the items that were available at that time, including a few that are totally unknown to today's collectors.

character ever had so many different designs used simultaneously. From 1933 until 1941, the comic strip Popeye and the animated Popeye remained basically consistent with each other; then, with World War II looming, the Fleischers drafted Popeye into the navy and gave him a new white uniform that matched what all the other sailors were wearing. The newspaper strip did not, however, so from that point, the screen Popeye began to resemble the newspaper version less and less each year. Famous Studios eventually redesigned Popeye's entire face, making him look even more different. As for the comic strip, after Segar's death in 1938, the artwork was handled primarily by Bill Zaboly, whose way of drawing Popeye's head and mouth made Zaboly's style immediately identifiable. At the same time, the Popeye comic books were being drawn by Segar's former assistant, Bud Sagendorf, who had yet a different way of depicting the characters. Things really got confusing in the 1960s, when King Features produced a new series of Popeye cartoons for television, using alarmingly simplified designs for the cast. Sagendorf took over drawing the newspaper strip in the late 1950s, and a decade later the comic book art chores were handed over to George Wildman. Thus, any given piece of Popeye merchandise could feature any one of these various character designs—or a strange combination of them. There are examples of a Zaboly Popeye interacting with a Famous Studios Bluto, or a King Features television version of Popeye in the same place as one based on Sagendorf's rendition. Some merchandise even went off into other directions and didn't resemble any other specific Popeye.

What really caused an avalanche of merchandise based on all of these theatrical cartoon characters was the sale of their film libraries to television in the 1950s. Older cartoons had been syndicated to local stations since the early 1950s, but in 1956, both the Warner Bros./Bugs Bunny and Paramount/Popeye packages were made available, and suddenly their already-vast merchandise lines stretched from coast to coast. Similar reactions occurred when any of the other veteran characters made their television debuts, reaching more kids in one broadcast than ever saw their cartoons in theaters.

But that was only part of the story. In 1957, MGM disbanded its animation division and William Hanna and Joseph Barbera were forced to look for other cartoon pastures. They responded by developing a severely streamlined form of "limited animation" and batting out TV cartoons at a rate and cost that was a mere fraction of what they had been spending on *Tom and Jerry*. Beginning with *Ruff and Reddy*, the Hanna-Barbera Studio launched one success after another, with *Huckleberry Hound*, *Quick Draw McGraw*, and *Yogi Bear* in syndication for Kellogg's and *The Flintstones*, *Top Cat*, and *The Jetsons* as prime-time series on ABC.

There is no way to overestimate the importance of merchandising in establishing Hanna-Barbera's reputation in the late 1950s and early 1960s. Since all of their TV shows were distributed through Columbia's subsidiary, Screen Gems, that company was responsible for overseeing the many licensees who wanted a piece of Yogi Bear's pie, and the executive in charge at the New York offices was Ed Justin, with not-inconsiderable help from his assistant, Myrna Masour.

A February 1963 *TV Guide* article illustrated Justin's success with some astounding figures and some jaw-dropping photographs'. According to the article, at that time, an estimated seventy-five hundred different licensed products bore the images of the characters Hanna-Barbera had created up to that point. The retail value of all Hanna-Barbera merchandise sold during 1961 totaled some eighty million dollars, and Justin estimated that figure would surpass one hundred million dollars once all the numbers for 1962 were turned in. Within Justin and Masour's office was a simulated store that displayed samples and prototypes for thousands of different toys, books, and clothing items.

Myrna Masour has warm memories about her days as second in command of Hanna-Barbera's licensing. She likes to tell one story about how merchandise actually came to control the content of the shows. When Fred and Wilma Flintstone were about to have a baby, the original plan was for the kid to be a boy, Fred Jr.. (In fact, that name had already been used in a *Flintstones* Little Golden Book.) Ed and Myrna, in conference with the tycoons at Ideal Toys, determined that girl dolls sold far better than boy dolls. Informed of this fact, Joe Barbera immediately switched the unborn baby's gender, and thus Pebbles Flintstone was foisted onto the world—another triumph in Hanna-Barbera merchandise ranging from dolls to breakfast cereal.

Even the combined power of Justin and Masour could not completely control every aspect of the early Hanna-Barbera merchandise, though, and nowhere was this better demonstrated than in the matter of color. You see, the older, established cartoon stars had been seen on theater screens in glorious Technicolor for years,

The original sponsor for the Hanna-Barbera cartoons was Kellogg's, and this *Huckleberry Hound* record was one of the many ways the cereal maker promoted the shows.

Quality control was not much of a concern in the early days of Hanna-Barbera merchandise. Barney Rubble with green hair, a blonde Betty, a puffy-faced Wilma, and an orange, duck-billed Dino were only a few of the quirky off-model toys that are highly prized by collectors.

but even though the Hanna-Barbera cartoons were produced in color, they aired almost exclusively in black and white, at least in the beginning. So while most consumers knew what colors were correct for Woody Woodpecker and Donald Duck, sometimes the early Hanna-Barbera toys were subject to various manufacturers' imaginations.

Take Huckleberry Hound, for example. Officially he was blue, to match his name. However, one of the best-selling Huck items was a plastic bank manufactured by the Knickerbocker company, and it was red. So was the

plush Huck made and sold by the thousands by the
same company. In other places, Huck might appear orange, green, yellow, or gray. White horse Quick Draw
McGraw turned up in blue, orange, and other non-official colors. Things really started looking stoned
in the Stone Age world of *The Flintstones*, where the
first toys on the market in 1960 had Betty Rubble as
a blonde and husband Barney with green hair (likely
because in molded 3-D form, Barney's hair resembled
a huge fig leaf, so the color stylists simply went with
what they thought they saw). As color television became more common, and also perhaps as embarrassment mounted over some of these early "off-model"
designs, Hanna-Barbera's toys began matching their

screen images more closely, although every now and then another anomaly
would slip through.

At about the same time Columbia, via Screen Gems, began handling Hanna-Barbera's TV product, the studio was phasing out its relationship with
the former supplier of its theatrical shorts, United Productions of America
(UPA). This was surely the most ambitious of any animation studio, formed
with the express purpose of rebelling against the type of storybook-inspired
artwork and violent gaggery of all the others. Although the UPA artists disdained the idea of being limited to any single continuing character, to their
everlasting annoyance, audiences took to their only creation that fell into
that format: the nearsighted Mister Magoo. (UPA's second-most-famous
character was Gerald McBoing Boing, but even he could not hold a candle
to Magoo in popularity—and Magoo could not have even seen the candle if
Gerald had been holding one.)

While UPA was still producing theatrical cartoons, entrepreneur Henry
Saperstein was charged with licensing Magoo and McBoing Boing for merchandising purposes; at one time or another, he had also done such work
with *Lassie*, *The Lone Ranger*, and *Dick Tracy*, to name a few. After television
caused the demand for theatrical shorts to drop, Saperstein bought the entire UPA studio—and the general consensus is that he did so primarily to
gain complete control over potential Magoo merchandise. If that were the
case, Saperstein's dreams certainly did not work out as he had planned, because while there were usually a few Magoo toys on the market at any given
time, they were extremely few and far between.

Saperstein produced a new series of five-minute Magoo misadventures

Henry Saperstein bought the
United Productions of America cartoon studio in the late 1950s, reportedly because he had big plans
for merchandising Mister Magoo.
This board game was one of the
toys that resulted shortly thereafter.

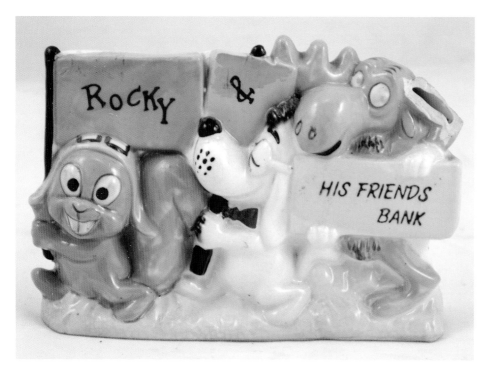

This ceramic *Rocky and His Friends* bank (yes, Bullwinkle is missing an antler) was one of the early pieces of merchandise from Jay Ward's witty and satiric TV series.

for television and supplemented them with a similarly formatted series of Dick Tracy shorts (no doubt stemming from his earlier experiences with licensing that property). Dick Tracy toys abounded in the early 1960s, featuring not only the square-jawed gumshoe but the zany sidekicks with whom UPA saddled him: Hemlock Holmes the bulldog, Joe Jitsu, and Go Go Gomez, the latter two of which were ethnic stereotypes that caused the cartoons to age poorly. Once the Dick Tracy TV cartoons had run their course, most Tracy merchandise reverted to being based on Chester Gould's original newspaper comic strip.

Kellogg's was enjoying so much success with the Hanna-Barbera shows it sponsored that rival General Mills decided it wanted to jump into the bowl, too. The result was Jay Ward's hilarious *Rocky and His Friends*, "starring that jet age aerial ace, Rocky the Flying Squirrel, and his pal, Bullwinkle the Moose," as narrator William Conrad often phrased it. While Ward and writer Bill Scott handled the creative end of the show, licensing was arranged through the distributor, Producers Associates of Television (PAT), and executive producer Peter Piech, whose exact relationship with Ward seems as fuzzy as his name. Certainly the two of them did not always agree on the deals that were being made, but according to Ward studio historian Keith Scott, the first Rocky and Bullwinkle merchandise was in stores in August 1960, following the show's November 1959 premiere.

The Ward output was not the only cartoon product handled by Piech and PAT. His warm relationship with General Mills extended to sponsorship of the programs produced by New York–based Total TeleVision Productions (TTV). These shows had a similar "look" to the ones Ward produced, and for good reason—not only were they distributed by the same company for the same sponsor, but they were physically animated at the same cartoon studio in Mexico. TTV's first show for PAT was *King Leonardo and His Short Subjects*, followed closely by *Tennessee Tuxedo and His Tales* and then the studio's megahit, *Underdog*. It has been pointed out more than once that the TTV characters somehow managed to receive considerably more merchandising in the years after their shows went into reruns than when they were new.

One thing that undoubtedly did little to endear Piech to Jay Ward was his habit, which became more pronounced as time went on, of authorizing merchandise that mixed the Ward and TTV characters together as if they all sprang from a single source. In fact, their only real relationship is that General Mills owned them all, but many kids who grew up getting Bullwinkle and Underdog drinking glasses as part of the same set naturally assumed they were all Jay Ward programs. As we shall see in later chapters, this tradition extended well into the 1980s, and after Ward's death in 1989, his daughter, Tiffany, spent several years fighting to regain all the rights to his beloved characters.

Meanwhile, what sort of effect were all of these upstart TV cartoon series having on the long-established leader of the club, Walt Disney? Well, television had initially proven to be a great benefactor to Walt's world. After a couple of experimental specials in the early years of the decade, Disney plunged ears-first into a weekly ABC-TV series in the fall of 1954. It was no coincidence that the name of the show was *Disneyland*, as ABC was one of the partners Walt had talked into investing money in the theme park of the same name he was building in Anaheim, California. When that park opened in July 1955, it provided an entirely new subject for licensing; as park history buffs Jack and Leon Janzen have so accurately pointed out, Disneyland was the only one of the company's amusement parks to be merchandised as if it were a separate character, with games, coloring books, jigsaw puzzles, and all the usual items based strictly on its name and attractions.

Because Jay Ward's characters and those created by Total TeleVision Productions were all under the control of General Mills and promoter Peter Piech, they often appeared together even though they had no other connection to each other.

Since Western Printing and Lithographing was one of the early investors in Disneyland, the company issued an amazing number of storybooks, comic books, coloring books, games, jigsaw puzzles, and other toys based on the world's first theme park.

Mickey Mouse Club merchandise hit stores in advance of the show's October 1955 premiere. In the case of the Mickey Mouse Roller Skates, notice the results when a manufacturer, rather than Disney's artists, took on the task of illustrating one of the famous characters. (Raymond Keese collection)

Then, in October 1955, Walt and ABC unveiled the daily hour-long production known as *The Mickey Mouse Club*. Kay Kamen was long gone by that time, but his successors in Disney's licensing offices had learned their lessons well from his example of getting the merchandise into stores before the programming hit the public. By the summer of that year, stores were selling Mickey Mouse Club Records, though they did not feature the voices of the real Mouseketeers: the youngsters who were going to star in the show had not yet been cast. For the same reason, the earliest Mickey Mouse Club puzzles and books have artwork depicting generic Mouseketeers rather than specific kids. As the show and its stars grew in popularity, of course, Darlene, Cubby, Karen, Annette, and the rest of the gang found their faces smiling from store shelves nationwide.

Al Konetzni of Disney's New York licensing office came up with the idea for General Electric's Mickey and Donald nightlights by placing the head of a PEZ dispenser over a standard low-wattage bulb.

By that time, Disney's New York office was being run by Jack Smith, with art directors Lou Lispi and later Jim Tanaka handling that end of the business. The "idea man" was Al Konetzni, who had the job of coming up with merchandise concepts that had not already been tried. We will be encountering his name repeatedly as we move through the pages that follow, but in interviews later in life he never failed to mention one particular concept of his, because it was so simple yet was such a hit. One of the Disney licensees was General Electric, and during one meeting, Konetzni says he took the plastic head off a Donald Duck PEZ candy dispenser, placed it over a standard G-E nightlight, and turned off the lights in the meeting room. Before one could say, "We bring good things to life," the Donald Duck nightlight was born, and it was soon selling by the thousands along with a similar Mickey Mouse version. Keeping fresh Disney merchandise in stores year after year called for lots of ideas—and fortunately, Konetzni's fertile brain had a seemingly inexhaustible supply of them.

And speaking of keeping things fresh, in the early 1960s Walt began to get concerned that his position as king was beginning to be challenged. The Hanna-Barbera and Jay Ward cartoons were certainly not triumphs of fine art, and the money spent to produce their entire half-hour shows would have bought only a few minutes of typical Disney animation, but both kids and their parents were enthralled by Disney competitors' clever, satirical

Ludwig Von Drake joined the cast on the day *Walt Disney's Wonderful World of Color* premiered on NBC in September 1961, and he soon took his place as one of the most merchandised Disney characters of the 1960s.

attitudes and hilarious voices. In the vernacular of that time, they were "hip," and Mickey, Donald, and Goofy suddenly looked like old fogeys. When Disney's weekly prime-time TV series leaped from ABC to NBC in September 1961, heralding its new format with the title *Walt Disney's Wonderful World of Color*, it seemed like a good opportunity to show that he could be as funny as everyone else. The new animated star of *Wonderful World of Color* was Ludwig Von Drake, ostensibly Donald's know-it-all uncle, who delivered hilarious and topical lectures in an Austrian accent supplied by voice whiz Paul Frees. (It is ironic that at the same time Frees was playing Disney's newest creation, he was also supplying the voice for bad guy Boris Badenov for Ward, one of the studio's biggest rivals.)

Ludwig received the full "star treatment" in Disney merchandise, especially during 1961–62. Around the same time, another artist began picking up work from the New York office; he was George Peed, who had worked as an animator at the Burbank studios during the making of such cinema classics as *Pinocchio* and *Fantasia* in the late 1930s. (He was the brother of famed Disney artist and story man Bill Peet, who reportedly had changed the spelling of his last name because of the constant tasteless jokes from his fellow employees.) Peed's art style is immediately identifiable after seeing an example or two; no matter how static the scene, Peed's figures are always bursting with movement. He was also adept at depicting beautiful women, so his work on the *Mary Poppins* merchandise of 1964 often features a Mary who is cuter than even the real Julie Andrews.

Only occasionally did Peed's trademark style work against him; a 1961 Ludwig Von Drake coloring book is one of Peed's only attempts at that type of merchandise, and being confined to heavy line drawings meant to be colored by small hands wielding smaller crayons seems to have crippled his usual enthusiasm, resulting in some rather deformed ducks. After his Disney work ended later in the decade, Peed became known to a new generation of kids for his colorful, kinetic covers for the albums and 45s produced by Peter Pan Records. For those, Peed did not fail to sign his name prominently, belatedly giving himself the credit he had not received while toiling anonymously on Disney merchandise.

What would turn out to be one of Disney's biggest coups took place around the time Ludwig Von Drake began his TV lecture tour. In June 1961, Walt made a deal with Daphne Milne, widow of famed British author A. A. Milne, for the screen rights to her husband's most famous character, Winnie-the-Pooh. Once Walt had obtained those rights, however, there was a stitch in the stuffing. As we have already seen, the Disney studio was not about to

undertake any sort of project without being able to flood the market with merchandise ahead of time—and Walt's deal with the Milne family did not include the merchandising rights to Pooh and his pals.

We now must backtrack to the very different world of 1930, when A. A. Milne had assigned the American merchandise rights for his characters to New Yorker Stephen Slesinger. From that point on, there had been quite a number of Pooh toys, including board games and the ever-popular stuffed toys based on the Ernest Shepard illustrations for the Pooh books. Slesinger died in 1953, and his young widow, Shirley, continued her promotion of Pooh until Walt came knocking on her door. At some point in 1964, Disney apparently secured the rights to license Pooh merchandise, because the earliest items produced bear a copyright date of that year. (As part of the deal, Shirley would continue collecting royalties on any Disney Pooh items, a fact that will come back to haunt us all in the final chapter of this book.)

The first Disney animated Pooh story, *Winnie-the-Pooh and the Honey Tree*, did not reach theaters until February 1966. In the preceding months, Disney made a deal with retail giant Sears, Roebuck & Co. for an exclusive line of Winnie-the-Pooh branded children's clothing—shirts, pants, dresses, shoes, and the like—as well as toys that could be purchased nowhere else. Within days, it seemed, children's departments in Sears stores nationwide were

It's time to
hang stockings,
dream of sugarplums too..
in the
enchanted land of
Winnie-the-Pooh

Sears 173

Disney made a honey of a deal with Sears, Roebuck & Co. to be the purveyors of an exclusive line of Winnie-the-Pooh toys, clothing, and other merchandise beginning in 1965.

transformed into outparcels of the Hundred Acre Wood, and that was just the beginning. Non-Sears manufacturers turned out Pooh, too, all using the Disney redesign of the characters. (Since two future stars, Piglet and Tigger, did not appear in Disney's first Pooh film, it is easy to identify the earliest merchandise by the fact that those friends' design was still in a bit of flux.)

If your short-term memory has not yet shorted out, you may recall that this chapter started out by talking about merchandise based on newspaper comic strips. Admittedly, we veered off onto another road through the world of animation, but now the two paths converge once more. And of all the comic strips that inspired their own merchandise, none was a bigger winner than *Peanuts*, featuring that biggest loser, "good ol' Charlie Brown."

Charles Schulz's creation is such a part of American pop culture that it is difficult to realize just how long it took to enter the field of merchandising. For the first eight years of the strip's existence, the only merchandise—in a loose form of the term—was a series of reprint books. Finally, in 1958 a company called Hungerford took a chance and produced detailed plastic figures of the characters as they looked at that particular time; somehow, they all appeared "younger" than their later familiar forms, and the Hungerford Snoopy had a nose longer than his head. Schroeder came complete with a plastic piano, which is now difficult to find because kids tended to not keep up with it as closely as the yellow-haired prodigy who played it.

Even after Hungerford opened the *Peanuts* floodgate, merchandise still only trickled out. Coloring books took the newspaper strips and enlarged them (usually two panels per page) into a size fit for creative crayoning. Another company made a set of nodders (or bobble-heads, as people frequently

The worldwide *Peanuts* merchandising phenomenon began innocently enough with these vinyl toys made by Hungerford in 1958. Pig-Pen is virtually unrecognizable without his customary coating of dirt and grime.

San Francisco entrepreneur Connie Boucher (right), founder of Determined Productions, probably did more to bring *Peanuts* from the newspaper page to the toy store and gift shop than any other individual.

refer to them today), which are interesting because each of them bore the character's name in the same format: "SNOOPY, of the *Peanuts* comic strip." At the time, it was still not assumed that everyone would know who these characters were without some extra identification.

If one person can be said to have broken down whatever real or imagined barriers prevented the proliferation of *Peanuts* merchandise, it was Connie Boucher, a former San Francisco window dresser who formed Determined Productions in 1961 for the express purpose of putting out *Peanuts* items. When Boucher died at age seventy-two in 1995, Schulz related the story of their partnership to the *New York Times*: "She kind of set a standard for licensing, which up until she came along had not always been that high." Staying with the idea that up until that time the only *Peanuts* books had been strip reprints, Schulz went on,

She had seen the strip I had drawn where Snoopy is being hugged by Charlie Brown, and Charlie Brown says, "Happiness is a warm puppy." Connie said that maybe this could become a good book, and I said I didn't know if I could think of any more of those ideas. That day, after she left, I wrote virtually all the ideas in "Happiness Is a Warm Puppy" and it was the best-selling book of the next year.

Throughout the rest of the 1960s and 1970s, Determined Productions' line was not the only *Peanuts* merchandise, but it was always easy to identify by its "groovy" colors and lettering, which could only have originated in the San Francisco art scene. Just to show how long it took for everyone except Boucher to catch on, however, consider that it was 1967 before any *Peanuts* items appeared in that bible of licensed toy history, the Sears Christmas catalog. Even then, the only items were books—the ever-popular strip reprints and Determined Productions' various titles. Finally, in 1968 Sears devoted an entire section to *Peanuts* toys, and there was no turning back.

What happened between the early 1960s and late 1960s that caused such a sudden upsurge in merchandise based on this popular strip? Studying the dates that various items came on the market, it is obvious that their numbers increased once the first *Peanuts* animated TV special, *A Charlie Brown Christmas*, aired in 1965 and really exploded after the next two shows, *Charlie Brown's All-Stars* and *It's the Great Pumpkin, Charlie Brown*, were released in

June and October 1966, respectively. By that time, the mogul in charge of licensing *Peanuts* for United Feature Syndicate was Jim Hennessy; Schulz paid tribute to his work by making "Mr. Hennessy" an offscreen hardware store owner in the *All-Stars* special.

If one tried to pinpoint a moment in time when *Peanuts*, in all its various incarnations, was at the absolute peak of its popularity, that precise moment would have occurred on a certain date in December 1969. On that particular day, *A Charlie Brown Christmas* appeared on CBS-TV for the fifth time; the off-Broadway musical *You're a Good Man, Charlie Brown* was playing in New York; the feature film *A Boy Named Charlie Brown* was the Christmas attraction at Radio City Music Hall; and an uncountable number of people had read the daily installment of the strip in their local newspapers. Although *Peanuts* (and its merchandise) remained a phenomenon for the remaining thirty-one years of its life span, never again would such a pinnacle occur.

The week of Christmas that year, *Business Week* published a feature story on the worldwide success of *Peanuts* licensing. Naturally, Jim Hennessy was quoted extensively. "We get three or four calls a day, and at least one visitor," he told the reporter. "We turn them all down." There was a real concern that the quality of the merchandise not get out of control, and although Schulz was not always privy to everything that was being done, he tried to stay as involved as possible. One anecdote from *Business Week* shows just how this could go:

> At J. Chein & Co., which makes Peanuts toys and housewares, Lyle Johnson, director of marketing, tells of a Schulz-ordered change in an illustration on a Peanuts wastebasket. One side showed Charlie Brown with an F on his report card. The other had Snoopy with a college diploma. Schulz said that Snoopy was not *that* much smarter than Charlie Brown—so Charlie's grade was raised to an A-plus and Snoopy's diploma was marked magnum cum laude.

This story hints at a secret concerning the *Peanuts* items that was kept confidential for many years: not all of the artwork appearing on the merchandise was actually drawn by Schulz. Beginning with a lunch box sold by the Thermos company, a "ghost artist" named Nick LoBianco drew the characters for some licensed products, supposedly the only other individual approved by Schulz to do so. Now, some historians have taken this to an extreme and claimed that Schulz's actual artwork was never used *anywhere* except the newspaper strip, but that too would be as false as saying that he personally illustrated every toy, greeting card, and board game. With a practiced eye,

PEANUTS and his gang

(11 and 12) Combed cotton knit. Pullover style pajamas can be worn in or out. Ribbed knit neck, cuffs and ankles.

Charles Schulz never liked the name *Peanuts* for his strip, knowing that first-time readers would expect to see a character by that name. Apparently Sears had not learned any better by 1967, when these boys' pajamas were advertised as "Peanuts and his gang."

A well-guarded secret was that not all Peanuts merchandise of the early days featured genuine Schulz artwork. The 1965 lunch box was illustrated by ghost artist Nick LoBianco; the instruction booklet for Kenner's battery-operated Snoopy toothbrush had a cover with Schulz's signature, but the drawings did not even begin to resemble his style.

one can usually spot telltale signs—an occasional distortion in a character's facial features, for example—to show whether one is viewing Schulz, LoBianco, or even some other commercial artist whose name was allowed to molder in the shadowy recesses of the licensing business. Actually, this was probably as much Schulz's preference as anyone else's; as he told the *Business Week* reporter, "Some of the licensees have trouble understanding that I need time to think. If I had more time, there would be new episodes in the strip, and new ideas that would give the licensees new material."

Not every newspaper strip could enjoy the same kind of merchandising success as *Peanuts*. One characteristic that seemed to hold true, though, was that their licensing jumped whenever a strip was adapted into another form, whether animated or live-action, for television or movies. For a few examples, let's take the many characters owned by King Features Syndicate (which began as one facet of William Randolph Hearst's empire).

We have already considered the matter of Popeye, of course, who was a special case because of his long-running film and TV career. Even at that, there were bursts of Popeye merchandise whenever a new version of the character debuted, especially in 1978, when Hanna-Barbera made arrangements to produce a new series for Saturday mornings, and a couple of years later, when Paramount released the love-it-or-hate-it live-action feature starring Robin Williams. Next to Popeye, KFS's most licensed property was undoubtedly *Blondie*, the strip begun in 1930 by Chic Young.

Even though in the 1940s, *Blondie* was possibly the most-read comic strip in the world, featuring situations that resonated with people in a multitude of countries and cultures, its merchandising success may well have been spurred along by the series of live-action movies produced by Columbia for more than a decade. About the time those ended, there was a short-lived TV series, and *Blondie* was again adapted for television in 1968. The merchandise produced at that time made it a point to promote the new show, with the live cast pictured alongside Chic Young's drawn characters. Unlike the *Peanuts* merchandise, which strove mightily to look like it was drawn by Charles Schulz even when it was not, there were many *Blondie* items—especially jigsaw puzzles and coloring books—that only bore the most superficial resemblance to the comic strip.

Most newspaper comics seemed to receive their biggest merchandising efforts when adapted for TV or animation. *Blondie* became a short-lived sitcom in 1968, and a number of items included photos of the live-action cast along with the cartoon characters.

At times, the artwork on merchandise licensed by King Features Syndicate only barely resembled the source comic strip, as with this odd style of drawing on a *Blondie* jigsaw puzzle.

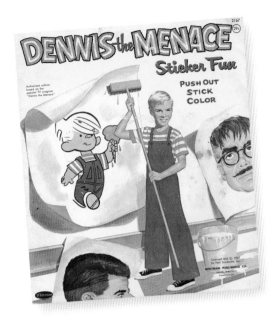

Hank Ketcham's *Dennis the Menace* followed a similar path into the merchandise mart. After the strip's debut in 1951, there were scattered attempts at licensing over the next few years, not always aimed at kids; for example, boxed sets of cocktail napkins bore reprints of selected newspaper panels. Not until Dennis became a live-action prime-time sitcom in 1959 did the merchandise really began to roll off the assembly line. Unlike the Blondie merchandise, which referred to the TV cast almost as an afterthought, Dennis items of the late 1950s and 1960s could picture either Ketcham's original cartoon characters or TV star Jay North and his castmates. Sometimes a single item used both, as with a storybook that has a photograph of North on the cover but Ketcham-style illustrations inside.

Ketcham was an avid golfer, and that hobby led directly to the next big push for Dennis merchandise. How, you ask? IMG Marketing was formed in the early 1960s to handle licensing and promotion for various sports stars, one of whom was golfing great Arnold Palmer. (Among other things, IMG

When *Dennis the Menace* became a popular TV program, the licensed items could depict either Hank Ketcham's original comic strip characters or the live-action cast of the situation comedy—or sometimes both at the same time.

In 1967, Hank Ketcham's licensing agency, IMG Marketing, arranged for Dennis the Menace to become the mascot for the Sears catalogs, and the company issued many exclusive pieces of Dennis merchandise during that association.

licensed Palmer's name for a chain of miniature golf courses across the country.) Ketcham was impressed by IMG's work with such sports celebrities, and in 1966 he arranged for that agency to handle the Dennis licensing as well.

Arthur Lefave, who was responsible for the Ketcham/Dennis account, remembers that one of their first deals was with Sears. Perhaps hoping to repeat Sears's success with Pooh, Lefave and IMG arranged for Dennis to become the mascot for the Sears catalogs in 1967. This also led to the last (to date, anyway) huge influx of Dennis merchandise, as Sears sold clothing, toys, and many other items bearing the towheaded brat's mischievous visage. That arrangement ran out in the early 1970s, however, and Dennis retreated to his own backyard while Pooh continued to reign supreme at Sears.

In 1963, buoyed by the success of the made-for-TV Popeye cartoons, King Features authorized three more series based on Mort Walker's *Beetle Bailey*,

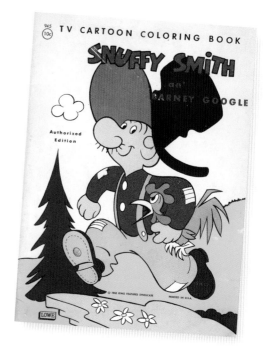

It was obvious that Mort Walker was not responsible for the illustrations in this *Beetle Bailey* coloring book, which was also issued in conjunction with a 1963 series of made-for-TV cartoons.

Fred Lasswell's *Barney Google* and *Snuffy Smith*, and George Herriman's *Krazy Kat*. The choice of *Krazy Kat* was a bit odd, since the strip had not been in print for twenty years, so the merchandising stemming from these new television toons concentrated primarily on Beetle and Snuffy. As with *Blondie*, many items only marginally resembled the comic strips, although as a new twist, some coloring books deliberately used the character designs whipped up specifically for animation.

In a truly odd clash of two completely separate worlds, Fred Lasswell and Shirley Slesinger married in 1964, around the same time she assigned the Winnie-the-Pooh merchandising rights to Walt Disney. If there are two other fictional characters as opposite in every way as Pooh and Snuffy Smith, they were never related by marriage as those were. As for Mort Walker, he was quoted in the same 1969 *Business Week* article that exposed the inner workings of the *Peanuts* merchandising machine: "It's the strip that pays off. The papers each pay from $5 to $500 a week, and you have to sell an awful lot of products before the royalties come near that." Of course, *Peanuts* was indeed selling an "awful lot" of products, while Walker considered some of the *Beetle Bailey* items simply "awful." With the eye of a father watching over his children, Walker could tell if Beetle's nose were the wrong shape or positioned on his face incorrectly, but most comic strip artists had no real control over whom the syndicates chose to produce the designs for much of the merchandise.

One cartoonist who refused to go along with that line of thinking was Walt Kelly, whose *Pogo* was one of the most erudite strips on any newspaper's comics page. Even though it dealt quite often (though not all the time) with political and social satire, the characters and their designs were appealing enough that manufacturers often approached Kelly about licensing them for one project or another. Kelly refused far more of those offers than he accepted, for the simple reason that he did not want anyone else trying to duplicate his style. In future chapters we will see how sometimes the temptation got to be too strong, and Kelly usually regretted the results when it did, but at least a couple of others should be mentioned here.

In 1968, Poynter Products made a set of six plastic figures of the Pogo characters, with each one having fake fur glued on in one spot or another. This was fine for fuzzy mammals such as Pogo Possum, but when reptiles such as turtle Churchy La Femme were required to wear a coat with a fur collar, that just seemed wrong somehow. Kelly was furious and tried to have the entire toy line scuttled, but apparently enough of them were sold that they do turn up occasionally as collectibles today. (It probably says something about the integrity of the Poynter company that around the same time it was involved in a blowup regarding its unauthorized reproductions of some of Dr. Seuss's characters.)

In 1969, Kelly had cause to gnash his teeth again when he teamed with former Warner Bros. director Chuck Jones to produce the first animated version of *Pogo* for an NBC-TV special. Kelly was most dissatisfied with the results, but at least he managed to stay more involved in the show's related merchandise. Sponsor Procter and Gamble offered plastic mugs with decals of the Pogo characters—apparently Kelly's own artwork—as well as a new set of plastic figures totally unlike the Poynter toys. To ensure that the Procter and Gamble figures would be faithful to the strip, Kelly reportedly sculpted the model for each one in clay, from which the molds were made. That story was told on more than one occasion by Kelly's widow, Selby, so who are we to deny it?

Most other major comic strips—and a surprising number of minor ones—fell somewhere between the two extremes of *Peanuts* and *Pogo* when it came to merchandise. With the notable exception of *Calvin and Hobbes*'s Bill Watterson, who actively and repeatedly stated that he wanted no part of the

Walt Kelly highly disapproved of the 1968 Poynter Products renditions of his beloved *Pogo* characters, each of which had fake fur glued on in one spot or another.

When Procter and Gamble wanted to issue a new series of *Pogo* toys in conjunction with a May 1969 animated special, Walt Kelly reportedly headed off any trouble by sculpting the originals in clay to be used for the molds.

merchandising machine, most strips took whatever they could get. Probably the nearest rival *Peanuts* had in sheer number of licensed items was *Garfield*, but since that strip did not begin publication until 1978, its toys and other related items are somewhat outside the baby boomer years that are this book's main focus. Whether they were 1930s and 1940s classics such as *Li'l Abner*, *Prince Valiant*, *Henry*, or *Joe Palooka* or part of the 1960s–70s trend toward more offbeat subjects including *The Wizard of Id* and *Broom Hilda*, most strips inspired at least a few items, and we will encounter a number of them in future chapters.

Li'l Abner produced its own merchandising phenomenon. A few licensed items had been created during the 1930s and the first half of the 1940s, but creator Al Capp was not totally happy with United Feature Syndicate's apparently halfhearted efforts to generate more. In 1948, Capp negotiated a new deal that gave him control of merchandise, and *Li'l Abner*–related products soon were being turned out faster than Abner could outrun Daisy Mae on Sadie Hawkins Day—and most of it was produced by subsidiary companies owned by members of Capp's family.

All of this took place just in time for the Shmoos' debut in the newspaper strip in August 1948. The cuddly Shmoos, which provided all of man's needs, including food, clothing and entertainment, were the subject of hundreds of different types of merchandise—clocks, drinking glasses, records, plastic banks, ceramics, and several dozen other categories. The Shmoo merchandise continued even after the characters' storyline had run its course, and Capp periodically brought them back for further appearances. Each Shmoo story invariably ended with the all-purpose creatures being destroyed by either the government or big business, both of which they threatened to make obsolete, so it was ironic that in 1948–49, Shmoo merchandise was one of the biggest categories of licensing.

Now, what about characters that originated in comic books rather than newspapers or animated films? With only a few exceptions, their merchandising would also gain extra strength when they were adapted into some other medium—and since most of them were superheroes, no doubt they greatly appreciated that burst of power.

Naturally, the grandpa of all the superheroes and the most super of them all (hence his name) was Superman, who burst through his first brick

Hal Foster's artistic masterpiece, *Prince Valiant*, enlisted young would-be Knights of the Round Table with this eye-pleasing board game.

wall into the public's consciousness in 1938. He must have made an impact far beyond that of ordinary mortals, because it took very little time for merchandise bearing his chiseled physique to appear. His official chronicler Les Daniels reports that the first Superman items appeared in 1939. And then,

> in 1940 a flood of Superman products was issued, including such items as puzzles, paint sets, paper dolls, games, greeting cards, coloring books and bubble gum (complete with trading cards). Kids could wear the image of Superman on playsuits, socks, shirts, moccasins and underwear, while keeping their cash in a Superman billfold and dining on Superman bread. Licensing would eventually prove to be twice a treasure trove, because each time the Man of Steel was adapted by broadcasters or filmmakers, the ensuing publicity would create an upsurge in the market for other licensed products.

As with the early Hanna-Barbera items, sometimes manufacturers seemed to be a bit hazy about the color of Superman's uniform, variously picturing him in green and in yellow with a red cape (the color scheme Mighty Mouse would claim as his own a few years later). And, as Daniels points out, Superman was brought to the big and small screens so often that it was never long before a new round of licensing broke out. The 1952 George Reeves television series, Filmation's 1966 Saturday morning series, and the 1978 Christopher Reeve big-budget theatrical feature were only a few of these productions. By the 1990s, even an episode of ABC-TV's reboot of the Superman saga, *Lois and Clark*, built its storyline around Superman/Clark Kent's self-conscious embarrassment at the plethora of merchandise based on him. (He is especially upset when he finds his adoptive mother, Mrs. Kent, playing with a nauseatingly cute plastic windup walking Superman.)

When Superman's fellow National Periodical Publications crime fighter, Batman, came to television in January 1966, it, too, sparked an explosion of licensing. Batman had less of a built-in audience from prior media exposure, so the TV show went after a goofy, over-the-top feel (usually described by the overused term "*camp*"). The merchandise, however, generally followed the more serious format of the comic books, which did not make ham actors out of villains such as the Joker and the Penguin. The number of Batman items—both licensed and unlicensed, as the image of a bat was fairly easy to utilize even for those who did not wish to pay a licensing fee—threatened to make even Superman's inventory look weak, but the biggest difference was that Batman's white-hot popularity blazed during 1966 and part of 1967 and then dimmed, while Superman just kept on flying. Batman would see future

The most famous superhero in history, Superman, became the subject of merchandising within a year or two of his comic book debut, and the mighty tide has not yet subsided. For this 1970s game, he was joined by his fellow DC Comics superheroes and their nemeses.

ABC-TV debuted its tongue-in-cheek *Batman* TV series in January 1966, and it did wonders (Boy Wonders, that is) for the amount of *Batman* merchandise on the market. (Steve Reisiger collection)

Marvel Comics' *The Incredible Hulk* became another hit TV series in the late 1970s, and with this calculator, kids found they could literally count on the not-so-jolly green giant.

revivals of merchandising beginning with his own big-screen success in 1989, and it has continued in fits and spurts ever since.

After Batman's TV ratings proved they could beat the guano out of his network rivals, the same producers briefly considered giving the same treatment to National Periodicals' third big star, Wonder Woman. A half-finished pilot film showed how misplaced that notion was, and Ms. Woman had to wait until she was included in the animated cast of Hanna-Barbera's *Super Friends* series in 1973 to begin making regular TV appearances. As with Batman, Wonder Woman merchandise had occasionally appeared since the 1940s, but even when *Super Friends* began generating licensing interest, she was still just part of the crowd. In March 1974, there was a lukewarmly received TV movie starring Cathy Lee Crosby, whose talents were many but did not include resembling the comic book Wonder Woman. Finally, in 1975 ABC cast the jaw-dropping Lynda Carter in first a series of TV movies and then her own series, and the dam blocking the flow of Wonder Woman merchandise burst like the heroine herself plowing into a nest of Nazis. Les Daniels's definitive history of the character includes plenty of examples of late 1970s items that were less than flattering to Wonder Woman's image; unlike the Batman merchandise, a healthy number of items pictured Lynda Carter in character instead of the cartoon Wonder Woman.

Marvel Comics must have been somewhat green with envy at its biggest competitor's success in both TV and merchandise, so in 1977, Marvel threw its biggest green guy into television to show he had what it took. *The Incredible Hulk* differed from all the other superhero TV shows in that the title character was played by two different actors, Bill Bixby as mild-mannered Bruce Banner and bodybuilder Lou Ferrigno, smothered in green makeup, as the semi-inarticulate Hulk. As expected, the TV show increased the amount of Hulk merchandise to be found, but years would pass before other Marvel stars, including Spider-Man, would get the big-screen treatment and really leave a mark in toy stores (as well as on their adversaries).

The 1970s were not a good time to be the Walt Disney Studios. Some Disney historians

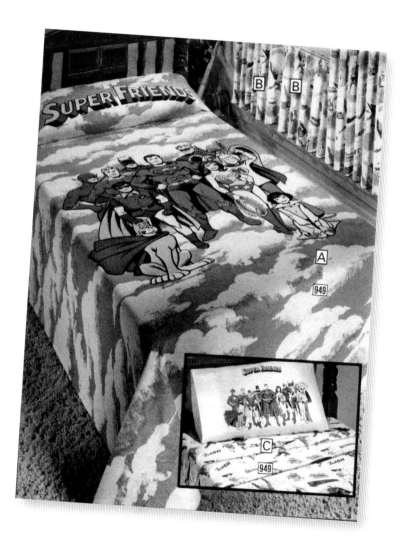

When the *Wonder Woman* TV series became a hit in 1976, some of the merchandise depicted its striking star, Lynda Carter, while other items (such as this release from Peter Pan Records) stuck to the original comic book designs.

Many of DC Comics' superheroes joined forces for Hanna-Barbera's *Super Friends* Saturday morning series in the 1970s. Kids could sleep securely under these bed linens, knowing their powerful pals were on the job.

28 OF WALT DISNEY'S MOST FAMOUS CHARACTERS DECORATING YOUR CHILD'S ROOM!

© Walt Disney Production

IMAGINE! ALL OF US FOR ONLY $1.00

Children love the magic of Walt Disney characters. Snow White, Pinocchio, Donald Duck and 25 other all-time favorites will make your child's room as gay and colorful as Disneyland. These characters are printed in full color on luxurious durable art-board. They are so big they easily decorate a 10-foot wall. They're easy to punch out and put up, and your child will have loads of fun arranging them.

The only way to appreciate the color and charm of these superb Walt Disney character wall decorations is to see them on your child's wall. Be the first in your neighborhood to transform your child's room into a magical Disneyland.

Send just $1, plus 25¢ for postage and handling. That's just a fraction of what you would expect to pay for wall decorations of such outstanding quality. This amazing offer may not be repeated this season in this publication—ORDER NOW!

Mickey Mouse, Pluto, Goofy, Donald Duck, Huey, Dewey and Louie, Snow White and the Seven Dwarfs, Mary Poppins, Jiminy Cricket, Pinocchio, Geppetto, Figaro, Peter Pan, Bongo, The Little Pig, Tinker Bell, Bambi, Winnie-the-Pooh, Thumper, Dumbo.

Golden Press, A Division of Western Publishing Co., Inc., North Road, Poughkeepsie, New York 12601

These cardboard Disney wall decorations were advertised in family magazines from the mid-1960s through the 1970s. However, the most recent characters included in the lineup were Mary Poppins and Winnie-the-Pooh. For an amazing length of time after Walt's death, the studio he founded seemed incapable of developing any memorable new characters.

have said that when Walt died in December 1966, his timing was perfect (even though he undoubtedly would not have planned it that way, if he had any say about it). Within a couple of years, the type of entertainment and view of life exemplified by the Disney movie and television output came to be derided by pseudointellectuals as a hoary relic of a bygone era. One of the low points came when Mickey Mouse's picture was removed from the dial of his own watch because it was felt that kids no longer thought he was cool; it was sold as a "Mickey Mouse watch" merely because the words "Mickey Mouse" appeared under the *12*. (Proving that Mickey was not alone in disgrace, Cinderella, Snow White, and Alice in Wonderland watches also featured only the names and no artwork. All three, however, made up for that flaw by coming packaged with a detailed ceramic statue of the namesake character.)

Fortunately, Mickey got his picture reinstated on the watches in 1968, in time for his fortieth birthday celebration. In chapter 4, we shall see how the nostalgia for collecting early Disney memorabilia got started at about the same time. As far as the general public was concerned, though, Disney was something that was more or less taken for granted. The animated features of the 1970s (*The Aristo-Cats*, *Robin Hood*, *The Rescuers*) were well received but seemed to produce nothing revolutionary in terms of tie-in merchandise. The opening of Walt Disney World in October 1971 did not produce the same type of "park as character" merchandising that had accompanied Disneyland, but some items—storybooks, coloring books, jigsaw puzzles—used its attractions as their basis. It is easy to identify the earliest Walt Disney World items, because the park logo had an extra element that was soon dropped: a tiny pennant with the word "*Florida*" just above the main lettering. There must have been a feeling that the public needed to be educated that there was now a park that was not in Southern California.

In the 1970s, Mickey Mouse was viewed primarily as a corporate logo and ambassador for the theme parks rather than as a viable cartoon character. In early 1975, edited reruns of the original *Mickey Mouse Club* shows were syndicated and raised the public's collective nostalgia. In 1977, an all-new *Mickey Mouse Club* was produced for syndication, starring a new crop of cute kids in multicolored uniforms. Many merchandise items were licensed, and unlike the earliest 1955 Club items, these made it perfectly clear that they were using the actual Mouseketeers' names and likenesses. (Magazine writer

Mickey Mouse   Alice in Wonderland   Snow White

Cinderella Sets . . Watch with figurine; Pendant with coach

The ultimate indignity came when Mickey Mouse's picture was removed from the dial of his own watch, leaving only his name for brand identification. His fellow stars Snow White, Cinderella, and Alice in Wonderland met the same humiliating fate.

Spencer Grendahl seemed to take diabolical glee in pointing out that Disney's contracts with the new Mouseketeers included all rights to their faces and images; thus, they received no extra compensation for the merchandise on which they appeared.) It all led up to Mickey's giant fiftieth birthday observation in November 1978, for which many more licensees signed on.

Other than the merchandising and the animated features, the Disney company was foundering under its own weight and seeming inability to connect with its audience. Although many Disney fans were shocked, the 1984 takeover of the company by Michael Eisner and his minions really turned it around; by the late 1980s, the children of the baby boomers were as avid Disney fans as their parents had once been, and the amount of merchandise connected with every production certainly proved that someone had indeed wished upon a star when things looked their bleakest.

The opening of Walt Disney World in October 1971 inspired some merchandise, if not as much as Disneyland's debut in 1955. Both of these books have the earliest version of the Walt Disney World logo, with a tiny pennant bearing the word *Florida*.

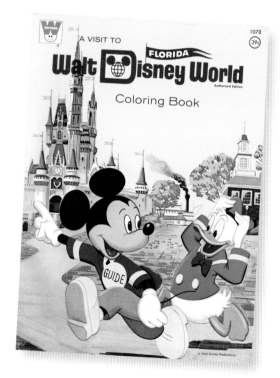

The first *Mickey Mouse Club* merchandise in 1955 had largely depicted generic Mouseketeers. When *The New Mickey Mouse Club* hit TV screens in 1977, the tie-in items went out of their way to accurately depict the actual kids who starred in the series.

Superman, Batman, Wonder Woman, and their fellow heroes from DC and Marvel Comics were translated from the printed page into various forms of merchandise over the years, including these highly prized Aurora model kits from 1966. (Donnie Pitchford collection)

Chapter Two

FUNNY BUSINESS

Okay, faithful readers, we need to get one point out of the way right here at the beginning of this chapter. There have been millions of words written on the history of American comic books—analyzing them, criticizing them, or simply giving credit to the innumerable writers, artists and editors responsible for them. There are people whose expertise in comic books enables them to identify whether two different artists worked on a single panel. There are people who know the intimate history of every major and minor comic book company and have published their research for all to read. So, why would this author and this publisher even attempt to cover the subject in a single chapter? The fact is that we will not.

Comic books were such a major part of cartoon licensing that they could not be left out of any discussion of the subject, no matter how much had already been written about them. We will be giving a tip-of-the-tip-of-the-iceberg look at how they influenced other licensed products and then moving on. So, this chapter exists only because it *has* to—got that?

Most of those histories agree that what we now think of as comic books grew out of publications that reprinted newspaper strips of their day. Somewhere during the 1930s, while that former style continued, companies began producing original stories and artwork not based on any preexisting character. No one has to be told that this was the true birthplace of Superman (Krypton notwithstanding), and he was soon followed by his costume-clad cohorts Batman, Wonder Woman, and all the rest. For these characters and their superheroics, plus the seemingly infinite number of Marvel Comics stars, comic books would not have been considered licensed merchandise—mainly because the comic books were their first home. In other words, anything *other* than comics required a license from the publisher. We will be seeing examples of their escape from between printed covers as we continue through the rest of this book.

In the next chapter, we will see how the Western Printing and Lithographing Company of Racine, Wisconsin, had the foresight in the early 1930s to secure a license for publications featuring the ever-growing output of the Walt Disney Studios. Among the various items published under Western's imprint was a periodical known as *Mickey Mouse Magazine*. It primarily featured storybook-like text pieces concerning the doings of the Disney cast, with reprints of newspaper comic strips thrown in. Perhaps responding

DONALD DUCK
Pin-Up Pictures

Free!

7¾" by 10¾" in Full Color

Of All Your Favorite Characters Given With Subscriptions to

WALT DISNEY'S COMICS AND STORIES

Together With Attractive Gift Card Bearing Your Name

3 Year Subscription $2.50
(4 Free Pin-Ups)

2 Year Subscription $1.75
(2 Free Pin-Ups)

Each **1 Year Subscription $1.00**

Everyone, young and old, loves comics. And everyone loves **Walt Disney's Comics & Stories**, filled with the hilarious antics of Donald Duck, Mickey and Minnie Mouse, and all the rest of the Disney gang. Clean and wholesome, it is *tops in comic entertainment*, suitable for everyone, from 3 to 90.

Mail to: K. K. PUBLICATIONS, Inc.

DEPT. 6   POUGHKEEPSIE, NEW YORK

Gentlemen:
Enclosed find $_____ for which please enter the following subscription to **Walt Disney's Comics and Stories** for _____ monthly issues beginning with _____ issue. (Please print)

Name _____

Street and Number _____

City or Town _____ Mailing Dist. No. _____ State _____
☐ Check here if this is a new subscription

Donor's Name _____

Address _____

Walt Disney's Comics and Stories was the most successful comic book in history, reportedly selling three million copies of each issue by the mid-1950s.

The comics produced by Western Printing and distributed through Dell produced their own merchandise lines. Dell offered these Disney squeak toys, and many others, during the 1950s and 1960s.

to the growing interest in the superhero comics in the late 1930s, the comic strip reprints gradually began to outnumber the text features, and in October 1940 the publication received a new identity: *Walt Disney's Comics and Stories*, a fully realized comic book. (It and most comic books that followed in the coming decades, retained at least one or two pages devoted to text pieces, as that somehow affected the postage rate paid to mail them to subscribers.)

While *Walt Disney's Comics and Stories* (or *WDC&S*, as collectors abbreviate it) was produced by Western Printing with input from Disney writers and artists, it was distributed by Dell Publishing. The Western/Dell/Disney association would have far-reaching and very profitable effects for all three of its participants and lasted for decades. Besides *WDC&S*, Western and Dell worked on other publications, including a long-running comic book series known unpretentiously as "Four Color." These were used to test out characters or formats before committing to a continuing series, and one of the historic moments in Disney comic book history took place under this banner.

The studio had made plans to star Donald Duck in his own animated feature, but World War II and its demand for military training films put a damper on any such thoughts. Unwilling to let a good story go to waste, di-

BRAND NEW from DISNEYLAND

Newly Designed WALT DISNEY SQUEEZE TOYS

Featuring YOUR FAVORITE DELL COMIC CHARACTERS!

LOOK FOR THEM IN YOUR LOCAL STORES NOW!

Brought to you by **DELL** too!

rector Jack Hannah and writer Carl Barks were assigned to turn the film's story into an original comic book. The result was published as the ninth in Dell's Four Color anthology series, *Donald Duck Finds Pirate Gold* (1942). It would today be considered a "graphic novel" in that the entire sixty-four pages were taken up by a single story. In fact, much of it resembled an animation storyboard, with many consecutive panels containing no dialogue. (This, no doubt, was a remnant of its origins as a proposed animated cartoon, since Donald Duck's voice could never be counted on to carry important plot exposition.)

Shortly after finishing his work on *Pirate Gold*, Barks decided to leave the full-time employ of the Disney Studio, as most of what was being produced for the screen was now war-related. Before long, though, he was back working with the beloved Disney characters, although not directly for the studio. He heard that Western Printing was looking for artists who could produce new material for *WDC&S*, and he submitted some Donald Duck material as samples of his work. Barks was hired on a freelance basis, and his long career as a comic book artist began. According to Donald Duck biographer Marcia Blitz,

> Western sent him the script for a story that had Donald protecting his victory garden from some nasty crows, and Barks, the consummate story man, asked for permission to edit and correct plot errors. The Western people were so impressed that they asked Barks to write and illustrate his own ten-page Donald Duck story. With that, he was off on a spectacular career that would take his imagination—and those of adult and child readers—where no comic book artist's had gone before.

Throughout the 1940s, Barks crafted those ten-page Donald stories for *WDC&S* and simultaneously created the longer, graphic-novel-type adventures for Donald's one-shot Dell comic books. Barks's influence on future Disney projects (and merchandise) would come about in those stories. In Dell's Four Color #178, *Christmas on Bear Mountain* (1947), Barks needed a rich relative of Donald's for plot purposes, and the result was Uncle Scrooge McDuck. At first simply a cranky miser, Scrooge's personality evolved over the next few years until he was rewarded with his own Dell comic book series in 1952. The next year, *WDC&S* reportedly became the most successful comic book of all time, selling a record three million copies each month.

Uncle Scrooge became the first Disney character originating in comic books to become a major merchandising factor. His first animated appearance was a brief cameo in the opening title sequence of TV's *Mickey Mouse Club* (1955), and by the end of that decade he was being included in toys and on records and books quite separate from his ongoing comics. This was as much a surprise to Carl Barks as anyone else; as a freelance writer and artist, he said years later, he literally had no idea whether any of his old comrades at the studio—Walt Disney included—were even aware of what he was doing. Not until Uncle Scrooge began being accepted into the cast with the rest of the Disney characters did Barks realize that his work was being recognized. Even at that, Barks had to endure the forced anonymity of all the artists who

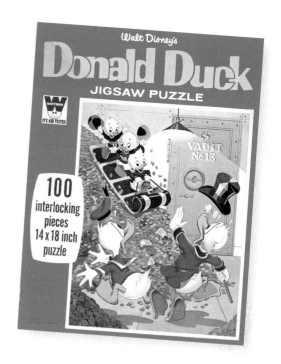

Uncle Scrooge McDuck, created by Carl Barks in 1947, was the only major Disney character to originate in comic books and subsequently be merchandised along with Donald, Mickey, and the rest.

Western Printing issued digest-sized reprints not only of its earlier Disney publications but also of the Warner Bros. and Walter Lantz characters, among others.

Members of the Dell Comics Club could obtain one of these posters to hang on their wall. All the major licensed characters appearing in Western Printing's comics got together for this publicity shot—except the ones from Disney, who were obviously felt they were too good to hobnob with the common horde.

worked on Western/Dell's licensed properties. Only when fans discovered his identity did a new phase of his life—that of comic book visionary—begin.

(Barks's merchandising success with Uncle Scrooge was pretty much a one-time event. Although his other additions to Donald's family, including the insufferably lucky Gladstone Gander, straitlaced Grandma Duck, and mad inventor Gyro Gearloose, remained prominent comic book figures, they did not translate into merchandise as frequently or as successfully as Uncle Scrooge. It is possible, however, to see at least some hereditary lineage between Gyro Gearloose and future TV/merchandising star Ludwig Von Drake.)

Of course, Barks was far from the only artist to work for Western Printing on its Disney comics; in fact, he was not even the only one to create the Donald Duck stories. But, none of the others came up with original characters that approached Uncle Scrooge's popularity outside the comics. It was not for lack of trying; one senses that any time a new comic book character was introduced, there was a hope they would find success across a wide variety of platforms. Take, for example, the case of Super Goof, Western's response to the 1960s craze for superhero comics. Introduced in 1965, Goofy's alter ego was a most entertaining character and his misadventures were published for years, but there was never a Super Goof lunch box or Halloween costume.

(Historian Jim Korkis tells of one story that took on a hilarious form of self-parody. In it, the villainous Beagle Boys attempt to brainwash the nation's children by printing counterfeit Super Goof comic books in which they win and the klutzy hero loses'.)

The friendly relations between Western and Dell extended to the many other cartoon (and noncartoon) properties in Western's seemingly bottomless bag of licensees. The Warner Bros. cartoon studio had been represented in Dell's comic line since 1941 by a diverse number of separate series, including *Looney Tunes and Merrie Melodies, Bugs Bunny* (of course), *Porky Pig, Tweety and Sylvester*, and *Beep Beep the Road Runner*. Yes, in that last one, "Beep Beep" was actually specified as the blurry bird's name; the *Road Runner* comic books probably took the greatest liberties with their source material of anything Western Printing ever generated. Not only did the Road Runner (alias Beep Beep) talk, but he did so in rhyme. He had a wife and children, who also sounded like their dialogue was written by Dr. Seuss, while Wile E. Coyote gave up his similarly mute ancestry and became a know-it-all braggart. In the cartoons, it was frequently not made clear whether the Road Runner actually realized his status as prey, but with all the new, fleshed-out personalities in the comics, his relationship with the hapless predator became quite clear. Significantly, in years to come, when Western needed to produce other

This 1950 ad for the Dell Comics Club shows the certificate that members received, decorated with many of the characters appearing in the comic books of that period. (Donnie Pitchford collection)

Oswald the Rabbit continued to appear in Western Printing's comic books long after his last cartoon had been released and even longer after Walt Disney had lost him to Universal Pictures.

This background painting from the Woody Woodpecker cartoon *Well Oiled* (1947) cleverly incorporated an ad for Dell's *New Funnies* series. (Jim Bennie collection)

Road Runner stories—for Big Little Books, Little Golden Books, Whitman Tell-A-Tale Books, and the like—the company used this "talking Road Runner" format.

The other Warner Bros. comics did not stray too far from their source material except that certain characters that were at best minor players in the theatrical cartoons enjoyed print careers that lasted much longer. Beaky Buzzard and Sniffles the Mouse were never screen stars of anywhere near the magnitude of Bugs, Daffy, or Porky, but their comic book appearances kept them prominent in coloring books, records, and other merchandise for years. Sniffles in particular departed from his animation origins to team up in the comics with a human girl, Mary Jane, who seemed more than a little inspired by *Alice in Wonderland*. Using magical powers to make herself tiny, Mary Jane and Sniffles would get into and out of one difficulty after another that the Warner Bros. animators never brought to the screen. That did not mean the studio was completely unaware of the comics; in fact, since many personnel were involved in both media, such a separation would have been next to impossible. At least one cartoon depicted Elmer Fudd reading an issue of Dell's *Looney Tunes and Merrie Melodies*, and other examples undoubtedly were used as inside jokes over the years.

(Noel Blanc, son of Warner Bros.'s vocal star Mel Blanc, has related many times that one of his fondest childhood memories is of when he would bring home a new Dell issue, and Papa Mel would have a field day reading it to him and acting out all the roles in the proper voices. One cannot help but speculate on what happened when Mel would run into characters he never played on the screen, such as Sniffles and Mary Jane.)

Western also had the Walter Lantz characters in its grip. The catchall title was *Walter Lantz New Funnies*, with other characters gaining and losing their own series over the years. Other than Woody Woodpecker's established personality, many of the other Lantz characters were basically blank slates, and their Western-created personas would be used in other merchandise. For example, Lantz had been producing cartoons with Oswald the Rabbit ever since he inadvertently inherited the hare from Walt Disney. By the 1940s, Oswald was almost dead as an animated character, but he was just beginning his comic book stardom. In the Dell comics, Oswald had two youngsters, Floyd and Lloyd, and together they had adventures that smacked heavily of Uncle Remus's stories of Brer Rabbit. Andy Panda also found new life in comics long after his final cartoon, usually teamed with sidekick Charlie Chicken. Country bumpkin Homer Pigeon had appeared in exactly one cartoon before becoming a comic book mainstay.

As with Uncle Scrooge, some Lantz characters began in the comics and then became part of other licensed items. Preeminent among these was Space Mouse, who never even appeared in an animated cartoon—at least, not one that was released. The intergalactic rodent was strictly a Western Printing creation, under the auspices of the Lantz studio, and after several appearances in comic books, coloring books, jigsaw puzzles, and so on, someone at Lantz decided maybe it was time to actually animate him. A pilot for a Space Mouse series was completed, but the series never happened, and audiences only saw the pilot after it was folded into the syndicated package of Lantz cartoons.

Judging from the number of Lantz characters that appeared together in merchandise, one would think the studio had practically the largest cast of any cartoon studio. It is ironic that while they all continued to be merchandised throughout the 1960s and into the early 1970s, by that time the studio was down to producing only three or four actual series; no doubt the licensing fees Lantz received from Western for all of those characters were largely keeping the studio in the black.

Popeye was such a major cartoon character that Western and Dell could not ignore him, either. As with some other characters, the old squint was

Walter Lantz created Space Mouse especially for Western Printing, and the character's only cartoon appearance occurred in an unsold TV pilot. His adventures continued in comic books, coloring books, and jigsaw puzzles for most of the 1960s.

Popeye became a Western Printing/Dell Comics regular in 1948, and his comics would continue without a break until 1966. (Donnie Pitchford collection)

By the time of this 1953 Christmas-themed ad, Western and Dell had the majority of the most famous licensed characters in their stable. (Donnie Pitchford collection)

first tested out in some single Four Color issues before gaining his own series in 1948. Drawn by Bud Sagendorf, Dell's Popeye comic books read more as an extension of the newspaper strip than an extension of Paramount's theatrical cartoons. Elements such as Popeye pulling out a can of spinach and eating it to gain an extra burst of strength were rare in the comic books until after the cartoons were sold to television and shot to the top of the ratings charts. Even then, Sagendorf hesitated to stray too far away from Popeye's print roots, and the comic book stories were often masterpieces of adventure and humor blended seamlessly.

Another newspaper strip that enjoyed a more unlikely run in comic books was *Peanuts*. This was unusual since Charles Schulz was notoriously insistent on trying to do everything himself. At first, the *Peanuts* comic book appearances were limited to reprints of the newspaper strips published through United Feature Syndicate. Just when these began has been a matter of dispute, but in Schulz's October 5, 1951, daily strip—coincidentally, just three days past the comic strip's first anniversary—he included two of the titles, *Tip Top* and *Nancy*, in his artwork of a drugstore comic book rack.

After a brief sojourn at the St. John company, the former United Features comics were absorbed by Western Printing and Dell in late 1957, and for the first time, new *Peanuts* material was produced to meet the demand. Four issues in Dell's Four Color series were devoted to *Peanuts*, after which the strip gained its own regularly published books. With all of this going on, there was no way Schulz could keep up with the books as well as his regular strip, so he reluctantly (it was like pulling Snoopy's teeth to get him to admit it) turned the comic book work over to some artistic assistants, first Jim Sasseville and later Dale Hale. Historian Derrick Bang tried to trace the evolution of the non-Schulz *Peanuts* stories and found that as Dell continued the series into 1962–63, the art and writing resembled Schulz's less and less as time went by. It probably did not disturb Schulz in the least when Dell finally discontinued the *Peanuts* comic books.

Western also grabbed the rights to the MGM cartoon studio's characters beginning in the 1940s. The big stars, of course, were Tom and Jerry; like the Road Runner series, Western decided that the cat and mouse had to talk in their comic books, and that carried over to most of the other merchandise in which they appeared over the years. Barney Bear and Droopy, MGM's other characters, made regular comic book appearances, some created by Carl Barks in between his Donald Duck projects. For the comics, Barney was paired with Benny Burro, another of those characters that had appeared in only one animated cartoon but lived on in merchandise thanks to Western.

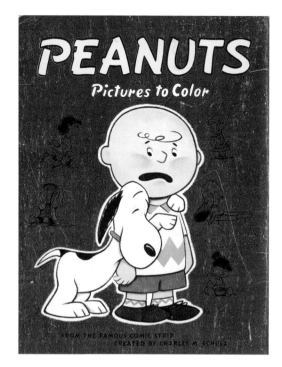

Dell's *Peanuts* comic books were not drawn by Charles Schulz, and it is obvious that neither was the cover of this coloring book that was issued at about the same time.

For their comic book stories, Tom and Jerry learned to talk. Their issues also included features with their fellow MGM stars Barney Bear and Droopy.

In 1962, Western Printing pulled its comic book license from Dell and began publishing its own highly successful line, Gold Key Comics. Most of the same series continued unabated, and new ones were frequently added.

When MGM closed its cartoon studio and Tom and Jerry's creators, William Hanna and Joseph Barbera, began making cartoons for TV, Western was standing by to lasso those new characters, too. Dell published several issues each of *Ruff and Reddy*, *Huckleberry Hound*, and *Yogi Bear*, but about that time, something occurred that would drastically alter all of the aforementioned characters' offscreen careers. According to comic book historian Joe Torcivia,

> One day in the early 1960s, the unthinkable happened. When most newsstand comic books sold for 10 or maybe 12 cents, Dell Comics raised their cover price to an apocalyptical FIFTEEN CENTS! THREE CENTS more than the competition! As a result, sales plummeted. Western Publishing ended its distribution arrangement with Dell, and Gold Key Comics, a new imprint of Western, was born.

Torcivia speculates that the "Gold Key" name might have had something to do with Western's Little Golden Books, but that is unlikely considering that the sophisticated Golden Books editors would probably have considered comic books lower than dirt under their shoes. In any case, Gold Key Comics made their newsstand debut in the summer of 1962, with practically all of the

same titles and series Western had been furnishing for Dell. *Walt Disney's Comics and Stories* continued uninterrupted, and so did the Lantz, MGM, and Hanna-Barbera characters. Popeye, too, jumped ship to Gold Key, with his stories still supplied by Bud Sagendorf.

During most of the rest of the 1960s, Gold Key continued to unlock dozens more new adventures of all these characters as well as many of the new Saturday morning TV stars that made their debuts each September, but things soon began to fall apart somewhat. In 1966, King Features Syndicate abruptly decided to pull the licensing of all its characters away from Western Publishing and begin its own comic book company, King Comics. This affected not only *Popeye* but *The Phantom*, *Flash Gordon*, *Mandrake the Magician*, and *Beetle Bailey*. The experiment lasted just over a year, after which King Comics retreated into the Hearst castle and the characters fell into other hands—but not back into Western's.

The next stop for Popeye and his pals, to most observers' way of thinking, was something like moving from a Beverly Hills mansion into the Beverly Hillbillies' mountain shack. With decidedly inferior writing and artwork, Charlton Comics had not enjoyed the best reputation among comic book fans. Until the late 1960s, Charlton had never even been home to licensed cartoon characters; instead, it had filled the gap with series that were more than a little "inspired" by established stars from various cartoon studios. It does not require much imagination to figure out where Charlton got the ideas for its original characters Atomic Mouse, Pudgy Pig, and Timmy the Timid Ghost. Charlton's *Li'l Genius* did not even attempt to camouflage the fact that it was copying Dennis the Menace and his castmates. This, then, was the tough new neighborhood into which Popeye and his fellow KFS properties were moving.

Apparently the King Features characters enjoyed reading their own comic book adventures, even the little-remembered female hero, Girl Phantom.

King Features Syndicate took the bold step of withdrawing its licenses from other comic book publishers and starting its own King Comics division. The experiment lasted only about a year and a half. (Donnie Pitchford collection)

Once Charlton Comics assumed responsibility for the King Features properties in 1969, the company proudly displayed its new acquisitions on its delivery trucks. (Donnie Pitchford collection)

Popeye did have at least one advantage: King Features still had a very few Bud Sagendorf stories and art left over from unpublished issues of King Comics, so the transition went smoothly. The Charlton editor who had arranged the deal with KFS was Dick Giordano; soon, however, Charlton's new editor, George Wildman, took over the *Popeye* art chores, with the writing handled by staffers Joe Gill and Nicola Cuti. After some early rough spots in which brief stories would begin and end with no warning, Wildman and his writers got more comfortable with Popeye, and during the 1970s, the stories and art improved with each issue. The other King Features characters followed a similar path, and Charlton soon seemed like a particularly cozy old home for them all.

Unfortunately, such was not the case for the other major group of licensed characters Charlton inherited from Western. At about the same time Popeye was changing course, Western lost its rights to the vast majority of the Hanna-Barbera properties. (For a while, Western retained its rights to more current H-B TV shows, but since none of them were anywhere near as successful as the early stars, this was a somewhat hollow victory.) Veteran comic book writer Mark Evanier explained to interviewer Mark Arnold that this seismic shift in the licensing business came about partly because the huge Taft Broadcasting empire had purchased the Hanna-Barbera Studio, and suddenly there were business interests involved that had little to do with making entertaining Saturday morning cartoons. At the same time, the Gold Key stories and art that were being turned out were then sold to overseas comic book publishers, and everyone was making enough money to fill several of Yogi's pic-a-nic baskets. But, as often happens, too much was not enough for some. Taft and Hanna-Barbera wanted Western to publish even more comics to generate more material for overseas, but Western felt it had enough Hanna-Barbera titles on the market as it was. Evanier recalled,'

When Gold Key said no to publishing any more Hanna-Barbera comics, this gentleman at Taft Broadcasting went around to other comic book publishers and asked, "Hey, would you like to publish a whole bunch of Hanna-Barbera comics?" and Charlton said, "Yeah, sure." Charlton was willing to put out a lot of them and, of course, to have Charlton writers and artists produce all these pages. The guy at Taft thought they were going to make a fortune, and they might have except that the foreign publishers didn't like the Charlton material and many of them refused to buy it. They felt the characters were off-model, and they didn't like a lot of the scripts.

It is true that the Hanna-Barbera stories and art went into a tailspin in the hands of Charlton. At least Popeye had input from some of his longtime associates, but as Evanier indicated, Charlton's Hanna-Barbera comics were being produced by people who seemed to understand little about the characters. In our next chapter, we will see how Western's loss of the rights to these characters affected more than just comic books, as all of the other merchandise formerly being produced by Western also went to other, inferior companies.

(To wrap up the Hanna-Barbera story, after seven years of dealing with Charlton and the reluctant foreign buyers, those licenses moved over to Marvel Comics, which kept them going for another year and a half. Much later, Archie Comics made an attempt to revive some of the Hanna-Barbera titles, but by that time the market for comic books had shifted from kids in the corner drugstore to collectors in the local hobby shop.)

At least in the case of the Hanna-Barbera characters, moving from Western/Gold Key to Charlton Comics marked a decline in art and writing. This extremely off-model Yogi Bear on an early Charlton issue is a prime example.

Charlton no doubt began the Yogi Bear Fan Club (and similar promotions for some of its other titles) as a way to measure just how much interest was being generated by its new series.

Hanna-Barbera Parade was Charlton's equivalent to *Walt Disney's Comics and Stories* in its mix of characters. Why, however, is good guy Touché Turtle using his sword to steal food? Had Charlton reduced his paycheck to that level?

Around the same time Charlton acquired the Hanna-Barbera license, it also enlisted a group of characters that had never before made much of an impression in comic books. Dell and later Gold Key had published a few issues of *Rocky and His Friends* and then *Bullwinkle and Rocky* between 1960 and 1963, but Jay Ward's much-beloved TV output had otherwise been absent from comics. Its style of humor was extremely difficult to recapture in print, as most of the comic books demonstrated. Apparently through the efforts of our old friend Peter Piech, whom we encountered in the previous chapter, Charlton arranged to publish not only a *Bullwinkle and Rocky* series but *Dudley Do-Right* and (true to Piech's usual business practices) Total TeleVision's *Underdog*. Underdog had previously not appeared in any comic books, and his TV show was long out of production, but the enterprising Piech somehow got "humble, lovable Shoeshine Boy" his own temporary street corner at Charlton.

Charlton's staff had no better luck in re-creating the nutty humor of the Ward TV shows but at least played it safe by adapting most of the *Underdog* stories from the actual television scripts. The experiment did not last long, basically covering 1970 and 1971, before Piech's wards again became free agents. By the middle of the 1970s, Western had picked them up for the Gold Key line, and they remained in print until the end of the decade.

After the great Ward/TTV project expired, Popeye, too, walked the Charlton plank at roughly the same time as Yogi and the Flintstones. His fate was a much happier one, however. In 1978, most of the King Features properties went "back home" to Western Publishing and Gold Key, and everyone seemed very happy with the arrangement. George Wildman continued to provide the Popeye art, moonlighting from his regular job as Charlton's editor, and with some fine scripts by writers Bill Pearson and Nicola Cuti (also moonlighting from Charlton), the latter-day Western/Popeye material reached new heights of art and storytelling.

To be fair to all involved, the Charlton era for all of these characters might not totally deserve the universally bad rap it seems to have gotten. As Charlton expert and historian Michael Ambrose says,

Undoubtedly both Charlton and King made lots of dough from all the licensed comics, however despised they might have been by true fans, collectors or

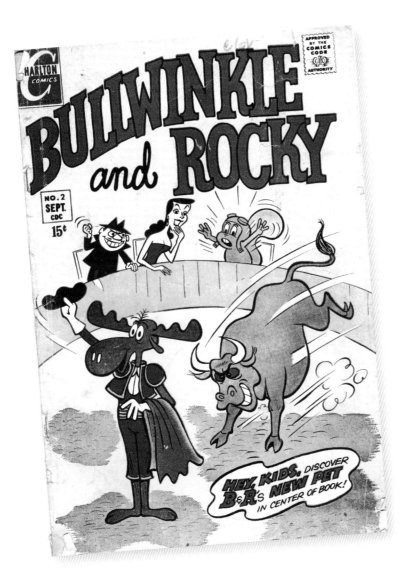

In 1970, Charlton acquired the *Bullwinkle and Rocky* license and began a series based on Jay Ward's *Dudley Do-Right*.

Thanks to their common representation by Peter Piech, Underdog joined the Jay Ward characters at Charlton in 1970. Strangely, the super canine had never before had his own regularly issued comic book title.

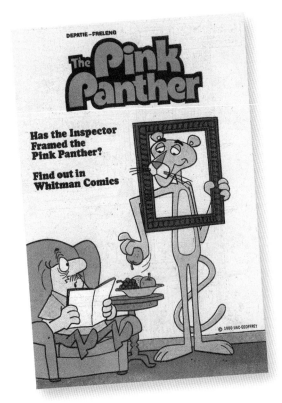

Like Tom and Jerry and the Road Runner in years past, Western Printing forced the formerly mute Pink Panther to learn to speak in his long-running comic book series. (Donnie Pitchford collection)

In the late 1970s, Western began issuing many of its comic book series under two imprints: Gold Key, for newsstand sales, and Whitman, for packing in cellophane bags of three and selling in variety stores and supermarkets. (Donnie Pitchford collection)

foreign publishers. They put out tons of them for almost a decade and they're still plentiful in the back issue market—and rare to find in non-beat-up condition, which if nothing else indicates they were read and reread by lots of kids.

Therein may lie the answer: kids did not care how simplistic a comic book story might be as long as they could read and understand it. Shortly thereafter, however, the changing face of the comic book market put a major crimp in the way comics were being sold, especially Western's. Although newsstand copies continued under the Gold Key imprint, Western began issuing alternate versions of the same comic books under its long-established Whitman logo. (Whitman had been responsible for an incredible number of licensed cartoon character books since the early 1930s, but this was the first time the brand name had been applied to comics.) The Whitman-labeled comic books were meant to be packaged in cellophane bags of three and sold in toy stores, supermarkets, and other places where spinning racks could be installed. This new sales approach applied not only to Popeye but also to Western's other major series, including the Disney and Warner Bros. titles. Collectors, who were becoming a major force in the comics industry by that time, were thrown into one tizzy after another because the dual identity of Gold Key and Whitman, with their now-unpredictable release schedules, made a mess out of trying to keep up with issue numbers and dates. Some books were issued and then reissued under different numbers a few months later, while

Western Printing might have temporarily lost its King Features and Hanna-Barbera licenses, but the company proved it could still deliver the goods with its series based on other studios' characters. (Donnie Pitchford collection)

After almost a decade at Charlton, Popeye returned to Gold Key in 1978, and ads such as this one confirmed that Western Printing welcomed back the prodigal sailor. (Donnie Pitchford collection)

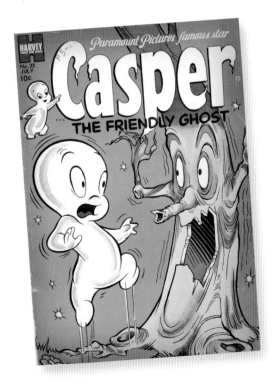

some issue numbers never appeared at all. Limping and mortally wounded, the legendary comic book career of Western Printing and Lithographing finally collapsed in 1984, by which time the last of the baby boomers were probably buying comics only as a financial investment (if they were buying them at all).

The preceding pages (and pages, and pages . . .) of discussion might lead one to believe that Western's various comic book escapades were the only ones that mattered. Oh, but one would be so, so wrong. As an example of a company that found its niche and stayed in it, we now turn to the saga of Harvey Comics.

With the exception of its comic books based on George Baker's World War II character Sad Sack and Chic Young's *Blondie* comic strip (about which more a little later), Harvey's licensed character lineup was derived from the properties owned by Paramount's cartoon studio. You will recall from an earlier discussion that Popeye was the big breadwinner for Paramount, but when it came to merchandising, he was a bit useless because he was 100 percent owned by King Features Syndicate, and the only green stuff Paramount saw was the spinach he consumed. In the early 1940s, Paramount had faced a similar problem with its highly successful animated adaptation of Marjorie Buell's Little Lulu, and by the latter half of the decade, the studio made a conscious attempt to develop characters it could control and license at will.

The first comic book company to license Paramount's original characters was St. John, but in 1952, the rights were transferred to Harvey Comics. Veteran Harvey editor Sid Jacobson explains that the company began taking deliberate steps to remold some of the Paramount properties into forms more suitable for the children's market. (Although adults could and still do enjoy the humor of the Harvey comic books, they were much more targeted at children than, say, Carl Barks's satirical Donald Duck/Uncle Scrooge adventures.) For the first few years of his screen career, Paramount had gone to great lengths to drive home the point that Casper the Friendly Ghost was indeed a dead little boy. His cartoons often showed him in his natural habitat, living next to his own tombstone in the cemetery, and some of the stories actually depicted supporting characters dying and then returning to cavort with Casper in the afterlife. This was hardly what Harvey wanted.

According to Jacobson, the Casper comic books did away with all of the macabre trappings and established the idea that in their world, ghosts were simply another type of fantasy creature on a par with elves and fairies. They had their own society, and they were born as ghosts, not the spirits of deceased humans and animals. This made it simple to take the next step and introduce other characters that could conceivably coexist in such a universe; Wendy the Good Little Witch; Hot Stuff, the ill-tempered devil; Stumbo the Giant; and so on. There were a number of additional ghost characters too, including Casper's tough guy friend, Spooky; Nightmare, the spirit horse; and the nefarious Ghostly Trio, those three obnoxious revenants who constantly wanted Casper to drop his namby-pamby niceness and be like them.

Of course, Harvey's comics also included Little Audrey, Baby Huey, Herman and Katnip, and the rest of the Paramount crew. By 1959, the comic books were doing so much better financially than the theatrical cartoons that Harvey made a deal to buy the whole cast of characters outright, making them Harvey's property instead of Paramount's. (Just to complete the story, Paramount continued producing theatrical cartoons for the next eight years, but since few people have ever heard of its latter-day characters such as Swifty and Shorty, Goodie the Gremlin, and Honey Halfwitch, it is obvious that the magic left with Casper—both figuratively and literally.)

Harvey rebranded all the existing cartoons with its new characters as "Harveytoons" and moved into the TV animation business. With its own creations such as Wendy and Spooky now introduced into the cartoons, the merchandising possibilities grew like Stumbo. Harvey introduced a staggering number of new human characters, too, including Richie Rich, Little Dot, and Little Lotta, each of whom had a personality quirk or gimmick that was good for story after story. Some of them were more successful in merchandising than others, but none could hold a floating candelabra to Casper, whose cheerful visage continued to enlighten toy shelves well into the 1980s.

Other cartoon studios' major characters enjoyed second careers in comics. One of those was Felix the Cat, whose offscreen antics have been nicely summarized by comics fan and historian Donnie Pitchford:

> Animator Otto Messmer gave life to Felix the Cat in the cartoons released by Pat Sullivan's studio, and is generally considered the creator of that silent film star. After the Sullivan studio's demise, Messmer continued to oversee the Felix the Cat newspaper comic strip, handling much of the pencil-and-ink work himself from its 1923 debut. Messmer's association with the newspaper strip

The 1954 line of Harvey Comics titles included not only the Paramount characters but some licensed newspaper strips and even a few original creations.

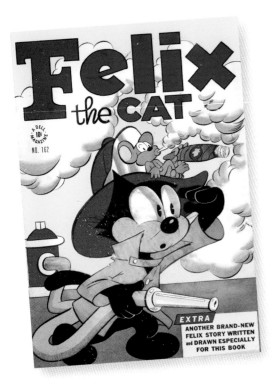

The character design Otto Messmer used for his Felix the Cat comics did not much resemble the way the cheerful feline had appeared in his silent cartoons, nor did it look like his later made-for-TV design. (Donnie Pitchford collection)

ended when assistant Joe Oriolo replaced him in 1954. Messmer's whimsical work with the cat continued in comic books. Dell Comics' Four Color series featured Felix newspaper strip reprints in scattered issues beginning in 1942, with new stories produced by Messmer beginning in 1946. Two years later, Dell introduced Felix the Cat's starring series with issue #1, still featuring the charming work of Messmer. Messmer was assisted in comic books by Joe Oriolo and Jim Tyer along the way. Toby Press (founded by Elliot Caplin, brother of Al Capp, creator of Li'l Abner) acquired the rights with issue #20 in 1951, publishing the title until the 61st issue (1955).

The numbering was continued with issues 61–118 (1955–1961) by Harvey Comics, with limited contributions from Messmer as his work in other media became more demanding. Felix returned to Dell in 1962, during the post-Western era, in a run that lasted 12 issues. By then, Felix was recognized by young viewers of the Joe Oriolo television series as a character quite different from his silent movie era concept.

At the same time, Pitchford also put together a brief history of the Terrytoons characters' journey through the revolving door of publishers:

Timely Comics (which eventually became Marvel) introduced its own imitations of animated cartoon characters before contracting with Terry and launching the Terrytoons title in 1942. It originally starred the now almost forgotten Dinky Duck, Little Roquefort, Gandy Goose, and Oscar Pig. Terrytoons' Mighty Mouse as a comic book has had quite a publishing history, leaping into his own title for four issues in 1946–47. St. John (named for publisher Archer St. John) trapped the mouse and published Adventures of Mighty Mouse from 1952–55. Art Bartsch, a Terrytoons staff artist, provided much of the art, providing the series with an authentic flavor. The mouse even leaped right off the pages in 1953, making history as the star of the first 3-D comic book! The process used glasses constructed of red and green cellophane lenses mounted in cardboard frames to convert the red and green printed images into a 3-D viewing experience. This helped the mouse issue to sell more than a million copies and inspired the competition to jump into all three dimensions with similar devices (others used red and blue).

Those movie magpies Heckle and Jeckle received their own title at St. John in 1951, enjoying a 24-issue span before Pines Comics picked up the Terrytoons titles from 1956–59. The Pines series featured the CBS-TV logo on the covers. It was 1959 when Terry's characters finally settled at Western and Dell, home of the most famous of all animated stars. They made the transition

to Gold Key when Western established that trademark in 1962 with Heckle and Jeckle and New Terrytoons, which eventually added "with Mighty Mouse" to the title. The title Adventures of Mighty Mouse was revived by Western in 1979, ceasing publication the following year.

The Fox and the Crow starred in theatrical cartoons from 1941 to 1950, but their long-running comic book series from DC lasted until 1968. (Donnie Pitchford collection)

Pitchford goes on to elaborate that both Felix and Mighty Mouse enjoyed brief revivals in the early 1990s, by which time they were of more interest to animation historians than the traditional audience for comic books.

We should also consider the case of the Fox and Crow, two battling characters created by Columbia's animation studio in 1941. Even though their series of theatrical cartoons lasted only until 1950, their comic book adventures published by DC continued until 1968, by which time no doubt few people even remembered they had ever been animated characters.

Before leaving this discussion, we need to look at one special licensed property that maintained a remarkable consistency during the years it was shuttled from one comic book publisher to another. That hardy survivor was

By 1957, the *Blondie* comic book series was celebrating its one hundredth issue. As you can see, the Bumsteads were in good company with the rest of Harvey's output. (Donnie Pitchford collection)

Blondie, which we have already seen was the most popular newspaper strip in the world during its heyday. It came to comic books early, with the David McKay company beginning a series reprinting the strip in 1942. In the early 1950s, Dagwood collided with Beasley the mailman in his haste to switch over to Harvey Comics, a relationship that endured until King Features pulled back all of its characters for the ill-fated King Comics series. For most of 1968, *Blondie* lingered in limbo (while its live-action TV series came and went), and then in 1969 the Bumstead family joined Charlton's line along with the other KFS stars. When that series ended in November 1976, so did *Blondie*'s comic book career, as for some reason Western/Gold Key chose not to pick it up. One remarkable aspect of this meandering journey is that for the vast majority of *Blondie*'s comic book life span, for all of those different publishers, a single artist, Paul Fung Jr., was responsible for keeping it going. Fung arguably came to understand the world of *Blondie* better than anyone except its creator, and he deserves much credit for keeping the look and flavor of the series consistent throughout its checkered publication history.

We told you at the outset that this chapter could do little but give a brief overview of the influence of comic books as both licensed merchandise and the inspiration for other licensed merchandise. So it has, and in the pages to come we will be returning to the characters and properties discussed here to see just what the future had in store for them. For now, put those comics back in the rack and follow us into the next chapter for a look at some completely different types of books.

Chapter Three

READ MORE ABOUT IT

Many kids no doubt learned to read via the comic books we just finished discussing. But another entire classification of books based on cartoon favorites was a bit more "literary" (but *only* a bit) than comic books, and since those have not received nearly as much historical attention over the years, we will now spend considerably more time examining them.

Actually, the early history of these books has been covered elsewhere, so we will only briefly give the basic background info here. Anyone wishing a comprehensive history is hereby referred to Leonard Marcus's lavish 2007 coffee table book, *Golden Legacy: How Golden Books Won Children's Hearts, Changed Publishing Forever, and Became an American Icon along the Way*. Wow, no pressure to produce something definitive there, huh, Leonard? Anyway, as with the comic book history, the story of cartoon-related children's storybooks really begins with Western Printing and Lithographing.

According to Marcus, this Racine, Wisconsin, printing company more or less got into the publishing business accidentally, when it took possession of a huge stock of children's books it had printed for the Hamming-Whitman Publishing Company of Chicago.

When Hamming-Whitman could not pay its printing bill, Western acquired the stock of books and did so well at selling them that Western's founder, Edward Wadewitz, bought the whole Hamming-Whitman enterprise, moved it to Racine, and gave it a new name, Whitman Publishing Company. Despite its name, by the 1920s, books were only a part of the Whitman output. As Marcus describes it, "After setting up a box department to streamline Western's shipping operation, someone suggested finding a product for the company to make and sell in boxes. It was on this basis that Western began manufacturing jigsaw puzzles and games."

At this point, Marcus introduces us to a Western Printing salesman, Samuel Lowe, who would, in effect, do for Western/Whitman what Kay Kamen did for the Disney studio. The first of his many successful and profitable ideas for the company was the Big Little Books series. Significantly, the two earliest Big Little Books came about because of Lowe's pitch to the Chicago Tribune–New York News Syndicate; in December 1932, Whitman published *The Adventures of Dick Tracy*, with *Little Orphan Annie* on the detective's trail in April 1933. Big Little Books certainly seemed to be a big little bargain to depression-era

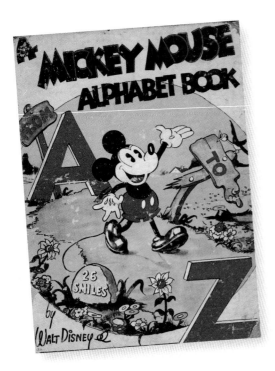

In 1933, Western Printing and Lithographing made a deal with Walt Disney and his studio to have the Whitman imprint publish storybooks featuring the ever-growing cast of characters.

shoppers. The tiny hardback volumes could contain more than four hundred pages each and retailed for a dime. The Big Little Book format was simple: the text was printed on the left-hand pages, while an illustration appeared on every right-hand page. Marcus reports that those first two comic-strip-based Big Little Books sold a combined total of six hundred thousand copies within four months, and that gave Lowe the courage to approach the big fish in the cartoon pond, Walt Disney.

Showing archival care that is surprisingly rare in the corporate world, someone thought to preserve a copy of the original letter Lowe sent to Walt on April 19, 1933, enclosing copies of the *Dick Tracy* and *Little Orphan Annie* books and proposing to license Mickey Mouse for a similar volume. The first Mickey books had appeared a couple of years earlier, but as Lowe persuasively wrote in his letter, "This 'Big Little Book' is unique in itself, and we are intending to follow up the books already published with other titles that will have appeal to the children."

That, friends, was the beginning of a quite monumental deal between Western and Disney that would eventually produce thousands of books, games, and puzzles, plus the world's first theme park—but we will get to that later. Back to the topic of Big Little Books, throughout the 1930s and 1940s (they were rebranded as Better Little Books in 1938 because other publishers were copying the format), their licensed subjects ranged into all corners of the known cartoon universe, with titles including *Popeye the Sailor Sees the Sea*, *Felix the Cat*, *Bringing Up Father*, *Li'l Abner in New York*, *Oswald the Lucky Rabbit*, *Mickey Mouse and the Sacred Jewel*, *Blondie: Papa Knows Best*, *Bugs Bunny and His Pals*, and *Andy Panda's Vacation*, among dozens more.

Whitman Publishing's Big Little Books were a big little success during the depression. For a dime, kids could have a four-hundred-page illustrated story based on every imaginable type of licensed cartoon or comic strip character.

Western/Whitman also published many other Disney books that were not a part of the Big Little series. One of particular interest is *Dippy the Goof* (1938), which came during the Dr. Jekyll–like metamorphosis of Dippy Dawg into Goofy. Even the anonymous author of this slim volume was unsure about what to call the title character. Take, for example, these lines that sound like a copy editor was badly needed:

"Hi, Goofy!" Mickey Mouse greeted his tall friend. "Whatcha doin'?"

"Diggin'," said Dippy the Goof. He paused in his labors and placed one foot wearily on his shovel.

Mickey whistled as he looked over Dippy's garden. The ground was full of holes. Goofy was digging.

"Watcha diggin' for?" Mickey asked.

"Aw," Dippy grunted, "I lost somethin' and I'm tryin' to find it."

By that point, if kids had not figured out whether Mickey were talking to Dippy or Goofy, they might have been feeling a bit goofy themselves.

In 1942, Western partnered with New York publishing house Simon and Schuster to launch a new series of children's books. Realizing that most hardbound full-color picture books retailed for around two dollars—a considerable amount to spend on an impulse purchase in those days—the publishers had decided to offer comparable quality for only a quarter. The books would be immediately identifiable by a strip of gold-colored foil on their spines and thus became known as Little Golden Books.

Not until 1944 did Simon and Schuster make use of Western's existing license with Disney, and even then it was for only two titles. In 1947–49, the Disney subset of Golden Books got fatter, with nine more volumes, all based on recent animated features. Somehow, the idea of coming up with original stories for Disney Little Golden Books did not hit until 1950, with *Donald Duck's Adventure*, penned by Annie North Bedford.

Now, Bedford could well qualify as one of the most prolific children's authors in the industry—if she had been a real person. She was not. The name was more of an inside joke than anything else, as Western Printing had a Los Angeles office on North Bedford Drive. It is somewhat odd that Disney's Little Golden Books usually credited the illustrator, but the author would be listed as simply "Walt Disney Studios" or the fictitious Bedford. (One author who posed as Bedford was Jane Werner, and sometimes she actually got to write under her own name as well.) Most of the illustrators were simultaneously employed working on the many comic book titles Western was

Donald Duck's Adventure (1950) was the first Disney Little Golden Book not based on an existing film. The credited author, Annie North Bedford (the name used for most of the Disney titles from Golden), was as fictional as Donald.

producing for Dell, and several of them were past or present Disney Studio staff, since they would obviously know more than anyone how to draw the characters properly.

When Golden Books published its first non-Disney licensed title, *Bugs Bunny* (1949), the company likewise employed Warner Bros. artists—in this case Tom McKimson and Al Dempster—to illustrate it. The story proved prophetic about how Western in general and Little Golden Books in particular would handle many characters. The Disney cast was a relatively innocuous bunch as a whole, but the rowdy characters from Warner Bros. (and, within a few years, MGM and Walter Lantz) were another story. Their usual behavior on the screen would not quite pass the critical eye of parents or especially the children's education professionals Golden Books employed to be sure all content was healthy and clean.

In his cartoons, Bugs Bunny normally triumphed over his adversaries by cunning and trickery, in the best Brer Rabbit tradition. The Little Golden Books, however, frowned on such antics. In his inaugural 1949 story, Bugs loafs when he should be helping Porky Pig plant a carrot patch; then, in a fit of jealousy, the wascally wabbit spreads tacks on the road to get revenge on Elmer Fudd for having a new motor scooter. Before the end of the tale, Bugs has instead stepped into the tacks and crippled himself, after which a kindly Elmer ignores the tacks' original purpose and helps Bugs home to bed. All in all, it is a much gentler take on the familiar characters, tempered only by the last sentence: "Bugs had learned his lesson . . . maybe."

M-G-M's
TOM and JERRY
and their Friends

128 PAGES IN FULL COLOR

A GOLDEN STORY BOOK

Western Printing licensed Tom and Jerry from MGM for Little Golden Books, Whitman books, and occasional other compilations such as this one.

Although the cover of this 1952 Little Golden Book says simply *Woody Woodpecker*, the title page reads *Woody Woodpecker Joins the Circus*.

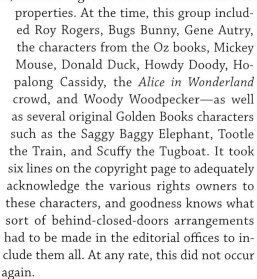

Golden brought MGM's biggest cartoon stars into the fold with 1951's simply titled *Tom and Jerry*. This battling pair was not sanitized quite as much as Bugs Bunny was in his Golden Books debut, although the story did carry over from the Dell comics the notion of having the usually silent characters talk to each other. As an example of not sugarcoating the usual conflict, on one page we read, "Tom Cat and Jerry Mouse were not good friends. Tom Cat would have liked to eat Jerry up. And Jerry didn't want that at all." The usual bash-'em-over-the-head violence was toned down, though, with Tom getting only grains of rice shot at his nose and a dunk in a nearby pond.

In 1952, one Golden Book bore the title *Woody Woodpecker* on the cover and *Woody Woodpecker Joins the Circus* on the title page. Either way, Woody's personality was flexible enough that the story did not ring any false notes—except the ones that came out of Woody's trumpet when he attempted to join the circus band and see the show for free. Andy Panda appeared in a cameo role.

Western made use of all its various licenses in a unique way in the 1951 Golden Book *Here Comes the Parade*. Although at its most basic it is a thinly disguised treatment of the annual Macy's Thanksgiving Day Parade, what makes the story so unusual for its time is that, more than thirty-five years before *Who Framed Roger Rabbit*, it mixes together all of Western's licensed properties. At the time, this group included Roy Rogers, Bugs Bunny, Gene Autry, the characters from the Oz books, Mickey Mouse, Donald Duck, Howdy Doody, Hopalong Cassidy, the *Alice in Wonderland* crowd, and Woody Woodpecker—as well as several original Golden Books characters such as the Saggy Baggy Elephant, Tootle the Train, and Scuffy the Tugboat. It took six lines on the copyright page to adequately acknowledge the various rights owners to these characters, and goodness knows what sort of behind-closed-doors arrangements had to be made in the editorial offices to include them all. At any rate, this did not occur again.

Even the addition of characters from other studios could not harm Western Printing's long and comfortable relationship with

Walt Disney. So when Walt decided to carry out his crazy idea of building an amusement park in Anaheim, California—one in which everything would be built around a theme, with no roller coasters, Ferris wheels, or games of chance—he approached Western about investing in his untested scheme. What did he have to lose? The bankers had already turned him down. Western Printing had enough faith in the Disney magic to invest in the new park to the tune of two hundred thousand dollars. The other major investor was the fledgling ABC television network, which poured money into the park in exchange for Walt producing his first weekly TV series. The show would be known as *Disneyland*, and the park would be known as—Disneyland.

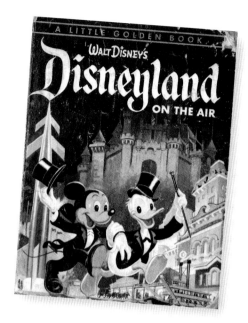

The TV *Disneyland* premiered in October 1954, and the amusement park opened in July 1955. With so much of its own money riding on the project, Western Printing was not going to waste an opportunity to promote it. During early 1955, the Little Golden Book *Disneyland on the Air* appeared. The short preface on the copyright page explained, "Disneyland, in southern California, is truly the land of childhood's dreams come true. Millions have visited this magic land on TV, and soon will in reality. Here for the first time some of its delights may be sampled in book form." The story involves Mickey Mouse apparently hosting the premiere episode of the television program direct from the Opera House on Main Street U.S.A. Naturally, Donald Duck is determined to be the star of the show but is thwarted at every turn by his costars Minnie, Goofy, Pluto, Tinker Bell, and Horace Horsecollar and even by the screening of 1933's *Three Little Pigs* short. "Those hams could never act," Donald grumbles to no one in particular.

Both of these Little Golden Books were published to introduce the new amusement park concept of Disneyland, in which Western Printing and Lithographing had made a major financial investment.

Shortly after that, Golden Books came up with an even more unusual take on the subject, *Little Man of Disneyland*. Set sometime before the first book, this one relates the tale of Patrick Begorra, a leprechaun who lives in a Southern California orange grove. He is understandably irritated when a group of

workers—namely, Mickey, Donald, Goofy, and Pluto—arrive to begin some sort of construction project. When they explain that it is going to be Disneyland, a new kind of amusement park, and that Patrick will be able to make his home somewhere within the acreage, he relaxes. Rumor has it that the Disneyland designers intended to hide a replica of the elf's home somewhere in the park as a way of tying in with this story, but that project somehow got put aside before opening day.

Just as one book showed the Disney characters as celebrities and the other made them out to be the crew that physically built the park, future books contradicted themselves regarding the cartoon characters' relationship with the place. In some stories they would visit and experience the attractions like any other tourists, while other books presented them as living in Disneyland all the time.

By this time, Western Printing was responsible for other series besides Simon and Schuster's Golden Books line. In 1945, Whitman had begun publishing the Tell-A-Tale Books, roughly half the size of Golden Books, but the licensed cartoon titles in the series began appearing in the early 1950s. Their style, in both text and illustrations, differed drastically from the treatment given to the same characters in Golden's line. A major reason for this is that the Tell-A-Tale books (and their eventual spinoffs, Top Top Tales and Big Tell-A-Tales) were marketed as strictly for fun, without the claim to being approved by educators, as Golden Books were.

One example of Whitman's more slam-bang (or maybe wham-bam) approach to humor is *Tom and Jerry and the Toy Circus* (1953). When Jerry and his sidekick, Tuffy, receive a toy circus—which actually seems more like a carnival, considering the miniature rides that are part of it—Tom decides to crash the party and take over the show. These paragraphs are a long way from Golden Books' gentle version of the characters:

> "We'll see about that!" Jerry said, running toward the Ferris wheel. "You'll never catch us!"
>
> "Oh, won't I?" Tom exclaimed. He stretched out a big paw. But Jerry was too quick. He pulled hard on the lever and the Ferris wheel began spinning, each little seat hitting Tom squarely on the head. "Ouch! Owww! Ouch!"

Bugs Bunny Hangs Around (1957) is closer in tone to the wabbit's first Golden Books story, but the smart-aleck hare gets to have a few characteristic moments. In one sequence, he volunteers to help Elmer Fudd weed his carrot patch, and Elmer is such a dope that he falls for it:

After a few minutes, Elmer went into the house. He made a pitcher of cold lemonade and cut a huge piece of cake. Then he went to the window and called, ''Oh, Bugs! Come on in and cool off. You've been working *so hard* out there in the garden.''

This two-page spread from *Bugs Bunny Hangs Around* (1957) demonstrates the Whitman illustrators' almost photographic approach to depicting beloved cartoon characters; Elmer's lemonade and chocolate cake look good enough to eat.

Bugs took the hoe and headed for the carrot patch. He pulled and pulled, but he didn't pull weeds! Not Bugs Bunny. He pulled carrots!

"Bugsy, ol' boy," he told himself, "I'm proud of you! This basket should hold enough carrots to last a whole week."

But true to suitable children's book tradition, Bugs gets punished for his trickery when Porky, Petunia, and a wised-up Elmer catch him in a rabbit snare that leaves him dangling from a tree branch. "Well, how about it, Bugs, old pal?" Elmer yells. "Have you had enough of HANGING AWOUND my garden?" (The authors were savvy enough to duplicate Elmer's unique speech pattern thwoughout the stowwy.)

In *Woody Woodpecker's Pogo Stick Adventures* (1954), we see the influence of the Dell comic books rather than the animated cartoons, as Woody encounters Andy Panda, Charlie Chicken, and Homer Pigeon in the course of the story. An uncharacteristically cranky Oswald the Rabbit puts in a brief appearance in *Woody Woodpecker's Peck of Trouble* (1951). *Woody Woodpecker Shoots the Works* (1955) has Woody accidentally set off an entire factory full of fireworks on Wally Walrus's birthday; social commentary is provided when we learn that "Woody often teased his big friend, but he didn't like to see him sad." (Definitely a different approach than the one taken to Woody and Wally's on-screen sparring matches.)

Of course, Whitman was also going to do its part to help promote its parent company's investment in Disneyland, and between 1955 and 1960, the company published several stories about Donald Duck's adventures in the

In the 1950s, some books made Donald Duck and his nephews into typical tourists, visiting Disneyland like any other family, while other titles had them living or working there.

This eye-popping array of Disney storybooks, coloring books, and other products from Western Printing was offered in 1963. At far right, the "Disney Starlets" boxed paper dolls anticipate the "Disney Princesses" merchandise line of the twenty-first century. The four "Starlets were Snow White, Cinderella, Sleeping Beauty, and Annette Funicello.

theme park. (Again, he was more of a tourist than a permanent resident.) In *Donald Duck Goes to Disneyland* (1955), he runs a-fowl (wak!) of Western baddie Bearclaw Bill, "the meanest outlaw who ever chewed cactus instead of chewing gum." The villain pursues Donald all over Disneyland until he is done in by the Rocket to the Moon ride. *Donald Duck in Frontierland* (1957) has him working as an employee, driving the stagecoach. Trouble rears its feathered head when Huey, Dewey, and Louie set him up with a team of oddly trained horses that run when Donald says "Whoa" and stop when he says "Giddyap." The artwork in all of these books was stunning.

The sudden influx of new created-for-television cartoon characters in the late 1950s and early 1960s further widened the canyon between Golden Books and the various Whitman series. (In 1958, Western Printing bought the rights to Golden Books from Simon and Schuster and began issuing them

under the imprint of Golden Press, but they retained their supposed educational goal.) Since these characters were completely unknown quantities before their shows premiered, it frequently seemed that the authors assigned to do the Golden Books adaptations had no clue as to what a particular program was about.

The best examples of this are the two Golden Books *Rocky and His Friends* (1960) and *Bullwinkle* (1961). The former reads as if the author (Ann McGovern) was told nothing beyond "write a story about a flying squirrel and a moose who are friends." The plot, such as it is, revolves entirely around Rocky's self-pitying concern that Bullwinkle, Mr. Peabody, and Sherman have forgotten his birthday, even weeping silent tears when they are not looking. Some distance removed from the TV show's satirical comments on the Cold War, government ineptitude, and the phoniness of show business, wouldn't you say?

The second Bullwinkle title strays even further from its source material, which is ironic considering that it was published the same year the cartoon series moved from weekday afternoons into a prime-time slot on NBC, in recognition of its appeal to both kids and adults. In Golden's 1961 approach, Rocky and Peabody make only token appearances on a couple of pages, while the rest of the story concerns Bullwinkle's desire to become a firefighter. Uh . . . do what now, you say? Yes, in a sort of *Rocky and His Friends* meets *Emergency!*, Peabody suggests that Bullwinkle travel from firehouse to firehouse until he finds a job, and then we get the lines that just might mark the lowest point these beloved cartoon icons ever reached in their printed careers:

> Bullwinkle put his head up. His great big ears flapped back and forth. He gave a long, happy honk.
>
> "HONNNNNKKKKK!"
>
> Rocky and Peabody held their ears. The moose's honk was louder than a thunderclap. It could be heard miles away.
>
> "Bully!" cried Bullwinkle. "I'm going to the city."

In contrast—and goodness knows, we need some after that scene—Whitman's *Rocky and Bullwinkle Go to Hollywood*, also published in 1961, takes its plot and some of its dialogue directly from a story line that played out on television. Posing first as an acting coach and then as famous movie director Alfred Hitchhike, Boris Badenov attempts to take the gullible moose for everything he is worth. Compare these paragraphs with that Golden Books excerpt:

These two Little Golden Book adaptations of Jay Ward's satirical TV cartoons read as if the authors had never been exposed to a single example of the source material—and it is very possible they had not.

The Hanna-Barbera TV characters starred in their own Little Golden Books beginning soon after their series premiered. The authors' unfamiliarity with the new programs meant that the books frequently presented plots and characterizations completely unrelated to the characters' usual personalities.

So the next day a poorer but no wiser Bullwinkle enrolled in the Thimblerig school of acting. He studied how to be brave, and how to show fear. He studied how to show surprise, and how to show sadness—all for one hundred dollars an hour.

Rocky really began to worry. "Bullwinkle, you are getting just terrible," he said.

"Yeah," said Bullwinkle. "When I get to be a complete mess, I graduate."

It should probably come as no surprise that the many Hanna-Barbera characters inspired almost as many Golden Books as Disney did. Just as with Jay Ward's clever creations, the H-B shows were so new that Golden did not always know how to handle them. *The Flintstones* (1961), with both story and art by Mel Crawford, bears no resemblance to the TV show at all other than being set in the Stone Age. Barney and Betty are nowhere to be found, and Fred and Wilma have a son, Junior, and a pet dinosaur, Harvey. (As we saw in our first chapter, Junior was originally planned to be a part of the series, but he was kicked out of the family before the birth of Pebbles in 1963.) And Fred never says, "Yabba-dabba-doo!"

Huckleberry Hound and His Friends (1960) presents an out-of-character Huck sulking because his titular friends (Yogi, Mister Jinks, and Pixie and Dixie) constantly take advantage of his good nature. *Yogi Bear* (1960) seems to be based on the wrong source, as Yogi eats honey to gain strength, just as Popeye did with spinach. *Quick Draw McGraw* (1960) is much more faithful to the original cartoons, with plenty of bumbling from Quick Draw and an accidental victory for him at the end. But it was back to bizarre with *Hokey Wolf and Ding-A-Ling* (1961), in which the two con men—uh, con wolves?—hire on for honest work helping Huckleberry Hound harvest his huckleberry fields, apparently without a thieving thought in their minds.

Over the next three years, Golden seemed to get a better grasp on the Hanna-Barbera characters and their most typical situations. *Top Cat* (1962), *The Jetsons* (1962), *Yakky Doodle and Chopper* (1962), *Touché Turtle* (1962), *Wally Gator* (1963), *Lippy the Lion and Hardy Har*

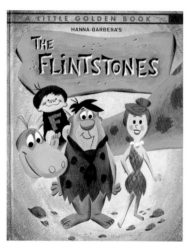

During the 1960s, both Little Golden Books and Whitman Publishing had to stay busy to keep up with the ever-growing number of new Hanna-Barbera shows.

Har (1963), *Magilla Gorilla* (1964), and *Peter Potamus* (1964) have no extremely out-of-character concepts in them other than their frequent indication that unrelated characters are acquainted with each other. Wally Gator visits his pal Yogi in Jellystone Park, for example, and Yakky Doodle earns money by cleaning Cindy Bear's house. Peter Potamus's adventure pauses for brief appearances by Mushmouse and Punkin Puss (oddly identified as friends instead of mortal enemies) as well as Ricochet Rabbit and Droop-A-Long.

Whitman gave its more rambunctious treatment to most of these same characters, with some hilarious results. *Peter Potamus Meets the Black Knight* (1965) sends the purple hippo into King Arthur's court; *Mushmouse and Punkin Puss: The Country Cousins* (1964) reestablishes the proper hillbilly feudin'-an'-fussin' milieu; and *Ricochet Rabbit: Showdown at Gopher Gulch Bakery* (1964) pits the hasty hare against outlaw Gosh Awful George, whom Ricochet put in jail "for robbing a bank after closing hours."

The Disney titles from Whitman in the late 1950s and early 1960s had some of the most elaborate and colorful versions of the characters ever drawn. They were often the work of the same artists responsible for Western's Disney comic book work.

Western's ongoing Disney books also kept up with the studio's changing emphasis. Golden's *Ludwig Von Drake* (1961) and Whitman's *Ludwig Von Drake: Dog Expert* (1962) tried to reproduce the new character's endearing eccentricity, no easy task without Paul Frees's masterful voice performance to fall back on. But Ludwig was not the only Disney duck getting more attention in book form. After spending the 1950s in the Dell comic books, Uncle Scrooge McDuck finally got to make some storybook appearances. The notable thing about his appearances in Golden's *Donald Duck and the Christmas Carol* (1960) and Whitman's *Uncle Scrooge, the Lemonade King* (1960) is that their illustrations were credited to Carl Barks. Considering that the comic books never allowed any such credits to be given, these stories mark the first time Barks's name was officially connected with his most famous creation. *Uncle Scrooge: Rainbow Runaway* (1965) is illustrated by Tony Strobl, another frequent contributor to the duck comics. In it, Scrooge rashly promises Huey, Dewey, and Louie a million dollars if they can find any gold at the end of the rainbow, only to find that the rainbow really does have an end, and it is on the roof of his own money bin.

Each new Disney animated feature brought another book adaptation, and several of the old characters were brought back for new stories. The Disneyland saga continued in *Donald Duck on Tom Sawyer's Island* (1960), with the nephews using a fish-shaped balloon to convince Unca Donald that he has finally caught the big one, and *Swiss Family Duck* (1964) in which the quacking quartet spends the night in Adventureland's Swiss Family Treehouse. *Goofy and His Wonderful Cornet* (1964) depicts a plethora of Disney veterans, including Clarabelle Cow and Horace Horsecollar, as the goof's irritated neighbors.

In 1965, the long-running tug-of-war among Golden Books' New York staffers over whether cartoon and television subjects were suitably high-class had a winner—at least temporarily. For the next six or seven years (the facts get foggy here), Golden Books stuck to original stories, and only occasionally would an entertainment-related one slip through. Whitman was under no such restriction and came up with some amusing takes on the cartoon shows that continued to debut during the 1960s. Among the highlights were *The Funny Company and Shy Shrinkin' Violette* (1964), based on the pioneering educational syndicated cartoon series; *Underdog* (1966), which would be banned from children's bookshelves today because of its emphasis on the heroic hound's Super Energy Pills; *Hoppity Hooper vs. Skippity Snooper* (1966), from one of Jay Ward's less-remembered shows; *Linus the Lionhearted: A Smile for Grouse* (1966), starring all the Post Cereals mascot characters; and *Gumby and Pokey to the Rescue* (1969), proving that Art Clokey's clay animation masterpieces still had audience appeal more than a decade after their debut.

Reminders of an even more distant past appeared in 1967, when Whitman revived the venerable Big Little Books series. As before, comic strip and animated cartoon characters received a heavy emphasis, although now they had to share space with adaptations of live-action TV shows such as *Bonanza, The Man From U.N.C.L.E.*, and *Flipper*. The illustrations were still on the right-hand pages and text on the left, but now the illustrations were in color and looked very much like the Gold Key comics Western was publishing at the time. Each of the new Big Little Books had a short blurb describing the plot on its back cover, and sampling a few of those makes one wish an old-time movie trailer announcer were on hand to deliver them in his best bombastic tones:

Whether a major network hit or a minor one-season wonder, many animated TV series of the 1960s were adapted for Whitman's various series. The Road Runner volume seen here was heavily influenced by the Gold Key Comics of the time.

Dick Tracy Encounters Facey, by Paul S. Newman
Jewelry theft! Bank robbery! Insurance fraud! Kidnapping! Same MO, but witnesses said otherwise! What was the answer?

Tom and Jerry Meet Mr. Fingers, by Carl Fallberg
Military jets sabotaged! Rails bent! Freeways mysteriously torn up! WHO or WHAT was behind these acts?

Bugs Bunny: Double Trouble on Diamond Island, by Don Christensen
Bugs and Elmer find more than they bargained for when they take an innocent space scooter ride.

Popeye: Ghost Ship to Treasure Island, by Paul S. Newman
A ghost ship! Buried treasure! Trouble galore! What would be the outcome?

Donald Duck: The Fabulous Diamond Fountain, by Carl Fallberg
Salty Sam appearing on TV sparks Scrooge, Donald and the boys to a diamond hunting adventure. Unfortunately, the Beagle Boys are also attracted.

Woody Woodpecker: The Meteor Menace, by Don Christensen
A mysterious message from a pen pal is only the beginning! It leads Woody into strange adventure in a faraway land!

Whitman revived the Big Little Books series in 1967–68, with titles based on classic cartoon characters as well as their newer made-for-TV companions.

The release of the initial twelve volumes must have sparked some interest, because 1968 saw the publication of twenty-three more, including the first Hanna-Barbera titles: *The Flintstones and the Case of the Many Missing Things*; *Frankenstein Jr.: The Menace of the Heartless Monster*; *Space Ghost: The Sorceress of CYBA-3*; and *Shazzan: The Glass Princess*. Comic book superheroes were represented by *Batman: The Cheetah Caper*; *Aquaman: Scourge of the Sea*; and *The Fantastic Four: The House of Horrors*. Western's Disney license was alive and well with *Mickey Mouse: Adventure in Outer Space*; *Donald Duck: Luck of the Ducks*; and *Goofy: Giant Trouble*. The Warner Bros. entries were *Bugs Bunny: Accidental Adventure* and *The Road Runner: The Super Beep Catcher*, which continued the comic books' tradition of having the speedy bird (and his wife and children) speak in rhyme instead of merely beeping.

Big Little Books had more opportunities in 1976 and again in 1980, when several older titles, including some from the 1940s, were reissued in paperback and joined by a few new ones, among them *The Incredible Hulk: Lost in Time*; *Spider-Man Zaps Mr. Zodiac*; *Tweety and Sylvester: The Magic Voice*; and *The Pink Panther at Castle Kreep*.

Believe it or don't, Western Printing and Lithographing did not have a monopoly on cartoon-related children's books, even though it did have the licensing rights to most of the major characters. Sometimes such rights were not exclusive. We have already seen how for years, Western published the Popeye comic books while using the sailor man in coloring books and Big Little Books. However, Popeye never appeared in a Little Golden Book or any of the other Whitman series; his adventures of that type were published initially by Treasure Books and then by Wonder Books, both of which were Grosset and Dunlap subsidiaries.

The first story, titled simply *Popeye* (1955), was distinguished by its illustrations by Bud Sagendorf, who was employed at the time creating the Dell comic books but would not take over the newspaper strip until the end of the decade. In fact, the illustrations alone almost have to carry the plot, as the text is minimal. In a simple tale of how Popeye rescues Wimpy and Swee'Pea when they are adrift in a rowboat on a stormy sea, what would be the major scene in a typical Popeye cartoon is quickly done away with in fewer than ten words: "Popeye ate the spinach and it made him strong." Well, blow me down!

Popeye comic book artist Bud Sagendorf supplied the illustrations for the interior of this 1955 Wonder Book but did not draw its cover; the difference in style is immediately apparent.

The two fishermen were so busy trying to catch fish they didn't notice that a big storm was blowing in from the sea.

But Popeye knew because his pipe started to twirl whenever a storm was brewing.

These three Felix the Cat volumes from Wonder Books show the black and white feline's gradual evolution from Otto Messmer's comic book design to the version of Felix that appeared in the 1960 made-for-TV cartoons.

Sagendorf continued to illustrate the various sequels as they were published. *Popeye Goes on a Picnic* (1958) arrived just as the Popeye cartoons were becoming valuable property for local TV stations nationwide. The conflict over who created Bluto/Brutus affected *The House That Popeye Built* (1960), in which the villain is called Big Bill Bully and looks nothing like Popeye's usual foe. In *Popeye's Big Surprise* (1962), Olive, Wimpy, and Swee'Pea build a new boat for Popeye but somehow neglect to figure out how to get it out of Olive's cellar. Years after all of these, Wonder Books added one more to the series, *Popeye and the Haunted House* (1980). It was not illustrated by Sagendorf but at least featured Bluto's return to the cast.

Another character who made his way into the Treasure/Wonder Books library began with his self-titled story *Felix the Cat* (1953). Since Felix never had as strong a personality as Popeye, his character tended to change from book to book. In that first one, Felix is a stray who comes to live on Sunnyside Farm and somehow ends up working as the local veterinarian. In *Felix on Television* (1958), he is the pet of young Danny and has an overwhelming desire to do not-so-stupid pet tricks on the boob tube. He finally succeeds at balancing himself on a rubber ball. As a bonus, the corners of the pages feature a flip-book-style animated sequence of his act. *A Surprise for Felix* (1959) changes his design from the comic book style of the first two to the version used in the made-for-TV Felix cartoons of the time; now he is a responsible adult, looking after his wayward nephew, Inky.

Treasure Books and Wonder Books certainly got the most use out of their license with Terrytoons. Between animated films, comic books, storybooks, and records, perhaps no other cartoon character had as many different and conflicting origin stories as Mighty Mouse, and yet another version was told in Treasure Books' *Mighty Mouse* (1953). In this retelling, the abandoned foundling mouse infant is adopted by Dinky Duck, who soon enough finds that his ward has superpowers far beyond those of ordinary rodents (or birds). The adventures continued in *Mighty Mouse: Dinky Learns to Fly* (1953), in which Dinky's status as Mighty's foster father is already forgotten, and *Mighty Mouse and the Scared Scarecrow* (1954).

Terrytoons might never have been prime examples of art or humor, but they certainly had a huge repertory cast of characters. Some of the other books starring various stars and not-quite-stars were *The Terry Bears Win the Cub Scout Badge* (1955); *Heckle and Jeckle* (1957) and *Heckle and Jeckle Visit the Farm* (1958); *Gandy Goose* (1957); *Tom Terrific!* (1958), costarring villain Crabby "Rotten to the Core" Appleton; and *A Joke on Farmer Al Falfa* (1959). Considering that the bewhiskered old rube dated back to 1916 in silent films, at the time he must surely have qualified as the oldest cartoon character to have new stories written about him.

Wonder Books really seemed to enjoy cramming batches of Terrytoons characters into stories that forced them to interact with each other, such as *Mighty Mouse: Santa's Helper* (1955), *The Terrytoon Space Train* (1958); and *Mighty Mouse to the Rescue* (1958), which offers a brief appearance by Farmer Al Falfa's previously unmentioned wife. As new Terrytoons characters were developed in the 1960s, including Deputy Dawg, Hector Heathcote, Astronut, and Luno, the Soaring Stallion, they were all brought into Wonder Books' wonder-filled library.

Also during the 1960s, Wonder Books cultivated a relationship with Harvey Comics for a series of books based on that company's characters, a healthy percentage of which were still the ones Harvey had acquired from Paramount's cartoon studio. There were *Casper the Friendly Ghost* (1960); *Little Audrey and the Moon Lady* (1960); *Herman and Katnip* (1961); *Baby Huey* (1961); and *Buzzy the Funny Crow* (1963). Late in the decade, a few titles imitated some of Harvey's multitude of comic book subseries: *Casper in Ghostland* (1965) and *Casper and Wendy Adventures* (1969) were a couple of these.

But that's not all, folks. Treasure and Wonder Books also had volumes based on King Features Syndicate's newspaper properties. *Henry in Lollipop Land* (1953) and *Henry Goes to a Party* (1955) had the mute comic strip star talking, not unlike the Tom and Jerry stories of the same era. *Prince Valiant* (1954) did a masterful job of duplicating the look of Hal Foster's richly illustrative Sunday pages, while *Blondie's Family* (1954) concentrated on pet dog Elmer, with Blondie and Dagwood appearing only on the cover. Wonder Books published *Mister Magoo* (1958) and *Crusader Rabbit* (1958), with plots based on some animated cartoon episodes. Finally, there were *Alvin's Lost Voice* (1963) and *Clyde Crashcup and Leonardo* (1965), with the characters from the formerly prime-time *Alvin Show*.

Wonder Books and its predecessor, Treasure Books, enjoyed a long association with Terrytoons, often mixing various characters together in the adventures.

With Western Printing having already grabbed most of the major cartoon licenses, Wonder Books had to be content with what it could get, primarily the King Features comic strip characters and the Harvey Comics cast.

In our brief chapter on comic books, we saw how in the late 1960s, Western Printing gave up its long-running license for the older Hanna-Barbera characters (some of the newer ones continued to appear in Gold Key comics for a few more years). But what happened to all of those characters' storybooks once they were cast out into the non-Western world to fend for themselves? They ended up with a company known simultaneously as Unisystems, Ottenheimer Publishing, and Modern Promotions; for the sake of simplicity, we will simply refer to this publisher as Modern. Beginning in 1972, Modern launched its own series of Hanna-Barbera stories in much the same format as the Little Golden Books, only much more carelessly written and illustrated.

Earlier we met—or did not meet, according to how you look at it—the nonexistent Annie North Bedford of Golden Books renown. Have you ever heard of Horace J. Elias? This was the author's name assigned to every one of Modern's Hanna-Barbera stories over the next several years; although it is possible that he was an actual living, breathing writer, it seems more likely that this was a nom de plume for whatever staff member was assigned to the project. If the mysterious Elias happens to be reading this, we welcome a correction from him.

One sign that Modern churned out its Hanna-Barbera stories at a pace that even the mass production animation studio would have found grueling is their somewhat pedestrian titles, which sound like they came before the stories. Even the most creative individual might have had trouble coming up with entertaining tales called *Huckleberry Hound Puts the Fire Out*, *Yogi Bear Teaches Boo Boo Some Ecology*, *The Flintstones on a Picnic*, and *Yogi Bear and the Colorado River* (all published in 1972). There were occasional breaks from the ho-hum routine, such as *The Jetsons: Sunday Afternoon on the Moon*, in which Elroy finds the golf ball that had been whacked by one of the Apollo astronauts of an earlier century, and some rather pointed political satire in *Top Cat: Candidate for Mayor*.

In 1976, Modern began subleasing its Hanna-Barbera rights to Wonder Books, which kept the same basic format but used traditional hardcover bindings. *Huckleberry Hound and the Big Blooming Rosebush*, *Magilla Gorilla and the Super Kite*, and *Fred Flintstone's Surprising Corn* did not deliver any more than their titles promised, although *The Flintstones: Wilma's Busy Day* at least distinguished itself by giving Mrs. Flintstone a nude scene on the cover. Yabba-dabba—duh, HUH?!

Modern also tried to imitate the Big Little Book format, with five Flintstones titles (one of which was a reprint of Whitman's *Case of the Many Missing Things* with new, inferior illustrations), two Yogi Bear tales, and one with Huckleberry Hound. *Yogi Bear Saves Jellystone Park* (1977) has some very odd humor for a story of its type, as Yogi and Boo Boo try to discover what is making the ground shake and the lake waters roil in the neighborhood. Their search leads them to a crabby elf who identifies himself as Oliver, the Jolly Green Midget, and tells them that his big brother—his *really* big brother—in the next valley is causing all the trouble:

> "I'm not at all jolly. I'm cranky and irritable most of the time. But that big, dumb brother of mine—he's really jolly! He goes stomping up and down his valley all day long, hollering 'Ho! Ho! Ho!' And that's the noise you hear. It sounds like thunder because he's so big and his voice is so deep."
>
> Yogi looked at Oliver. "Then if you're the Jolly Green Midget, even though you're not really jolly," he said slowly, "that would make Mr. Ho Ho Ho over there the Jolly . . ."

Since Western Printing had lost its Hanna-Barbera license in the late 1960s, those characters' adventures were chronicled by Modern Promotions by the early part of the next decade. Modern made the risky move of giving Wilma Flintstone a nude scene on one cover.

Look for all these exciting, new adventures about your favorite T.V. cartoon characters . . . from Rand McNally and Hanna-Barbera Productions, Inc.

In the mid-1970s, Rand McNally arranged with Modern Promotions to issue a new line of stories based on more recent Hanna-Barbera properties.

Since the actual panels from Walt Kelly's *Pogo* would have been too complex for young children to color, this 1953 coloring book was illustrated by Kelly assistant Wally Wood. (Steve Thompson/Pogo Fan Club collection)

"Exactly!" said Oliver. "My brother is the real, genuine, Jolly Green Gi . . ." He broke off as a series of thunderous "Ho ho ho's" drowned out whatever he was going to say.

Between 1975 and 1977, the Hanna-Barbera characters and shows that had not been part of Modern's acquisition process were given over to Rand Mc-Nally, which published a set of sixteen titles during those three years. The Great Grape Ape, Hong Kong Phooey, Jabberjaw, Speed Buggy, and their contemporaries might not have had the star power of their ancestors, but at least Rand McNally could boast of having Scooby-Doo, and the company made good use of the timorous Great Dane by devoting four of the sixteen new books to his adventures.

Up to this point, we have been dealing only with books that presented beloved (and otherwise) cartoon characters in new stories. Another class of books that deserves discussion, however, is the volumes that collected newspaper strips. Walt Kelly's *Pogo* was one of the most successful series of this type, beginning only a couple of years after the strip's debut in 1949 and continuing even after Kelly's death in 1973; the final volume reprinted some of the last strips he drew.

Simon and Schuster, the *Pogo* book publishers, treated each title with tender loving care; many of them contained essays and other original work by Kelly that was prepared especially for them rather than reprinted from an earlier source. Entire volumes, including *Uncle Pogo So-So Stories* (1953) and *The Pogo Stepmother Goose* (1954) were made up of new material instead of strip reprints. Some of the books gave Kelly a chance to make his satire a bit sharper than nervous newspaper editors might have allowed; *The Pogo Poop Book* (1966) has stories taking on, among other topics, the Ku Klux Klan (parodied as "the Kluck Klams") and the John Birch Society ("the Jack Acid Society").

These were still the exceptions to the rule, and as volume after volume collecting the newspaper strips accumulated, readers caught on to an interesting aspect of them. More than one person has commented that reading the strips collected into book form gave a much better understanding and appreciation of Kelly's art and wit than seeing a few panels each day and then having to remember what was happening when the next day's newspaper was published. No doubt the Pogo books made many new fans for the strip, and many subsequent cartoonists would come to depend on book collections of their strips to supplement their income.

Even the number of Pogo books paled next to the number of *Peanuts* reprint books, but that long-running series had its beginning because of

Fawcett had enormous success with small paperback books reprinting *Peanuts* strips that had already appeared in Holt, Rinehart, and Winston's larger volumes. The books particularly appealed to kids, in part because of the reprints' compact size and low price.

This impressive spread from 1969 shows the multitude of available *Peanuts* reprint books plus other examples of that strip's ever-expanding merchandise line.

a hunch. John Selby, who was editor in chief at the Holt, Rinehart, and Winston publishing house (then known simply as Rinehart and Company) had been following *Peanuts* in one of the early newspapers that had signed up to carry the new strip, the *New York World Telegram*. In January 1952, after reading the strip for a few months, he came up with the idea of doing a collection and suggested as much to Charles Schulz. There was a twist: since the strip's debut in October 1950, Schulz had been tinkering with his cast, their personalities, and the "voice" of *Peanuts*, and by the time that first book collection went to press, some major changes had occurred. Therefore, Schulz personally selected the strips for that and most of the other early volumes, making sure nothing seemed out of character.

The *Peanuts* book series grew slowly. After that first volume (naturally titled simply *Peanuts*) appeared in July 1952, *More Peanuts* followed in September 1954, *Good Grief, More Peanuts* in October 1956, and *Good Ol' Charlie Brown* in August 1957. From 1958 on, at least one and usually two books were issued per year.

It is somewhat remarkable that Holt, Rinehart, and Winston maintained basically the same uniform format for the Peanuts books for twenty-three years. A typical book measured 5" × 8" and contained approximately 160 daily strips and 40 Sunday strips. (The earliest books separated the dailies and Sundays into separate volumes, but that format was eventually discarded.) Strips from as many as three different years could be found lumped together, often by theme. In other words, rather than a strict chronological reprinting, strips about, say, baseball from several different years were grouped to make up a seemingly continuous story line. The earliest books had new cover art supplied by Schulz, but as their numbers grew, art taken from individual comic panels became the most common.

Holt released approximately thirty-five volumes in this format; after the first few, most contained Charlie Brown's name in the title (*The Unsinkable Charlie Brown*; *You're You, Charlie Brown*; *But We Love You, Charlie Brown*; and many more). The last one in this series was *Win a Few, Lose a Few, Charlie Brown* (1974).

In 1975, Holt dramatically revamped the *Peanuts* format. The volumes now measured 9" × 10", and each one contained approximately 275 daily strips and 50 Sunday strips. Another huge change was in the titles. Now, they were taken from dialogue in some particular strip in that volume, often seeming arcane or meaningless until one read the whole volume to find the title's source. The first in the new style was *Speak Softly and Carry a Beagle*, and they continued with such puzzling covers as *Don't Hassle Me with Your Sighs, Chuck* and *Here Comes the April Fool*.

With the series getting somewhat top-heavy, Holt finally discontinued its *Peanuts* reprints around 1986. Other publishers picked up the fallen banner off and on throughout the remaining fourteen years of the strip's (and Schulz's) life.

Those were not the only *Peanuts* reprint books available, though. As a 1970 article about the strip's phenomenal popularity noted,

> After Holt has had a year or two to sell a Peanuts book at $1, the paperback rights are turned over to Fawcett World Library, which takes the Holt volume, splits it in two, and sells each copy for 40 cents. To date, Fawcett has sold 12 titles and 10 million copies.

Judging from the number of copies that turn up in antique stores, the Fawcett printings must have been the ones most kids grew up reading in bed before turning out the lights. With a retail price of less than half of the Holt printings, this seems only natural.

Besides the gift-shop-type books published by Connie Boucher and her Determined Productions and discussed in chapter 1, *Peanuts* was represented by another type of book that the vast majority of other comic strips did not have: storybook adaptations of its many animated TV specials. It began with World Publishing's version of *A Charlie Brown Christmas* in 1965, and that first book differed greatly from any of its successors.

First, the illustrations in the book are most definitely *not* Charles Schulz's artwork. However, they also are not taken directly from the TV special. In fact, in some cases—particularly the final scene, in which the gang decorates Charlie Brown's spindly Christmas tree—the illustrations bear practically no resemblance at all to what TV viewers saw. The drawings might be the work of ghost artist Nick LoBianco, early in his association with Schulz and *Peanuts*, but that is by no means certain. The front cover illustration does look like Schulz might have done it, even though his signature does not appear.

(It might be just as well to note that all of the book versions credit Schulz as the author. This may or may not mean he actually wrote the text that appears in them; his authorship may be based solely on the fact that he crafted the original story for each special.)

The book series continued with *Charlie Brown's All-Stars* (1966), and this time the illustrations look like they very well could be Schulz's, albeit colored with what looks like crayon or colored pencil. From that point on, beginning with the publication of *It's the Great Pumpkin, Charlie Brown* in 1967 (following the TV special's 1966 premiere), World Publishing's illustrations were reproduced from the animation cels and backgrounds created by Bill Melendez's studio.

The rather minimal text for each book remained well written, regardless of whether Schulz was knocking it out during his nonexistent spare time or a staff writer was responsible for it. The book versions occasionally would read differently than the TV versions. The script for *You're in Love, Charlie Brown* (1967) has a subplot in which Peppermint Patty unwittingly sets Charlie Brown and Lucy up on a blind date, to their eventual horror; Patty does not even appear in the book adaptation. In the TV version of *He's Your Dog, Charlie Brown* (1968), Patty locks the recalcitrant Snoopy in the garage for the night, only to be awakened by his howling. Opening the door to check on him, she is body-slammed by the beagle, who makes his escape. In the book, he simply unlocks the garage door from the inside and returns to Charlie Brown's house.

World Publishing maintained this consistent stream of TV show adaptations through 1972's *You're Elected, Charlie Brown*, which was retitled *You're Not Elected, Charlie Brown* for all repeat broadcasts, because he wasn't. After that, World went out of business. (In the interim, Holt, Rinehart, and Winston had done the book versions of the two *Peanuts* theatrical features, *A Boy Named Charlie Brown* [1969] and *Snoopy Come Home* [1971], using a format virtually identical to that of World's books.)

Beginning with *There's No Time for Love, Charlie Brown* (1973), Random House took over the job of turning the *Peanuts* specials into books but chose a vastly different approach. Now, instead of text with illustrations, the books appeared to be reproductions of Bill Melendez's preliminary storyboard sketches, shown in TV-screen-shaped frames. The "text" consisted of the show's dialogue printed underneath the drawings, just as the staff of an animation studio would have read it. Authorship was still credited to Schulz, loaning extra strength to our earlier theory that he was merely responsible for each show's story, not what was printed in the books.

Eventually, Random House went back and redid World Publishing's eight original volumes in this same storyboard style. It made for some interesting moments when it came to the 1978 special *What a Nightmare, Charlie Brown*; after a few lines of dialogue from Charlie Brown in the opening scenes, the rest of the show was a pantomime by Snoopy, meaning that the illustrations alone had to carry the story from that point onward in Random House's version.

Of all the comic strips other than *Peanuts* that enjoyed long runs in reprint volumes, surely none could approach Reg Smythe's British import, *Andy Capp*. Fawcett used virtually the same format for its *Andy Capp* books that it used for *Peanuts*, even down to the style of choosing titles (such as *Take a Bow, Andy Capp*). *The Wizard of Id* also worked its magic in paperback reprint form, and *Dennis the Menace* made trouble for anyone who attempted to accumulate a complete set of the books featuring its daily panels. Others including (but not limited to) *Beetle Bailey*, *The Family Circus*, and *Marmaduke* got similar treatments at some point in their careers.

Other types of books brought cartoon characters into avid readers' homes, and we will finish up this chapter by briefly examining some of them. There were novelty items, such as Golden Books' series of "Golden Shape Books" from the mid-1970s. Just as the name implied, the pages were cut into the shape of the front cover illustration. Inside, the stories differed from standard Golden Books fare only in that they were written for very young readers. *The Bullwinkle Book* (1976) rivals the original Bullwinkle Golden Books of the early 1960s in its wildly inaccurate depiction of the characters' personalities; just the idea of Boris and Natasha joining Rocky and Mr. Peabody at Bullwinkle's house for a game of hide-and-seek seems so wrong somehow. The Golden Shape Book adaptation of Disney's *The Jungle Book* sets some sort of record for the retelling of Rudyard Kipling's tale, since most of the pages have fewer than ten words each. *Cinderella's Castle* (1972) is one of Western Printing's few attempts to do for Walt Disney World what the company had done for Disneyland in the mid-1950s. The thin plot has Cinders staging a party attended by Snow White and the dwarfs; Peter Pan, Tinker Bell, Wendy, Michael, and John; Dumbo and Timothy Mouse; Bambi; Alice in Wonderland, the White Rabbit, the Queen of Hearts, and the Mad Hatter; and Pinocchio and Geppetto.

Most of the original book adaptations based on the *Peanuts* TV specials were illustrated with cels and background art from Bill Melendez's animation studio. The text was credited to Charles Schulz, whether or not he actually took time from his schedule to write it.

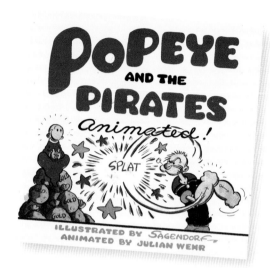

Conspicuous by their absence are Mickey, Donald, Goofy, and their usual gang. *The Bugs Bunny Book* (1976) again has Bugs being punished for tricking his cohorts out of carrots rather than triumphing via his scheming.

Another novelty in the publishing industry has been the pop-up book, with intricately designed scenes that unfold when the pages are turned. Sometimes the illustrations would also have moving parts triggered by a lever or some other method. The fragile nature of these, especially in the hands of eager kids, has ensured that intact, working copies are difficult to find. Maybe it was because of his name, but Popeye was a particularly popular pop-up pop star. As far back as 1945, Bud Sagendorf was creating animated illustrations for Duenewald Printing's *Popeye and the Pirates*. With a little manipulation, Wimpy could sprinkle salt on his hamburgers, Popeye's boat rocked back and forth on the ocean, pirates ran their fingers through stolen loot, and the spinach-fueled sailor man socked a bulky buccaneer right in his buckteeth.

Some of these Popeye pop-up books with animated illustrations date from the 1940s, while others are from the 1980s, proving that good ideas have a way of coming back to life.

Popeye's pop-up career continued in 1980 when Random House issued four tiny books that were translated from their original publication in Colombia (of all places). *Popeye and the Ghost*, *Popeye and the Magic Flute*, and *Popeye and the Treasure Hunt* were all fairly standard, but *Popeye and the Spinach Burgers* was a bit unusual in that Wimpy got to eat spinach (unwittingly, not by choice) for the climax.

Whitman came up with its own series of oddball books in the early 1960s. Billed as "Whitman Comic Books," they were hardback volumes containing what appeared to be reprints from the Dell comics of the time. However, the covers promoted Whitman's titles as "New, exciting picture stories," so perhaps the comics were indeed written and drawn especially for them. Hanna-Barbera characters populated six of the eight books available, with Bugs Bunny and Donald Duck the only interlopers from other studios. As we saw in the last chapter, in the late 1970s, the Whitman brand would be applied to true comic books, the first time it had been used in that manner.

If you were ever a kid, you will remember the books that required one to punch out stickers and place them in the appropriate spots on the pages, then color in the rest of the scene. Western Printing was responsible for dozens of different styles of these; when issued under the Golden imprint, they were branded as "Stickum Books," and when Whitman was on the cover, they were "Sticker Fun Books." Either way, the format was the same. Many times the stickers-to-be-punched featured stunning artwork, thereby frustrating us kids who could not possibly color the rest of the page to match them. Seemingly every character ever licensed by Western—and as we have seen, that's a big group—made it into a sticker book at some point or another.

And so, whether one was in the mood to read a story (or have one read to them), catch up on the newspaper comics, or do something a bit more creative, a licensed cartoon book was waiting to fill the void. The popularity of the Little Golden Books and their various imitators on today's collectors' market clearly indicates former children's warm feelings for them, and the more odd the format of the rest, the more sought-after they are. And who knows? Some kids who read these books just *might* have grown up to write books of their own. Can you imagine that?

Whitman published a series of hardback "comic books" in the early 1960s, but the experiment seems not to have extended beyond the titles seen here.

Whether "Sticker Fun Books" published under the Whitman brand or "Stickum Books" from Golden Press, these are some of the most difficult-to-find types of collectibles since once they were finished, most parents and kids saw no need to hold onto them.

Somewhat unusually for the time, this Underdog jigsaw puzzle from Whitman and board game from Milton Bradley were obviously based on the same piece of promotional art. However, a lighted match cannot hold a candle to Simon Bar Sinister wielding a hypodermic needle.

Chapter 4

TOYING AROUND WITH YOUR FRIENDS

Our last couple of chapters have dealt quite heavily with the output of Western Printing and Lithographing in the field of books. That company was also responsible for an amazing number of toys, and its dozens of cartoon licenses gave it the freedom to use those characters in any of its other merchandise lines. Since this chapter deals with toys in general, perhaps we should begin with the two largest categories Western had in its catalog, jigsaw puzzles and board games.

There would seem to be little connection between these playthings and the book printing business, but Western kept its many staff artists busy turning out artwork to be used in all of its products. The puzzles Western marketed, primarily under its Whitman brand, had some of the most stunning art ever found in cartoon merchandise. Examining them provides a stark contrast to today, when most licensed merchandise uses the same corporate-approved stock poses of each character over and over again; rarely did Western use the same cartoon art more than once. There are some isolated examples of, say, puzzle art on the cover of a coloring book, but these were exceptions rather than the rule.

The most unusual thing about Western's puzzle line is that it had to share its most valuable licensee, Disney, with another company. Jaymar was the second-largest producer of cartoon puzzles, but how it and Western came to jointly produce Disney puzzles at the same time is a question for which there seems to be no real answer. Even Disney's longtime merchandise creator Al Konetzni found himself at a loss when asked how such a situation could have occurred. Konetzni's best guess was that it had something to do with the retail prices assigned to each company; Jaymar could produce Disney puzzles that sold for a lower price than Western's line, for example. This is only an expert guess, but if there were ever an expert with firsthand knowledge of Disney's licensing efforts, Konetzni would be it, so we must pay attention to his view on the matter.

Jaymar tended to release its boxed puzzles in a sort of series, such as one group with the overall theme of "Donald Duck in Disneyland" (an even

Western Printing used toys as well as its books to promote its investment in Disneyland. In this example, Dopey is practicing how he will drive on the Southern California freeways.

Disneyland's Haunted Mansion had not yet received its official name when this Whitman boxed puzzle made it onto the market.

In this masterpiece of a Jaymar puzzle from 1962, the core Disney cast members are seen welcoming newcomer Ludwig Von Drake.

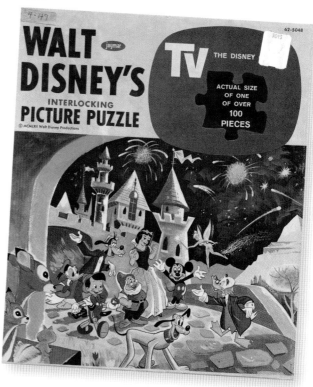

more unusual move considering that Western had published at least two different books under similar titles). In the grand old tradition of combining the Disney cartoon stars with the theme park's attractions, Donald was seen driving the Casey Jr. circus train in Fantasyland, with passengers including Mickey, Minnie, Jiminy Cricket, Tinker Bell, and Timothy Mouse. Donald barely missed being swallowed by one of the hippos on the Jungle Cruise ride on the Adventureland puzzle and served as a sheriff in the Frontierland scene. The Tomorrowland installment depicted the Autopia ride, with Donald, Mickey, and Minnie crammed into one car and Snow White and Dopey piloting the one behind. (Apparently not all the dopey drivers can be found on the nation's highway system.)

Western/Whitman also produced a number of theme-park-themed puzzles, including one that has become legendary among toy collectors. It showed Mickey and Goofy running in terror through the "Haunted House at Disneyland," marketed before the attraction later known as the Haunted Mansion had opened to the public. Once Walt Disney World in Florida came along, there were also a few puzzles based on its own attractions, but somehow these never seemed to garner the same attention as the ones featuring the original park.

When the 1961–62 TV season made such a big deal out of the introduction of Ludwig Von Drake as a regular contributor to *Walt Disney's Wonderful World of Color*, both Western and Jaymar wasted no time incorporating the eccentric genius into their merchandise. Perhaps the masterpiece of it all was Jaymar's puzzle picturing an assortment of characters—including not only Mickey, Donald, and Goofy but Pinocchio, Snow White, Doc, and Bambi—emerging from the Fantasyland castle to welcome Ludwig into their midst.

Western and Jaymar also shared joint custody of the Warner Bros. characters for puzzle purposes. It should have not been surprising that Whitman's puzzles of the gang greatly resembled the covers of the Dell comic books of the era. Jaymar's Warner Bros. characters, however, more closely approximated the look of the Bugs Bunny newspaper comic strip.

Jaymar apparently had an exclusive when it came to Popeye, because while Western for decades held the license for the sailor man's comic books, that company produced very little nonprint merchandise featuring him until the

Jaymar's jigsaw puzzles depicting the Looney Tunes characters strongly resembled their designs as seen in the Dell comic books as well as the daily *Bugs Bunny* newspaper comic strip.

This Popeye jigsaw puzzle art seems to combine the designs from the Fleischer animated cartoons with just a hint of Western Publishing's comic books.

In the 1970s, Whitman doubled its fun by combining comic books and jigsaw puzzles into single packages. (Donnie Pitchford collection)

late 1960s. Before then, Jaymar had a long series of Popeye puzzles that are somewhat remarkable in that their artwork did not actually resemble any specific rendition of the Popeye cast. It certainly did not have the look of the newspaper strip during its Zaboly or Sagendorf periods, but it also did not look like the theatrical cartoons produced by Paramount or King Features' made-for-TV series (except for the occasional inclusion of Bluto). That did not seem to matter to anyone, as the puzzles remained on sale from the 1950s right into the 1980s, with the same scenes endlessly recycled into different formats.

Boxed puzzles were great for older kids, but those who were just getting used to putting pieces into place were often entertained by another type that had roughly two dozen pieces contained inside a frame of sorts. Whitman's name for these was "Frame-Tray Puzzles," while Jaymar went with the more literally descriptive term "inlaid puzzles." Jaymar, much more so

than Western, tended to issue the same scenes as both boxed and inlaid puzzles, while Western preferred to have new art created for each individual piece, although in a few cases, Whitman used the same art for both formats.

A very special breed of collector seeks out and purchases the original artwork for items such as these. Since there can be only one original for each mass-produced puzzle or other piece of merchandise, this supply is obviously rather finite. Most of the commercial artists involved were anonymous, but a knowledgeable historian can usually identify their differing styles. For example, both Western and Jaymar produced puzzles in conjunction with Disney's 1964 megahit *Mary Poppins*, but Jaymar's featured the unmistakable artwork of George Peed. His *Mary Poppins* scenes are among the best he ever created, with his trademark animated style; the fact that none of the characters look like the actors who portrayed them on the screen (Julie Andrews, Dick Van Dyke, Ed Wynn, et al.) is completely beside the point.

Two other subgenres of puzzles should be mentioned briefly. Remember the type with the tiny plastic sliding tiles that had to be manipulated to correctly form the picture? The primary manufacturer of those was a company called Roalex, and during the 1950s and 1960s, it seems to have grabbed practically any license it thought could be adapted to that format. Roalex puzzles included Superman, Batman, the Jetsons, Magilla Gorilla, Snuffy Smith, Huckleberry Hound, and Mighty Mouse, plus many more obscure characters rarely seen in merchandise, such as Courageous Cat, the Mighty Hercules, Space Ghost, and Dino Boy. Roalex puzzles contained fifteen plastic tiles; since one space had to be left open to permit the pieces to be manipulated, this meant that most of the puzzles pictured three tall figures and one shorter one. (Rarely but occasionally, as with the Superman puzzle, the picture was a single image.) Some creative license had to be taken to force familiar character designs into this rigid format, with characters sometimes appearing to have been stretched vertically and/or squashed horizontally to fit into their four (or three) pieces. Surviving Roalex puzzles, especially if still on their original store display card, command jaw-dropping prices today—a far cry from when our parents would grab one at Stuckey's to bribe us brats into keeping quiet in the backseat for ten minutes.

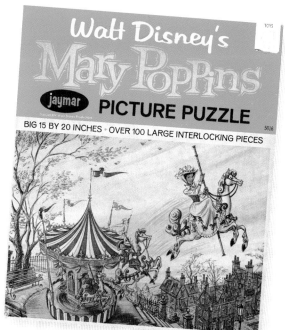

George Peed's incredible artwork made Jaymar's line of *Mary Poppins* puzzles a true joy to behold, even if the characters did not in the least resemble the actors in the movie.

The Roalex company manufactured these sliding tile puzzles for every imaginable licensed character. Here, Secret Squirrel, Squiddly Diddly, and Winsome Witch get four tiles each, while Morocco Mole is shorted with three.

ALL YOUR FAVORITE *Walt Disney* CHARACTERS
IN **3-D** MAGNETIC PUZZLES

*FLEXIBLE PLASTIC SEGMENTS WITH
BUILT-IN PERMANENT MAGNETS NEST INTO
A COLORFUL 3-D BACKGROUND*   Ages 2 to 7

THEY'LL LOOK GREAT
ON ANY CHILD'S WALL!

2101 MICKEY MOUSE
2102 DONALD DUCK   2103 PLUTO   2104 PINOCCHIO
2105 SNOW WHITE   2106 CINDERELLA   2107 PETER PAN   2108 GOOFY
2109 WINNIE THE POOH   2110 TINKERBELL   2111 DUMBO   2112 BAMBI

WINNIE THE POOH © MCMLXV WALT DISNEY PRODUCTIONS
MADE IN U.S.A. BY CHILD GUIDANCE PRODUCTS, INC. NEW YORK 10472
© WALT DISNEY PRODUCTIONS
3-D BACKGROUNDS MADE IN JAPAN. PATENT PENDING

Child Guidance was responsible for these puzzles that used separate plastic pieces with magnets affixed to the back to form the beloved Disney stars.

Whitman's Woody Woodpecker's Crazy Mixed-Up Color Factory (1972) had beautiful artwork on the box, but the game was so complex that it confused adults and kids alike.

Another odd variety of puzzle was marketed in the 1960s by preschool toy titan Child Guidance. The plastic pieces of these puzzles were the various body elements making up a character of some sort; the background was metal, so tiny magnets affixed to the back of each piece helped hold it in place. Child Guidance made these puzzles in dozens of designs ranging from public domain nursery rhyme figures to various generic animals, but the company's line of Disney characters produced in this style are the most impressive.

Western/Whitman also produced board games, as did such other giant companies as Milton Bradley, Transogram, and Ideal, all working under separate licensing agreements. Cartoon character games could range from the simple "whoever arrives at Point B first wins" type to ones whose rules were so complicated that even an adult would have trouble following them. (The prime example of this is a 1972 Whitman release, Woody Woodpecker's Crazy Mixed-Up Color Factory, which features beautiful artwork on the box and board but is virtually unplayable.)

Making up for their otherwise simplified rules, often the instructions would set up the premise of the game as a sort of ministory, reinforcing their relationship to the source material. One of the best examples comes from Milton Bradley's 1971 Yogi Bear Game. This is how its theme is introduced:

Walter Lantz WOODY WOODPECKER'S crazy mixed-up color factory game

HELP POOR CONFUSED WOODY
STRAIGHTEN UP HIS CRAZY
MIXED-UP COLOR FACTORY

The game board for Milton Bradley's 1971 Yogi Bear game is full of amusing poses and dialogue as Yogi tries to beat Ranger Smith to the ranger station.

Yogi and Boo Boo were at home in their cave. It was a nice day and the door was open. The aroma of fresh baked cakes and doughnuts drifted through the open door. Yogi knew it came from Ranger Smith's headquarters and he was determined to get a taste of those goodies. Boo Boo told Yogi he could get in real trouble if he tried to get them. Yogi said he would go alone, but Boo Boo knew he would help his friend if he could. In this game each player moves both Yogi and Boo Boo through many adventures to be first to get to the Ranger Station and all the sweets there.

In contrast, that same year, Milton Bradley also marketed a Flintstones game that went to considerably less trouble to establish the scene. In fact, it sounds rather like the person who invented it—or at least whoever wrote the instructions—had only the foggiest notion of its source:

Milton Bradley issued this Flintstones game the same year as its Yogi Bear installment, but in stark contrast, the characters look like their artist had never seen them before. Why is an unusually tall Barney wearing his turtle shell hard hat while on vacation?

Parker Brothers sold a Winnie-the-Pooh game from the 1930s right up into the 1970s. Here we see the late 1950s version bearing Stephen Slesinger's copyright and the 1964 edition released soon after Disney bought the merchandising rights. Tigger and Piglet had not yet received their Disney makeovers.

Based on the TV series The Flintstones, in which Fred Flintstone always manages to "mess things up." In this game everyone is invited to come along on a vacation full of Fred's bungling ideas. Try to be first home in spite of all the hazards.

Most cartoon games remained for sale for only a year or two, quickly replaced by the "next big thing" that came along. Some were survivors, though; Milton Bradley's Casper the Friendly Ghost Game was first sold in 1959 and was still available into the 1970s. One game that received periodic face-lifts over at least three decades was Parker Brothers' version of *Winnie-the-Pooh*. Introduced in 1933, while author A. A. Milne was still living, Parker's Pooh was somewhat a forerunner to that postwar baby boom favorite, Candy Land. Designed so very young children could play it without being able to read or count, the game involved drawing colored disks (originally wood, later plastic) out of a bag and then moving one's Pooh character piece to the next square of a matching color on the board.

Parker Brothers must have been proud of its Pooh game, because a beautiful new version of it was issued in 1956. Then, after Disney got the merchandising rights for Pooh away from the Slesinger family in 1964, Parker brought out a re-redesigned version using the character models Disney planned for its first Pooh film. At this preliminary stage, some of them looked a bit different than they would end up—and since neither Piglet nor Tigger was animated in the initial film, they remained in their Ernest Shepard designs for this game. In all of the versions, the rules and path of multicolored squares remained the same, with only the artwork changed to reflect the new look.

Parker Brothers had a long and profitable relationship with Disney. When Disneyland opened in 1955, Parker was on hand with a game themed to each of the four lands (Adventureland, Frontierland, Tomorrowland, and Fantasyland) and sold them for a buck apiece in the park and in stores nationwide. The box lid for the Fantasyland game is especially interesting, using artwork primarily from Little Golden Books to illustrate a horde of cartoon characters entering the famous castle. Somehow, buried within the mob is an unauthorized appearance by Bugs Bunny, wearing a red sweater in an apparent attempt to pass himself off as Brer Rabbit.

Although Parker Brothers did not market as many cartoon-related games as some other companies, the ones it did offer tended a bit toward the unusual. Its 1969 Li'l Abner game was a bit of a throwback in that it pictured Daisy Mae in hot pursuit of her lunkheaded lover, even though the two had been married in the comic strip for more than fifteen years by that time.

The Transogram company is all but forgotten by everyone except vintage toy collectors, but in its day it produced some of the most attractive cartoon games of them all. Transogram got on board the Hanna-Barbera express early on and within a few years had produced games based on *Ruff and Reddy*, *The Jetsons*, *Touché Turtle*, *Snagglepuss*, *Lippy the Lion*, and—of course—*The Flintstones* ("the game that rocked Bedrock!").

Western Printing's Whitman brand also had some terrific artwork in its games, frequently throwing Disney projects to that trusted merchandise artist George Peed. He outdid himself with the illustrations for Whitman's Wonderful World of Color Game, with Ludwig Von Drake and the rest of the crew perched on a spinning, multicolored globe. Peed also brought his unique style to Whitman's 101 Dalmatians Game, among others.

If one company can be said to have dominated the market for licensed games, it would have to be Milton Bradley. Its Yogi and Flintstones games were only a microscopic part of its cartoon catalog, as the company seemed bent on producing a game for nearly every major or minor character or series that was not under an exclusive license to someone else.

Its games could be amazingly complex, too. Consider the 1971 Good Ol' Charlie Brown game, which took about as long to set up as to play (and was just about as much fun). No mere foldout board here; players first had to assemble a three-dimensional replica of the *Peanuts* neighborhood, including

Get out your magnifying glass and look closely at the illustration on this 1956 Fantasyland game from Parker Brothers, and see if you can spot Bugs Bunny making an unauthorized appearance.

Milton Bradley issued these two Warner Bros. board games in the late 1960s. Both mixed characters who rarely if ever shared the screen in the original cartoons.

Transogram was a major Hanna-Barbera licensee in the early 1960s. This Touché Turtle game shows that even a relatively minor H-B character could shine at merchandising time.

George Peed was at work again on the *101 Dalmatians* game board, infusing the character designs from the 1961 animated feature with his trademark style.

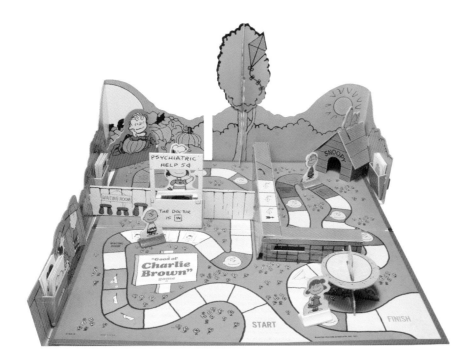

When Milton Bradley decided to create a *Peanuts* board game, the company did not take the easy way out. Players were first required to assemble a replica of the characters' neighborhood, complete with 3-D models of Lucy's psychiatry booth, Snoopy's doghouse, Woodstock's birdbath, and the Kite-Eating Tree.

cardboard models of such landmarks as Lucy's psychiatry booth, Snoopy's doghouse, Linus's pumpkin patch, the kite-eating tree, Woodstock's birdbath, and the brick wall on which the characters were most often seen leaning. That same year, Milton Bradley also issued Lucy's Tea Party, in which players assumed the roles of Charlie Brown, Linus, Peppermint Patty, and the others and attempted to be the first one to have their plastic cup of "tea" (actually, water) overflow. With potentially angry parents in mind, Milton Bradley included a plastic tablecloth as the playing surface.

Although not strictly a board game, the 1970 Milton Bradley Snoopy vs. the Red Baron game also involved a three-dimensional playing surface. One player was to drop marbles down a chute that led directly toward a plastic model of Snoopy's doghouse, with the famed flying ace perched on the roof. The other player was to quickly open the top half of the doghouse to catch the white marbles while leaving it closed to ward off the dark blue ones—yes, this is one game that required some manual and mental skill, as opposed to sheer dumb luck. (On the box lid, Charlie Brown summed up what was probably the experience of many who played this game: "Good grief, I goofed!")

Milton Bradley's A Visit to Walt Disney World game, released at the same time the Orlando park opened, made the Parker Brothers Disneyland games

The long-running association of Disney and Whitman only seemed to grow stronger as the years whizzed by. These 1970s games showed that things had not yet slowed down. (Donnie Pitchford collection)

Second- or third-tier Walter Lantz characters Oswald the Rabbit and Space Mouse enlivened this game board with their ever-cheerful countenances.

look like cutouts from the back of a cereal box. Following the same format as the Charlie Brown game, the playing board required constructing a miniature model of the Magic Kingdom, with replicas of the Haunted Mansion, the castle, and other such landmarks.

Games were also turned out by the boxful by companies other than the huge manufacturers. Woody Woodpecker's Game Box (1964) contained a quartet of simple cardboard playing surfaces and sheets of punch-out pieces; although made by Saalfield instead of Whitman, it followed Western Printing's long-established habit of basing all of them on the Walter Lantz comic books far more than on any of the animated cartoons. Where else could one find Woody Woodpecker, Andy Panda, Chilly Willy, Wally Walrus, Oswald the Rabbit, and Space Mouse all running for president of the United States? Those who desired an end to the traditional two-party system could find comfort in this apparent six-way race.

Although Standard Toykraft and Lowell produced various Mister Magoo games during the 1960s, by 1978 the Magoo license had been passed along to the Warren company; its Oh Magoo, You've Done It Again game hearkened back to Milton Bradley's efforts of the early part of the decade. The board represented the generic cityscape through which Magoo was to blunder during the course of the game, with various buildings and structures to be assembled. Perhaps the most clever inclusion was a square labeled "Eye Doctor." The official rules solemnly instructed, "Magoo *never* lands on this space."

As much fun as it would be to stay here and play games, we now must move along to some of the other successful toys that depended on licensed characters for much of their appeal. Among those were the fondly remembered

Soaky bubble bath toys marketed by the Colgate-Palmolive Company. Since there was nothing new about the concept of bubble bath, this was one example of how the bottle in which the product was sold made all the difference. In fact, just over a year after the product was introduced, the venerable trade publication *Business Week* took notice, titling its article on the subject "How a Package Quadrupled a Market":

> The Colgate staff, together with its advertising agency, Ted Bates and Co., Inc., came up with the new packaging concept over a year ago, and introduced the first two characters, Mickey Mouse and Donald Duck, in January 1962. Colgate Vice-President Robert W. Young Jr., general manager of the company's Household Products Division, recalls: "We expected Soaky to do well, but instead of merely taking over leadership in its field, Soaky has quadrupled the entire market and is virtually revolutionizing the way children take baths in this country."

Colgate and Soaky might have been able to claim that responsibility, but the idea of cartoon bubble bath bottles had been tried before. As early as 1957, the Sears Christmas catalog offered bubble bath in (here they are again) Mickey and Donald bottles, so what exactly enabled Soaky to make such a splash? Probably it has to do with being sold in neighborhood supermarkets rather than department stores and with its bargain price—sixty-nine cents. Whenever suburban kids accompanied their suburban mothers to the suburban supermarket, they were confronted with a colorful array of character bottles—and if a product was likely to make grimy children willing to bathe, Mom might be willing to shell out for it.

In addition to Mickey and Donald, the rest of the early Soaky line was dominated by Disney characters. Goofy, Pluto, and Jiminy Cricket joined in the bath-time fun, with other licenses bringing in Bugs Bunny, Woody Woodpecker, Smokey Bear, Alvin (of the Chipmunks), Mighty Mouse, and Deputy Dawg. *Business Week* described one of the problems inherent in the production of these characters:

> Polyethylene presents a problem in decoration, because ordinary plastic paints will not adhere to it, and polyethylene containers had never been painted in the production quantities Colgate required for this program. A special coating had to be developed for the application. The paint had to be non-toxic and pass three tests specified by Colgate for adhesion to the plastic, a water-immersion test, and an elevated-temperature test in the detergent solution.

Colgate-Palmolive introduced its Soaky brand of bubble bath in January 1962, with Mickey Mouse and Donald Duck (who else?) as the first two figural bottles. (CartoonResearch.com)

Alvin and the Chipmunks, along with long-suffering David Seville, made a special recording as a Soaky bubble bath premium.

During the years it was in production, Soaky grabbed licenses from just about all the major and minor animation studios.

As it turned out, the winning paint was Poly-Fin, a product developed by the Bee Chemical Company, and the physical manufacture of the Soaky bottles was done by Imco Container Company. At the time of *Business Week*'s profile, Soaky bottles were being turned out by Imco at the amazing quantity of seventy thousand per day.

That original style of Soaky bottle was a single piece with a cap on top. Sometimes the cap would be covered with an appropriate decoration, such as Woody Woodpecker's topknot or Alvin's baseball cap, but at other times it was simply left exposed. After a couple of years, Soaky converted to the bottle type most people remember: the body of the character contained the liquid bubble bath, while the cap was covered by the character's screw-off plastic head. This change made it possible to more closely reproduce the licensed characters' true appearance, although some continued to look weird. Elmer Fudd and Harvey Comics' Wendy the Good Little Witch in particular are often unrecognizable to those who encounter them on the collectors' market. While most of the original one-piece characters were remade in this new image, some (notably Goofy, Jiminy, and Woody Woodpecker) never received the face-lift and were simply phased out.

Anything as successful as Soaky was sure to attract the attention of competitors, and in the bubble biz, Colgate's biggest rival was fellow soap maker Purex. Soon after Soaky bubbled up seemingly out of nowhere, Purex launched its own line of decorated bottles under the brand name Bubble Club. Here is where the story gets as murky as dirty bathwater.

The Soaky line included characters from practically every major cartoon studio—except Hanna-Barbera. Bubble Club was 99.9 percent pure Hanna-Barbera only. Why didn't Soaky grab the Hanna-Barbera license first? After so many years, it is impossible to find out. But wait, there's more. Of all the characters Soaky produced, its only Hanna-Barbera bottle was Top Cat. Of all the characters sold under the Bubble Club logo, the only non–Hanna-Barbera one was Beany's pal, Cecil the Sea Serpent. Did the two companies agree to try a swap, or did some loophole in their licensing agreements allow this to happen? Again, with all the parties involved long dead and any legal paperwork either destroyed or locked away in corporate archives, we will never know.

The primary way Bubble Club differed from Soaky was that it came in both liquid and powdered versions, and its character containers varied accordingly. Most were of the Soaky style, with a screw-off head covering the spout, but the ones that held the powdered bubble bath were molded as a single piece, with the contents dispensed through an opening in the bottom. A few containers (Huckleberry Hound, Yogi Bear, and Quick Draw McGraw) held the powdered form but had removable heads, and at least one Hanna-Barbera favorite, Touché Turtle, came in both versions. Standing upright, he held liquid Bubble Club, but another container had him lying on all fours like a real turtle, with powdered contents. Another character forced onto his stomach for this purpose was Wally Gator, who apparently was not made as a standing figure.

Bubble Club was promoted via print ads in *Parents* and other such magazines of the era, while Soaky went all-out with its animated TV spots. The Soaky commercials were miniature gems, usually produced with the original

Rival soap maker Purex fought back against Soaky by coming up with its own product, Bubble Club, which came in a line of bottles based almost exclusively on Hanna-Barbera's properties.

cartoon voices. In one, Alvin and the Chipmunks promote the three bottles made in their images; in another, Popeye and Brutus cheerfully slug it out to determine which of them will be the newest Soaky toy (as it turns out, they both receive that honor). The Soaky commercials also foreshadowed *Who Framed Roger Rabbit* by more than two decades by combining characters from different—and competing—cartoon studios. Superman rescues Tennessee Tuxedo in one adventure, while in another, Dick Tracy apprehends Deputy Dawg's thieving pal Muskie the Muskrat. Another commercial features both Donald Duck and Porky Pig, but perhaps because Disney and Warner Bros. were the two six-hundred-pound gorillas of the industry, the two characters do not interact or appear on screen at the same time.

The fact that Bubble Club's character bottles are somewhat harder to find on the collectors' market today may indicate that those products were less widely distributed than Soaky's.

Both Bubble Club and Soaky remained on supermarket shelves until the end of the 1960s, but production of any new characters seems to have ceased after 1966 or so. By then, both lines were so vast that they hardly needed new additions anyway. After disappearing for several years, both products made something of a comeback in the late 1970s, but in very different ways. Colgate produced a few new characters in 1977, no longer using the Soaky name. These bottle shapes and their decorations were minimalist in the extreme, almost to the point of being abstract in their depictions of Spider-Man, Popeye, and Scooby-Doo (Colgate apparently finagled another Hanna-Barbera license after all those years). The molds for several of the Bubble Club characters were used by a Mexican company known as Roclar to bring back the product under the name Flintstones Fun Bath, even though the Flintstone characters were not among the ones Roclar used. Some of the molds apparently had become lost or damaged, because in the Roclar line, Lippy the Lion's head was joined with Mushmouse's body to form a very runty feline with a very oversized cranium.

Usually considered close cousins to the bubble bath toys are the hundreds of characters produced for the candy containers sold by PEZ (the name always rendered in upper case lettering). Originally a German product, PEZ was introduced into the American market in 1952, but not until a few years later did the company get the idea of placing licensed cartoon character heads atop its slender dispensers. According to historian Margaret Mittelbach, the first character to be so honored was not, as might be expected, one of the Disney gang but Popeye. The exact date of this milestone seems to be uncertain, but an educated guess would be that it happened shortly after the Popeye cartoons' enormously successful release to local TV stations in 1956. Next, according to Mittelbach,

PEZ really began to expand into multiple lines of characters in the 1960s. Along with Popeye, some of the earliest licensed characters were Bozo the Clown, Casper the Friendly Ghost, and of course, Mickey Mouse. Within a short time,

In 1977, Colgate-Palmolive briefly tried to revive the figural bath bottle concept, but as Popeye and Scooby-Doo illustrate, the designs were so simplified as to be almost abstract.

In the 1970s, a Mexican company, Roclar, bought some of the former Purex molds and began using them to contain Flintstones Fun Bath. In this example, Lippy the Lion's head was incongruously joined with Mushmouse's body to create a beast of truly odd proportions.

PEZ is an example of a product that has kept going continuously since it first began using licensed character heads in the late 1950s. As new characters are introduced in movies and television, they are dutifully added to the PEZ line. (Larry Leshan collection)

PEZ was producing a full line of Disney characters, including such widely sought-after dispensers as Jiminy Cricket, Tinker Bell, Snow White and Bambi. (Interestingly, the Bambi head looks more like a space alien than a deer, and the same mold was used for Rudolph the Red-Nosed Reindeer.)

While Colgate and Purex got out of and then occasionally back into the bubble bath toy business over the years, production of new PEZ toys never stopped. They are still available in stores to this day, with new characters introduced regularly to supplement modernized versions of many of the old favorites.

Many kids talked to their toys, but it was thanks to Mattel that some of those toys eventually started talking back. In 1960, the home of Barbie introduced Chatty Cathy, now recognized as the first in a long line of talking dolls; when a string was pulled, a minuscule record player inside would spout a random phrase. Chatty Cathy became another Mattel star, appearing on puzzles and in coloring books, but soon after her debut she was joined by other characters that had gained their fame the old-fashioned way—through show business.

When Mattel took on sponsorship of *Beany and Cecil* in 1961, it was a good enough reason to produce a vast line of toys based on the show, and naturally those included talking versions of both propeller-topped Beany ("Help, Cecil, help!") and his serpentine buddy ("I'm comin', Beany Boy!"). The commercials were narrated by mascot moppets Matty Mattel and Sister Belle, which were also made into talking toys. Parents probably realized they had basically paid for an advertisement when they heard Matty bark, "You can tell it's Mattel! It's swell!"

They walk, they run, they're lots of fun!

Character Skediddles Each **$2⁹⁹**

Famous cartoon characters come to life as the cutest Skediddles ever. Their oversized heads wiggle from side to side when you attach their walkers and push. Each is 4⅓ in. tall; vinyl.
(6) 49 C 30416—**Goofy.** Shpg. wt. 5 oz... $2.99
(7) 49 C 30417—**Donald Duck.** Wt. 5 oz.. . 2.99
(8) 49 C 30418—**Mickey Mouse.** Wt. 5 oz.. . 2.99
(9) 49 C 30413—**Snoopy.** Shpg. wt. 5 oz.. 2.99
(10) 49 C 30414—**Lucy.** Shpg. wt. 5 oz..... 2.99
(11) 49 C 30415—**Charlie Brown.** Wt. 5 oz.. 2.99
Disney characters 6, 7, 8 ©WALT DISNEY PRODUCTIONS
Peanuts characters 9, 10, 11 © 1968 United Features Syndicate

In the late 1960s, Mattel introduced its Skediddlers, which used a control rod in the back to make them "skediddle" across a table or floor. The Disney and *Peanuts* characters received this oversized-cranium treatment.

Mattel really started people—and their toys—talking when it introduced pull-string dolls beginning with Chatty Cathy. By the time of this 1963 ad, several licensed characters were also speaking up for Mattel, and their numbers would increase over the next few years.

WE TALK

I like you!
You called?
What's up Doc?

From MATTEL.. Pull the Ring and listen to them talk

Beany. You never know which one of many phrases he'll say next. 17 in. rag doll has vinyl head, feet and hands. Painted face, hair. Wears shirt, coveralls, copter hat. Needs no batteries. Shpg. wt. 3 lbs. 4 oz.
49 N 3654..........$6.71

Cecil. Comical serpent says many different phrases at random. Rolling plastic eyes. Big 18 in. high.. fluffy, rayon plush. Bright green body with colorful cotton felt trim. Cotton filled. No batteries required.
49 N 4168-Wt. 3 lbs. $8.61

Bugs Bunny. Famous cut-up wisecracks funny phrases .. clutches a big orange carrot. Stands 26½ in. tall. Gray and white rayon plush, vinyl face, hands. Cotton filling. No batteries needed. Wt. 3 lbs. 4 oz.
49 N 4181..........$7.91

Mattel was the sponsor for the weekly *Matty's Funday Funnies* TV show starring the Harveytoons characters, so the company also made many toys in their likenesses.

The Mattel-O-Phone gave youngsters a chance to enjoy one-sided conversations with Charlie Brown, Lucy, Linus, and the rest of the gang.

During the rest of the 1960s, Mattel turned out one character after another in talking doll form. Most of them were logical choices: Bozo the Clown, Casper the Friendly Ghost, Mister Ed, Bugs Bunny, Linus the Lionhearted, and all the other usual suspects. A few defied all rational thinking, however: Why make a talking Tom (of Tom and Jerry fame) when that character did not speak? Mattel also enclosed its talking mechanism inside some hand puppets and toward the end of the 1960s came up with the Mattel-O-Phone, which operated on the same principle except that the talking records could be manually removed and switched around.

Although the Mattel-O-Phone records were necessarily a bit more complex than the ones inside Chatty Cathy and her talkative friends, the basic idea remained the same and is actually even more ingenious than any of us thought when we were youngsters. One popular Mattel-O-Phone allowed kids to have one-sided conversations with the *Peanuts* characters; although the tiny records have the same appearance as any other vinyl or plastic disks of the day, trying to play one on a real turntable exposes Mattel's secret process. In the case of the *Peanuts* records, the grooves on each side actually contain four completely different routines, the selection of which depends entirely on where the stylus hits the first groove. Labeled with generic topics including "Baseball," "Snoopy and the Red Baron," and "The Great Pumpkin," playing any of them produces four different gags, usually taken from the comic strip's own dialogue, on that given subject. Just as with the pull-string toys, the choice of which of the four routines is heard is completely arbitrary.

(Mattel must have done a rather poor job in keeping its trade secrets from getting out. By the late 1960s, Hasbro was also making a talking telephone with interchangeable records that enabled one to talk to Snow White and any of the Seven Dwarfs. Remco manufactured a talking Popeye hand puppet that operated on the same pull-string mechanism as Mattel's products.)

Of course, scores of stuffed cartoon characters did nothing but sit there and look appealing. These could be found in a wide variety of materials, from felt to plush to fake fur, and sometimes a combination of all of them. Some of the most unusual were made under Knickerbocker's Hanna-Barbera license in the late 1950s. They usually featured molded plastic faces on their plush bodies and kept up the grand old tradition of early Hanna-Barbera toys by having color schemes that did not resemble their TV appearances in the slightest. Most of the original casts of *Huckleberry Hound* and *Quick Draw McGraw* were rendered by Knickerbocker in this form. Beginning in 1964, Ideal Toys got into the act with its even higher-quality stuffed toys derived from its two Hanna-Barbera shows, *Magilla Gorilla* and *Peter Potamus*. If you look carefully at scenes during the *Bewitched* sitcom set in young Tabatha's nursery, you will usually see a number of examples of the Ideal Hanna-Barbera dolls being used as set dressing, thanks to the show's association with Screen Gems, H-B's TV distributor.

Closely related to stuffed toys were hand puppets, and Ideal also produced Magilla, Peter, and their costars in that form. A company called Gund, however, probably made the widest variety of cartoon puppets, including a huge cast of major and minor Disney characters. Gund also had the license for many others, including the characters from United Productions of America's *Dick Tracy* cartoons and King Features' early 1960s TV output starring Popeye, Beetle Bailey, and Snuffy Smith. In the earliest days, the

In this terrific 1948 photo, Walter Lantz poses with the stuffed dolls representing his most popular characters, including Woody Woodpecker, Andy Panda, and Oswald the Rabbit. (Jim Engel collection)

Ideal Toys sponsored Hanna-Barbera's *Magilla Gorilla* and *Peter Potamus* in 1964 and marketed a line of extremely well-done plush and rubber renditions of both shows' casts.

Popular character
Hand Puppets
Each
Set of 2 $1⁷⁷

Hand puppets with cloth bodies and rubber heads were some of the most interesting versions of characters from many different studios. Gund and Ideal were the two major manufacturers of this genre of toys.

Mattel revolutionized the old-fashioned jack-in-the-box by making famous characters spring out when the crank was turned. The artwork on the boxes was frequently more appealing than the figure hiding inside.

vinyl heads were practically the only clue as to who the puppet was supposed to represent, as the bodies were fashioned from generic cloth patterns. By 1961 or thereabouts, the bodies were printed with artwork representing the characters' own drawn torsos, often with their names included as part of the design.

One of Gund's best sellers was a Popeye doll that was marketed in conjunction with the old salt's burgeoning TV career in the late 1950s. Its head was the same as the one found on Gund's Popeye hand puppet, but the body was a well-made stuffed version of the sailor man, complete with vinyl arms sporting the requisite bulges and tattoos. An all-vinyl Popeye doll was made by Cameo and sold through Sears around the same time; the Cameo doll gained immortality of sorts by becoming the model for the much-loved and fondly remembered Popeye balloon that enlivened the Macy's Thanksgiving Day Parade for many years.

Mattel was responsible for a vast line of cartoon character musical jack-in-the-boxes beginning in the 1950s. These did not talk but in many cases played the character's theme song when the crank was turned. At the conclusion

of the musical piece, the lid would pop open and the character would emerge; toy-collecting experts have determined that forty-two different designs were made in this series between 1951 and 1992, including Mickey Mouse (of course), Popeye (naturally), Casper, Snoopy, the Cat in the Hat, Porky Pig, Bugs Bunny, Tom and Jerry, and one of the most obscure of all, the foghorn-voiced Super Chief from the *Funny Company* TV cartoons. While the pop-up figures were invariably well made, with molded plastic heads and decorated cloth bodies, the metal boxes in which they hid were even more attractive, with colorful artwork covering all sides.

Mattel used the same basic hand-cranked musical mechanism for its popular line of "Ge-Tars." Again, each one played a specific theme song related to the character pictured on the outside of the miniature instrument; the Popeye Ge-Tar also featured a removable pipe that could be used to strum the Ge-Tar's functionless strings. Over the years, many different other characters made it into Mattel's Ge-Tar lineup, among them Mickey Mouse, Casper, Beany and Cecil, Snoopy, Captain Kangaroo, and Doctor Dolittle.

With today's concerns about child safety, virtually every current toy carries a warning label to alert parents about possible hazards. Consider, then, the vastly different world that existed when Marx Toys introduced the Disneykins, dozens of hard plastic figures direct from Fantasyland, none of them over an inch and a half tall. Some of the smaller ones, such as Tinker Bell and Thumper the rabbit, measured less than a quarter inch. Many Disneykins no doubt ended up in younger kids' mouths, but they were popular for at least fifteen years. Marx also produced a line of much larger Disney characters, molded in solid colors that bordered on fluorescent. A hot pink Mickey Mouse or lime green Donald Duck was a sure sign that Marx was in the house. And, showing no favoritism, Marx also turned the Hanna-Barbera characters into "TV Tinykins," which came and went within only a few years, while the Disneykins just kept on going.

Obviously the goal of any toy company was to get its customers to spend as much money as possible, but during the 1960s, Hasbro did the altruistic thing and decided to help kids save money instead (no doubt hoping said kids would eventually spend said savings on more Hasbro toys). Surely anyone

Long, long before consumer groups oversaw child safety rules, the tiny Disneykins plastic figures made by Marx ended up in many homes—and undoubtedly in many kids' mouths. (Donnie Pitchford collection)

Anyone who watched Saturday morning TV in the late 1960s and early 1970s saw repeated airings of the commercials for Hasbro's cartoon character gumball banks: "Penny for a gumball, Mickey!" "Thanks for the gumball!"

Punching bags with cartoon decorations were consistent sellers, but the choice of characters to depict on them was sometimes a bit odd. What kid would want to punch Fred Flintstone or Bozo? And who at Disney ever approved these bizarre designs for Donald Duck and Mickey Mouse?

who grew up in the late 1960s or early 1970s remembers the incessant TV commercials for Hasbro's line of gumball-dispensing character banks: "Penny for a gumball, Mickey!" "Thanks for the gumball!" Like Mattel with its talking toys, Hasbro applied the same basic gumball bank mechanism to toys of many different licensed characters, whose clear plastic heads contained the candy. Judging from what is available today, Mickey Mouse and Popeye were the most popular, but other Hasbro banks included Fred Flintstone, Scooby-Doo, and the Pink Panther.

Various companies sold rubber punching bags under several different brand names, the most common being Punchos and Punch-Me's. Like the gumball banks, the basic toy was the same, differing only in the character whose image was printed on the front. In one of my other books, *Christmas Wishes: A Catalog of Holiday Treats and Treasures*, I note that it seems odd that the toy companies made punching bags out of characters that normal, mentally healthy kids would really have no desire to hit. Think about it: if given the chance, wouldn't you have liked to have Yogi Bear, Bozo, Fred Flintstone, Mister Magoo, and Woody Woodpecker as friends rather punching them in the snoot? They were friendly, funny, and always doing or saying something interesting, yet the punching bag manufacturers seemed bent on encouraging youngsters to whale away at them as if they were bad guys. Occasionally at least some attempts at reason were made; the Bullwinkle punching bag, for example, pictured the moronic moose in a boxing outfit and a pugilistic pose, as if he were encouraging being bopped, but most of the others bore their usual cheerful countenances. Strangest of all were the punching bags

that pictured Popeye, Superman, or Batman, characters with which no kid in his or her right mind would ever deliberately provoke a fight.

For those who had peaceful rather than fighting personalities, an endless variety of toys might all be considered to fall under the category of arts and crafts. However, even today's most sensitive, artistic dreamer might stand slack-jawed at the low-tech nature of those toys. First, we take up the subject of Rub-Ons. You do remember those, right?

Hasbro must have been especially aggressive when it came to pursuing licenses for its Rub-Ons, as the total line included practically every major and minor cartoon character in existence—except the Hanna-Barbera properties, for reasons about which I speculate below. The idea of Rub-Ons was stunningly simple. They were paper transfers that could be "rubbed on" a pre-printed background scene to form a complete picture; that was it. The backgrounds had empty white spaces where the rubbed-on pictures were to go, so the whole effect was much like that of the "sticker fun" books Western Printing had made into such a big deal. When done well, the completed Rub-Ons pictures were attractive enough that some parents framed them to use as wall decorations, but therein was the toy's main drawback. Rub-Ons could only be used once, after which it was either frame the picture, toss it into the toy box, or throw it away. This lack of "repeat play" was a great thing from Hasbro's point of view, as it kept parents constantly buying new Rub-Ons sets, but it contributed greatly to the toy's scarcity today, as few people took the time to hang onto a box of pictures that had outlived their useful purpose.

As stated above, Rub-Ons were made for multiple Disney subjects, the Warner Bros. characters, Casper and his Harveytoons crowd, and the DC Comics superheroes, among many others, but no representatives from Hanna-Barbera. This may well be because another toy company already had the market in the basket for artsy Hanna-Barbera products, and that company was Kenner.

In the next chapter we will revisit the Kenner/Hanna-Barbera association and how it applied to Kenner's megahit Give-A-Show Projector and other such optical toys. When it came to arts and crafts, though, Kenner was ready to get its hands dirty right along with the kids. Or, more correctly, perhaps we should say it got its hands gloppy. Uh—what was that again, you say? Yes, Gloppy was the brand name the mad scientists at Kenner chose for their modeling clay that took the most famous elements of Play-Doh and Silly Putty and combined them with the company's valuable and long-established Hanna-Barbera license.

RUB-ONS™...just a rub makes a picture

The most wonderful toy for every girl and boy!

Hasbro's Rub-Ons were a prime example of the type of toy that was rarely saved after it was played with, as there was really nothing left to do with it except look at the pictures that had been created.

Kenner's version of Play-Doh was known as Gloppy and came in plastic molds of the Hanna-Barbera characters. Few kids had the artistic ability to duplicate the models of Magilla Gorilla, Astro the dog, and the other figures shown on the box.

Gloppy sets came in varying sizes, but each one contained between three and six clear plastic molds in the shapes of Secret Squirrel, Yogi Bear, Space Ghost, and other Hanna-Barbera stars. The substance was tinted in shades of blue, yellow, and hot pink, and the instruction sheet enthusiastically promoted the idea that the molds could be used to fashion characters in multiple colors to more closely approximate their TV appearances ("the head in one color, the body in another and the feet in the third color"). In addition to the main molds, there were smaller molds of characters not fortunate enough to be represented full size, including Touché Turtle, Wally Gator, and Peter Potamus.

One has to wonder just how many kids mastered Gloppy's most challenging concept. Each set included cardboard "Figure Forms" that created basic, skeletal shapes of still more characters, including Magilla Gorilla, Astro (the Jetsons' dog), and Boo Boo. The idea, according to the instruction sheet, was to

> Fill in the shapes with Gloppy, smoothing the surface with your fingers or the modeling tool. With a little skill, the figures can be rounded to give them full dimension.
>
> Extra touches can be used, such as stroking the figure of Boo Boo with a comb to give the effect of hair, or applying little dabs of Gloppy to make him look shaggy. Suspenders, ties and collars can be added.

It would have taken an artist of considerable skill to duplicate the finished figures of these characters that appeared on the instruction sheet and on the box. Perhaps sheer frustration was responsible for Gloppy's relatively short shelf life; despite its sticky nature, it certainly has not stuck around in the memories of as many people as Kenner's other products.

Kenner also appealed to the innate artist in each kid with its collection of Sparkle-Paint Sets, Presto-Paint Sets, and for the true nonconformist, Presto-Sparkle Paint Sets. And just what were these sets? The advertising for Presto-Paints coyly stated, "Paint brilliant water colors without water or brushes—no dipping, no spilling. Just pick up and paint!" Notice that Kenner never said exactly what Presto-Paints were, but they sure sound like close relatives of felt-tip markers. Sparkle-Paints were a bit easier to describe, as kids were to use tubes of glitter to highlight specified areas of the pre-printed pictures that came with each set. Yes, Sparkle-Paints were no doubt one of those toys your parents had better sense than to buy for you, although there was a strong possibility you might get them from another kid at your

Assembling model kits of airplanes was a popular hobby, made even more interesting when the subject was Snoopy in his World War I Sopwith Camel.

With Mattel's Picture Maker, kids could practice drawing the *Peanuts* crew. The Barbie and Hot Wheels designs involved no licensing fees because they were Mattel's own properties.

Kenner's Presto Paints, Sparkle Paints, and Presto-Sparkle Paints provided hours of quiet but messy fun for kids with an artistic bent. (Steve Reisiger collection)

birthday party (if her parents hated your parents, for example). Toy historian Tom Frey has wittily described Sparkle-Paints: "While kids took a shine to their finished artwork, their artwork put a shine on them."

For reasons unknown, Kenner seems to have ignored its own Hanna-Barbera license when it came to these particular toys. Presto-Paints starred Popeye and Mighty Mouse and in 1966 jumped on the Batman batwagon with a set featuring those "TV favorites," as the box described them. Sparkle-Paints cast their lot with the United Productions of America Studio, calling on Dick Tracy and seeing what Mister Magoo could do for them. Then, Presto-Sparkle Paints combined the elements of both previous toys and gave kids a chance to make a huge mess out of Rocky and Bullwinkle and the Three Stooges.

If one thought Kenner's Presto-Paints and Hasbro's Rub-Ons were low-tech, they had not yet been exposed to the miracle of Colorforms. Unlike the others, Colorforms were not a product nestled among a vast line of other products from the same company: Colorforms were made by the Colorforms Company and originally had nothing to do with licensed characters. Harry Kislevitz and his wife, Patricia. invented the disarmingly simple idea of sticking vinyl pieces onto a laminated background in 1951 and originally marketed Colorforms as a form of art. They were considered equally entertaining for both kids and adults, and the small vinyl pieces were made in simple geometric shapes that could be arranged according to the user's creative whims. Toward the end of the 1950s, Kislevitz began licensing characters for the Colorforms kits, and what had already been successful became even more so. Since Colorforms kits sold for one dollar for a basic set and two dollars for the deluxe model, parents could load up their progeny with several different kits, all designed with the tantalizing promise of "quiet play." (If any kids heard that slogan, they could well be expected to try their best to prove it wrong.)

It was no small selling point that Colorforms' licensed character sets were known as "Cartoon Kits," with the appropriate title ahead of that description. Most of the early 1960s Hanna-Barbera stars, a long line of Disney subjects, Dick Tracy, Bozo the Clown, Popeye, and numerous others made their way into the Cartoon Kits. The TV advertising was even more creative than the actual toy, using the Colorforms pieces animated via stop-motion to make Popeye, Olive Oyl, and Bluto act out a simple story, for example. Throughout the 1960s, it seemed there would never be an end to Colorforms' successful formula.

At this point in our story, we must introduce Mel Birnkrant, a freelance commercial artist who came to have a tremendous influence on the world of licensed merchandise. Along with John Fawcett, Robert Lesser, Ernest Trova, and a few others, mostly Manhattanites, Birnkrant had been one of the first individuals to recognize the value of early character toys, particularly the Disney ones, and begin collecting them. The general public first became aware of this phenomenon around 1968, and even then it was almost a joke more than anything else. Birnkrant likes to describe how there was not even a name for what he and the others were doing: the items for which they were searching in New York junk shops certainly did not fit the accepted "one hundred years old" definition of antiques, but no one knew how else to refer to them. Finally, Birnkrant says, someone invented the word *collectibles* to describe artifacts that were not old enough to be antiques but that people were buying for nostalgia (and as an investment). The term stuck.

Would-be hipsters and anti-Establishment types began sporting Mickey Mouse watches as a way of showing their contempt for the "normal" world. It did not take long for this jocularity to develop into a full-fledged collectors' market—and the toys, books, and other memorabilia of the depression years sported the sometimes primitive image of Mickey and his friends they sought. Most of them expressed public disdain if not outright hatred for the more streamlined and humanized Mickey, Donald, and so on that had become the norm in the early 1940s. (Time, as is its habit, continued marching

Colorforms' Cartoon Kits of the late 1950s and early 1960s were paragons of simplicity: you stuck the plastic pieces onto a background sheet and removed them. That was all the entertainment needed in those days, though.

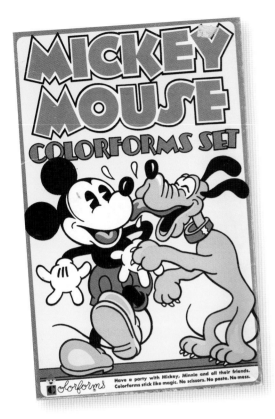

Pioneering Disney merchandise collector Mel Birnkrant was responsible for reviving the depression-era look of the characters in the Colorforms sets he created in the early 1970s.

on, however, and now the 1950s, 1960s, and 1970s Disney merchandise is eagerly collected by those who grew up during those periods.)

So it was that Birnkrant found himself assigned to come up with some new Disney products for Colorforms, and he was torn between his personal preference for depression-era Mickey and the mainstream version of the Disney characters that proliferated. He soon encountered two of the biggest wigs in Disney's New York licensing office, executive Jack Smith and "idea man" Al Konetzni. Birnkrant's exhaustive autobiography, published on his own website, describes how his ideas both dovetailed with what was happening with nostalgia buffs nationwide and perplexed Disney:

> Al was both fascinated and enraged that collectors were paying relatively big bucks for things that in his day sold for pennies. He loudly complained about antique dealers, and wracked his brain trying to figure out how Disney could either get a piece of that action, or put a stop to it!
>
> Because I was aware that Mickey had never been allowed to be seen in his original incarnation with pie-cut eyes and circular anatomy since 1939, I urged Harry Kislevitz to clear it with Disney before I set out on my hallowed task of bringing vintage Mickey back again.

Although Konetzni would later become an enthusiastic collector of Disneyana, his attitude here reflected the puzzlement of the whole Disney corporation; it had gotten its licensing fees four decades earlier, and now "collectibles" dealers were selling those same old toys for many times their original prices—and Disney got nothing. That feeling no doubt prompted the company to give a cautious go-ahead for Birnkrant and Colorforms to begin trying to re-create the old look. (Today, such a move would be called "retro," but it did not have a name in 1972.)

As a matter of fact, Birnkrant claims that at first he was plagued with clueless Disney secretaries complaining that some of his character art did not match the current model sheets, which of course was his entire point. This explains why some of Birnkrant's early Mickey/Colorforms kits have 1930s versions of Mickey, Minnie, and Goofy but 1940s (and later) renditions of Donald, Daisy, and Pluto. Come to think of it, since Daisy Duck was not introduced into the Disney world until 1940, it might have been difficult for Birnkrant to depict her in a form that would have matched his preferred long-billed Donald of the 1930s.

Whatever tribulations Birnkrant had to endure, his work created an entirely new market for Disney merchandise that still exists today. In his words,

Thus the flood gate was open. More attempts to rediscover vintage Mickey followed, not just from me but from others. A sweatshirt was produced with that overused image of old Mickey with his hands behind his back and one foot forward. Overnight it sold 50 thousand pieces. Disney was stunned and mystified; they couldn't understand it. Al Konetzni finally decided it was "Mod Mickey," and naming it accordingly, a new licensed property was born.

Carrying on with the theme of "re-creating" vintage Mickey merchandise that had never existed before, Colorforms branched out into home gardening territory in 1974 with a series of seed packets—both vegetables and flowers—with Birnkrant's depression-era Disney artwork on the packages. The idea was that once the seeds were planted, the empty packets could be used as row markers and, as Birnkrant put it, if the plants took too long to grow, at least the packets would be fun for kids to look at. However, the public did not seem to take to the idea of purchasing garden supplies from a toy company; according to Birnkrant, "When you plan to plant a garden, who would you believe, Mickey Mouse or Burpee Seeds? Well, I for one would choose Mickey seeds—provided a live Mickey Mouse is what they grew."

Also in 1974, Colorforms acquired the license for the *Peanuts* crew. Birnkrant's telling of the story leads once again to the question of just how much of the art on the *Peanuts* merchandise was Charles M. Schulz's and how

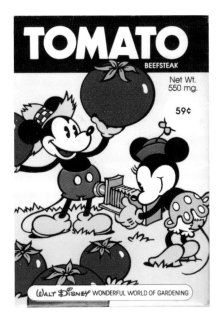

Colorforms made a brief excursion into marketing flower and vegetable seeds, assigning Mel Birnkrant to illustrate the colorful retro packaging.

much was ghosted. Birnkrant flatly states that Nick LoBianco was the only other artist to whom Schulz would grant the right to draw Charlie Brown and company for merchandise: for the many different *Peanuts* Colorforms kits, Birnkrant would do the original sketches, and then LoBianco would "trace over my drawings with his Schulz approved brush and ink line."

Returning briefly to Hasbro, whom we left rubbing on Rub-Ons a few pages back, we should mention that company's late 1960s innovation known as Lite-Brite. No baby boomer has to be reminded of how the toy operated, with clear plastic pegs that could be punched through a black paper background to form illuminated artwork via a light bulb housed inside the box. Although most Lite-Brite subjects were generic or abstract, the company did manage to get out a few sets that applied the same principle to Bozo the Clown, Bugs Bunny, and later the *Peanuts* gang.

We cannot forget what must have been the most basic yet most common art-related toys on the market. Does the term *Magic Slate* bring back any blurry memories? It should, because the pictures kids created with it were usually pretty blurry. A Magic Slate was nothing but a piece of gray plastic laid over a waxy background, so that whatever was drawn on the top sheet

Bozo the Clown was one of several characters represented in Hasbro's refill pages for its popular Lite-Brite toy. Others included the Warner Bros. characters, the *Peanuts* gang, and Popeye.

would create a picture that required only a lift of the plastic to erase it and start anew. (It was sort of the lower-tech version of an Etch-a-Sketch, if such a thing were possible.) The only feature that distinguished one Magic Slate from another was the cardboard backing, which came decorated with a more-than-wide range of licensed characters. Since Western Printing owned so many of those licenses, Whitman was one of the largest producers of Magic Slates. The product must have been sheer joy to the company, as no components had to be changed from example to example; once a new design was created, printing the cardboard backing was the only difference.

The vast majority of the toys discussed in this chapter fall under the "unisex" heading—in other words, they could be enjoyed equally by boys and girls, without the gender distinction that went with, say, G. I. Joe, Barbie, or the Easy-Bake Oven. Oh sure, the cartoon-decorated punching bags might have been considered primarily boys' items, but enough big sisters were sharpening their hitting skills on their little brothers to make even that point somewhat moot. For the most part, toy manufacturers going to the trouble and expense of paying for cartoon licenses wanted to market the resulting toys to as large a segment of the population as possible, not just one half or the other.

Does this chapter even begin to include all the different types of items one would find in any well-stocked toy department of the baby boomer years? No, but have no fear, Underdog is here—uh, that is, don't worry, because some of the other types will be getting chapters of their own. Don't get too engrossed in arranging those Colorforms pieces or working out the details of that Casper jigsaw puzzle . . . there is much more to come.

The Magic Slate was the most basic of all toys: the manufacturer (in this case, Whitman) needed only to secure a license and come up with some artwork for the cardboard backing, and the rest of the production process remained the same no matter what character was featured.

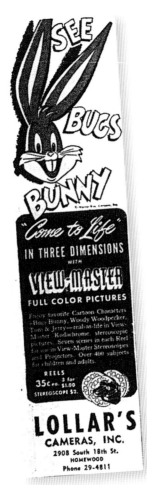

Although View-Master was originally developed as a diversion for adults and not a child's plaything, by the time of this 1953 ad, some very famous licensed cartoon characters were beginning to make their 3-D debuts.

The Tru-Vue Company originally owned the rights to make stereo slides of the Disney properties, but View-Master eventually bought Tru-Vue, mainly to gain that very lucrative license.

View-Master continued to release many of its reels as Tru-Vue slides well into the 1970s.

Chapter 5

WINDOWS INTO ANOTHER WORLD

If you were a part of the baby boom generation, surely you spent a goodly portion of your early years marveling at the intricate little scenes of View-Master reels. The special viewer brought the scenes into three-dimensional reality long before movie producers thought about doing the same thing—and with View-Master, you didn't have to wear those weird-looking red and blue glasses.

Most of us baby boomers did not realize that View-Master dated back to our parents' childhoods, and of course 3-D photography was invented even before that. In the late nineteenth and early twentieth centuries, stereopticon viewers were standard equipment in living rooms and parlors, with printed cardboard cards of two slightly varying views merging in the viewer to form scenes from the era's lavish World's Fairs and other scenic events. In 1931, the Tru-Vue Company of Rock Island, Illinois, began producing stereo slides and filmstrips; this company would eventually have a major impact on the better-known View-Master.

View-Master was invented in 1938 and made its public debut at the 1939 New York World's Fair. Its innovation was in having its pairs of stereo scenes arranged in a circle around the edge of a cardboard reel that could be inserted into a hand-held viewer. The combination of brilliant color photography and the luminosity that came from viewing the scenes with the light source projected through them from behind rather than from in front gave View-Master productions a quality unmatched by any competition. The parent company, Sawyer's of Portland, Oregon, knew it had something special, and contrary to our own childhood experiences, View-Master was *not* considered a toy. Viewers and reels were sold in photography shops and the photo sections of large department stores; they were not something for rambunctious youngsters to play with.

Likewise, licensing famous cartoon stars was not part of the original plan. For its first dozen years, View-Master concentrated on photographing exotic locales, fauna, and flora to be preserved in the 3-D format. A new line of fairy tale reels was eventually introduced, utilizing photography of miniature models and scenery. This led directly into doing the same thing with cartoon characters, although that idea

View-Master artist Joe Liptak was responsible for most of that company's Hanna-Barbera reels. Liptak was justifiably proud that no cartoon studio ever asked for revisions to his 3-D models of its famous characters.

began slowly. At first, View-Master reels were sold individually, rather than in the three-reel sets we remember so well. The first three cartoon reels, debuting in 1951, were Bugs Bunny and Elmer Fudd in "The Hunter," Tom and Jerry in "Cat Trapper," and Woody Woodpecker in "Pony Express Ride." As late as 1955, the View-Master catalog, included only these three cartoon subjects plus a Walter Lantz three-reel set that included a different Woody story as well as Andy Panda and Chilly Willy reels.

These early cartoon productions are still appealing, but they lack the detail to be found in later releases. The Tom and Jerry one, for example, features extremely simple backgrounds and scenery, and the 3-D models of the battling cat and mouse appear to be covered in some sort of flocking similar to that used on Christmas tree ornaments. The stories necessarily had to be brief—they had to be told in only seven frames—and they often resembled a single gag in a typical theatrical cartoon. The 1955 Woody Woodpecker set also showed the influence of Western Printing's version of the characters, with the comic book team of Andy Panda and Charlie Chicken running afoul (well, at least Charlie was a fowl) of Wally Walrus at the beach.

View-Master was well aware not only of Tru-Vue's existence but also that Tru-Vue had already managed to snare the lucrative license to produce Disney material in 3-D. To gain that and eliminate a competitor at the same time, Sawyer's purchased the Tru-Vue Company outright in the early 1950s. However, rather than discarding the line, Sawyer's continued to market Tru-Vue's product right up through the late 1960s, sometimes issuing the same stories and scenes on round View-Master reels and oblong Tru-Vue cards. Just to make sure everyone knew who was the boss, though, the Tru-Vue slides were produced on cheaper film stock that turned red after several years. In comparison, some View-Master reels have held their brilliant colors for nearly eight decades.

As the Disney characters joined the rest of View-Master's licensed cast, the creation of the miniature scenes rose to new artistic heights. View-Master historians Mary Ann and Wolfgang Sell have worked tirelessly to identify the artists responsible for creating these tiny glimpses into a fantasy world; some of the work was done in Hollywood, while some was created in Sawyer's Portland studios. The Sells identify the earliest of the View-Master artists as Florence Thomas, who began her work on the fairy tale reels and only occasionally ventured into licensed character work. Her working methods were the same as those of most of her successors:

Modeled in wet clay, each figure was subject to a certain percentage of shrinkage in drying. Therefore, it was necessary to make each figure a bit oversize to fit into the set and complement the other figures. Most difficult of all was the exact likeness of the same character. Tom Corbett in scene one had to look exactly like Tom Corbett on all the rest of the scenes and had to be close enough in appearance to satisfy his copyright owners.

Joe Liptak was primarily responsible for most of View-Master's (and Tru-Vue's) cartoon reels. The Sells identify him as creating most of the Disney subjects plus the early Hanna-Barbera reels starring Yogi Bear, Huckleberry Hound, and Quick Draw McGraw. As the Sells tell it, "Joe is justifiably proud that neither Disney nor Hanna-Barbera ever returned a test shot of a set he produced because of company dissatisfaction."

Whereas Thomas created all-new figures for each shot, Liptak and most of his contemporaries followed the precedent set by those who created stop-motion animation— that is, building figures that could be twisted and bent into new poses, perhaps with different heads for varying facial expressions. In the case of most of Liptak's figures, the clothing was made of the same plastic-like material as the rest of the character.

Other unsung View-Master artists included Lelia Pearson, who made something of a specialty out of creating

By the time of this 1968 ad, View-Master reels spanned every type of cartoon character, fairy tale, and famous roadside tourist attraction.

Self-lighted Stereo Viewer shows every scene uniformly bright   Low-cost unlighted Stereo Viewer

Although there could not be two more different cartoon properties than *Peanuts* and *The Road Runner*, the View-Master versions of both were sculpted by Lelia Pearson. Her *Peanuts* characters differ from most View-Master scenes in that the clay figures wore actual miniature clothing.

Not all View-Master scenes were created with 3-D models; some, such as *Mighty Mouse*, used overlapping layers of flat artwork to simulate depth. In later years, this became the preferred way of adapting animated characters to the medium.

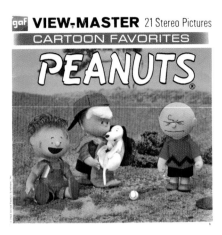

Peanuts reels. Pearson's approach differed from Liptak's in that the Schulz characters wore genuine clothing (miniature shirts, pants, and dresses) rather than molded clothes. Pearson was also responsible for what might initially seem to be the complete opposite of the introspective world of *Peanuts*: View-Master's *Road Runner* packet, in which some of the violent gags from the cartoons were broken down into seven frames each.

This might be a good spot to mention that not all cartoon View-Master reels used these modeled figures. Some used what the company referred to as "3-D drawings," looking much like animated cartoon cels but photographed in such a way that they still had depth. (The company steadfastly kept the method for doing this a secret, for good reason.) The reason or logic behind which cartoon properties were produced in which style was not always clear. Donald Duck, for example, was done with models, but Mickey Mouse was done with drawings. There were two different *Popeye* packets, one resembling Bill Zaboly's comic strip version and the other in the Bud Sagendorf style, not using models. In some cases, the two styles would even be combined: *Casper's Ghostland* has the Harvey Comics characters done as drawings but the backgrounds and any supporting cast as models.

The writers responsible for the miniature storybook that accompanied each three-reel packet received little recognition, but they, too, had the responsibility of remaining as close to the source material as possible. This was not easy, as with the *Bullwinkle* packet, where it was a challenge to simulate the wacky wordplay of the television show. A highlight of that packet's story booklet is its description of a delightfully evil Snidely Whiplash "rubbing his hands with Glee (a new washday detergent)."

As the years went by, all of View-Master's productions that had used the tabletop models were converted over to the drawn style, and of course, new ones are still being produced. Ostensibly the conversion occurred because the drawings more closely resembled the characters' screen appearances, but there was also the economic reality that it was expensive to create miniature scenes that were photographed once and then dismantled. Collectors generally prefer the modeled type for the sheer intricacy of their detail, but any View-Master production, new or old, gives a marvelous glimpse into a new dimension.

After View-Master, the second-largest producer of optical toys was Kenner, for which these toys were only a small part of the catalog. Unlike View-Master, which began as a product for adults and only gradually evolved into a plaything, Kenner was in the business of making toys, pure and simple. The cheaper they could be produced, the cheaper they could be sold, so Kenner was most successful with its simplest products. Few could have been simpler than the venerable Give-A-Show Projector.

Introduced in 1960, Give-A-Show was a molded plastic projector that ran on a battery-powered flashlight bulb. Its slides were not three-dimensional like View-Master's, but they were larger—the size of standard 35mm slides—and extremely colorful. At times it seemed that the Give-A-Show slides should have been viewed with black light rather than a flashlight bulb, so bright were their fluorescent colors. There was a similarity, though, in that Give-A-Show's stories were told in seven panels each, though they were arranged in a row like a comic strip rather than in disk form, with the dialogue in captions underneath each image. For most of its existence, the seven individual Give-A-Show slides were mounted in a cardboard strip bearing the title and copyright information; these strips were prone to warping over the years, so late in the product's life span, the slides became one continuous strip printed on film stock.

Apparently Kenner was not positive about exactly what direction Give-A-Show would take. The standard selection of sixteen different slides was established from the first set, but of those original 1960 sixteen, only six featured licensed cartoon stars. The remainder of the set comprised generic fairy tales, public domain characters (Annie Oakley, Buffalo Bill, Kit Carson, Wild Bill Hickok, and Wyatt Earp, all carefully divorced from any of their TV incarnations), and a couple of live-action series (Maverick and the Three Stooges). Since the actual cartoon slides numbered so few, perhaps we can take a closer look at them and see how they made use of their licensed properties.

In 1960, Kenner introduced its highly successful Give-A-Show Projector. Dozens of cartoon characters would be turned into seven-frame Give-A-Show slides over the next two decades, but Popeye was a fixture. (Steve Reisiger collection)

Popeye in "To the Rescue": This being the period in between Bluto and Brutus, the villain is neither one, but he tries to carry off Olive Oyl anyway. No prizes for guessing what Popeye does to not-Bluto after eating spinach.

Yogi Bear in "All at Sea": Yogi and good buddy Huckleberry Hound are adrift in a boat that is rapidly taking on water. Yogi's solution is to drill a hole in the bottom of the boat so the water can run out.

Huckleberry Hound in "Jinks' Surprise": Despite his star billing, Huck appears only in the opening panel before disappearing. Pixie and Dixie surprise Jinks with a spring-loaded boxing glove inside a jack-in-the-box.

Quick Draw McGraw in "Two Heads Are Better Than One": The dim-witted sheriff draws the fire of hostile Native Americans with a dummy head made to look like his own—and practically as empty.

Woody Woodpecker in "Go, Go, Goat": Rather unusually told in rhyme, this story has Woody trying to use a goat to budge a stubborn mule, only to end up riding the goat instead.

Oswald the Rabbit in "Bug Game Hunter": Another rhyming story; Oswald's butterfly net helps him escape from Reddy Fox. In a seeming nod to the

Kenner made good use of its left-over slides from past Give-A-Show sets by boxing them and selling them to those who had missed them the first time around.

For a number of years in the 1960s, Kenner would release two different Give-A-Show sets annually, one with the usual mix of cartoon characters, and another focusing exclusively on the Hanna-Barbera stars. (Steve Reisiger collection)

Uncle Remus tales, Oswald leaves the fox with the net over his head and the handle plugging the opening in a nearby hornets' nest. "I'll bet that pest / Stays close to that nest!"

The pattern was thus set for how most future stories would be handled. In 1961, obviously deciding that bigger was always better, Kenner introduced the Deluxe Give-A-Show, with twice as many slides included. Returning from the first set were Huck and Yogi, Popeye, and Woody Woodpecker, to be joined by new arrivals Rocky and Bullwinkle, Bozo the Clown, Mighty Mouse, Heckle and Jeckle, and others. Public domain stories continued to fill in gaps, including some Aesop's Fables and the story of the "Union Drummer Boy," aka Johnny Shiloh, just in time for the Civil War centennial. Perhaps the inclusion of that last one hurt the projector's sales south of the Mason-Dixon Line, because the Deluxe Give-A-Show sets are comparatively difficult to locate today, while the years of standard sixteen-slide boxed sets are plentiful on the antique and collectibles market.

Kenner returned to the normal-sized boxes in 1962 and began another tradition that year. Because Kenner was a huge Hanna-Barbera licensee, one of the two 1962 sets contained nothing but characters from that prolific studio, padding its sixteen slides by having two different stories each with Augie Doggie, Huckleberry Hound, Yogi Bear, Quick Draw McGraw, and Ruff and Reddy. The Flintstones rated three stories, while Snagglepuss and Snooper and Blabber were relegated to one each. The second set, as would become customary, was nonexclusive, mixing characters from many different studios with merry abandon.

As the older Give-A-Show sets were replaced by each year's newer collection on toy department shelves, what to do with the leftover slide inventory? Someone had a marketing brainstorm: package them in boxes of six slides each and sell them for less than a dollar per box. You have to give Kenner credit for milking every possible cent out of its slide show concept, and keeping up with the constantly multiplying list of Kenner's projectors in the mid-1960s would have required the services of those "eight maids a-milking" of Christmas fame.

One of the most ambitious was the Super Show Projector. This set came with fewer Give-A-Show slides but packed its box with multiple other activities. Super Show was an opaque projector (remember those from school?) as well as a slide projector, so one of its big selling points was that it came with flat puppets of the Flintstones, Popeye, Rocky and Bullwinkle, and other members of Kenner's licensed cast. These were controlled by rods from below in the fashion of shadow puppets and could be used to act out stories via

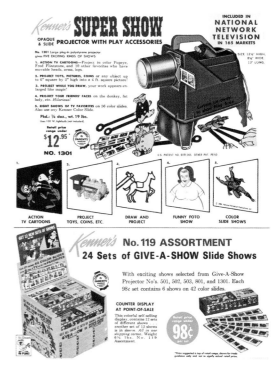

The Super Show Projector attempted to go Give-A-Show several ones better by including puppets and other paraphernalia for creating one's own productions. (Steve Reisiger collection)

Kenner's answer to View-Master and Tru-Vue was the See-A-Show viewer, with 3-D scenes printed on cards rather than on film stock.

In the early 1970s, yet another mutation of Kenner's projectors was the Screen-A-Show, which was somewhat like a drive-in movie theater.

Give-A-Show Projectors were still going strong in the mid-1970s, when new characters such as Hong Kong Phooey were sharing the billing with Kenner veterans that included Bugs Bunny.

Super Show's opaque capabilities. Apart from the cartoon elements, Super Show also came with blank Give-A-Show slides so kids could draw their own stories. Perhaps Super Show was a little too elaborate, because like the De-luxe Give-A-Show attempt, it did not have the lasting power of the original, simple Give-A-Show Projector.

Another new product was the See-A-Show Stereo Viewer. Yes, the name gave it away: this was Kenner's answer to View-Master, but it actually more closely resembled Tru-Vue. The See-A-Show stories were not on slides but were printed cardboard cards that hearkened back to the earliest 3-D stere-opticon viewers from more than fifty years earlier. To Kenner's credit, the company did not simply recycle the artwork from its Give-A-Show slides but created new stories, still told in the traditional seven frames. Let's look at a few examples.

Snuffy Smith in "Sky-High Still": While Snuffy catches "a leetle nap," Jughaid tightens the valve on the rustic's still, causing it (and its potent contents) to explode across the vicinity. One of Snuffy's bewhiskered neighbors comments, "You shore keep a messy still, Snuffy."

Superman in "The Eyes Have It": Bank robbers tie up Superman and leave him helpless in a room next to a Kryptonite chunk. But Supes uses his X-ray vision to melt a lead blackjack one of the miscreants has left behind, causing it to coat the deadly substance in time for him to punch out the crooks. "Aren't you boys glad I'm feeling better?" Um . . . but if Kryptonite neutralized Superman's superpowers, how was his X-ray vision still working?

Dick Tracy in "A Switch in Time": Detective Joe Jitsu traps the Mole, who is escaping by train, with the old cartoon trick of painting a tunnel on a sheer rock face and then diverting the locomotive toward it. Why would a set of tracks be built leading to a sheer rock face? In cartoons, it's best not to ask logical questions.

The See-A-Show sets also featured stories with Linus the Lionhearted in the days when he was still merely a cereal mascot and not the star of his own series. He was seen interacting with generic jungle beasts rather than his later TV cohorts Sugar Bear, Rory Raccoon, and Lovable Truly the postman.

In the early 1970s, Kenner's Screen-A-Show Projector tried to improve on what did not need improving by placing the usual Give-A-Show type slides into cassettes that advanced via rollers, much like an old-fashioned scroll. The toy projected the image onto a small screen, but kids apparently preferred their own bedroom walls or ceiling, because Screen-A-Show was relegated to the remnant shelves while Give-A-Show just kept on a-givin' and a-showin'.

Kenner made a big jump from slides to actual motion picture film with its Easy-Show Projector. Sure, the films were silent and in black and white, but many youngsters no doubt got their first rudimentary education in the mechanics of animation by observing the frame-by-frame progression of the moving images. The first Easy-Show Projectors were hand-cranked, with later models motorized. Either way, the film cartridges never seemed to work as well as promised, as threading them through the many troughs and crevices needed for operation was difficult for a parent, much less a five-year-old. Since the films were manufactured in a continuous loop, once they became snarled, th-th-that was all, folks.

Harry Reisiger was one of the major packaging designers for Kenner. For this 1966 edition of the Easy-Show Movie Projector, he used his son, Steve, and next-door neighbor, Diane Judge, as the kids enjoying Superman's latest animated adventure.

The best way to see how the Easy-Show movie film reels looked is to see them in their original packaging, since one or two trips through the projector usually resulted in a major tangle.

With Kenner's Change-A-Channel TV set, kids could switch back and forth between two unrelated cartoons playing simultaneously on the same reel of film.

With four cartoons instead of just two, the Change-A-Channel film reels were a better bargain than the ones for the Easy-Show Projector—at least for the brief time they functioned properly.

When they were working, the films presented a wide variety of animated—and sometimes live-action—subjects. Naturally, since they were short and silent, Kenner had to choose scenes that did not depend on dialogue to carry the story; for those moments when exposition was absolutely necessary, captions were superimposed across the bottom of the picture.

With Kenner's reliance on Hanna-Barbera, the films naturally leaned heavily in that direction. Yogi Bear starred in "Disguise and Gals," helping foil two bank robbers dressed as little old ladies. Huckleberry Hound's episode was "Freeway Patrol," and Precious Pupp helped his owner, Granny Sweet, become "Queen of the Road." Secret Squirrel and his archenemy, Yellow Pinkie, battled it out with ever-more-lethal weaponry, while Atom Ant had to wreck a rampaging robot and turn the resulting scrap pile into an amusement park ride. The Flintstones appeared in a short clip from a 1961 TV episode in which the family visited a prehistoric dude ranch (the Grand Canyon was a trickle of water) and Fred and Barney got a lesson on some bucking brontos.

Even some classic theatrical cartoons were licensed for this sort of toy use. Bugs Bunny and Porky Pig were seen in excerpts from their 1946 releases *Acrobatty Bunny* and *Mouse Menace*, respectively. Other characters represented in the Easy-Show line were Casper the Friendly Ghost, Bozo the Clown, and Alvin and the Chipmunks (in a "haunted house" episode from their prime-time TV series).

Then came Kenner's battery-operated Change-A-Channel TV Set, which used 16mm film but with a new twist: every frame was divided in half, with a different cartoon on each side, so when the films were run through the plastic toy television set, the channel could be "switched" from one cartoon to the other, with both playing simultaneously. Popeye and Rocky and Bullwinkle were on opposite channels; so were Bozo and Mister Magoo. Most of the same Hanna-Barbera stars represented in the Easy-Show Projector appeared on the Change-A-Channel network as well.

The other manufacturers did not let Kenner have the field all to itself. View-Master underwent a change of ownership from Sawyer's to the General Aniline and Film (GAF) Corporation in 1966. Under GAF's ownership, View-Master accelerated its evolution from a photography hobby to the toy market, and one of the products that resulted was the Talking View-Master. The

The Talking View-Master has become infamous for its extremely inaccurate renditions of every major cartoon character's familiar voice.

General Electric's Show 'n' Tell TV set was quite a novelty in its day, with a record turntable that triggered a film strip to wind its way through the viewing mechanism. Like most of the optical toys in this chapter, Show 'n' Tell could not survive the advent of home video.

Fisher-Price's film cartridges were an improvement over Kenner's in that they were self-contained and less likely to snarl. Many of them have survived in perfect condition to this day.

reels remained the same as always, but each Talking View-Master reel had a small plastic record attached that would play inside the viewer as each scene changed. The crummy sound quality of the Talking View-Master recordings was exceeded only by their horribly poor imitations of the various cartoon characters' voices, whether they be Yogi Bear, Popeye, or Bugs Bunny.

Another combination audio/video product that was somewhat lacking in faithful rendering of cartoon voices was General Electric's Show 'n' Tell. This was a combination record player and slide projector; each strip of slides would be inserted into a slot and would then automatically advance as the record played. The only voice characterizations were the ones the uncredited narrators felt comfortable in throwing into their stories. Disney was the primary source of licensed material for the Show 'n' Tell (with Captain Kangaroo hopping close behind). It is understandable that the Show 'n' Tell folks had their work cut out for them when condensing a Disney animated feature into fifteen slides and three and a half minutes of audio; General Electric's rendition of *The Sword in the Stone* may be the only version of that classic tale to make no mention at all of Merlin the magician.

Although not strictly toys, many theatrical and made-for-TV cartoons were licensed for 8mm and Super 8 home movie use. They were sold in the photography sections of large department stores rather than in toy departments, and the artwork on the boxes could range from beautiful to "What were they thinking?"

During 1978, View-Master belatedly got into the moving picture toy business with its Double-Vue Automatic Movie Viewer. Unlike the old Easy-Show films, this battery-operated toy's stories were contained in interchangeable cartridges that could not tangle; licensed characters leaned heavily toward the Warner Bros. output, plus the DC and Marvel superheroes. Perhaps not coincidentally, the same year, toy giant Fisher-Price came out with its own movie viewer, also with cartridges instead of film reels. Hand-cranked instead of battery-operated, Fisher-Price's was probably the more foolproof of the two, since its cartoon cartridges still turn up for sale in remarkably good condition. Like View-Master, Fisher-Price licensed excerpts from the Warner Bros. theatrical cartoons, but Fisher-Price also had segments from the animated *Peanuts* specials and the biggest ones of them all, Disney feature films, including *Cinderella* and *Snow White and the Seven Dwarfs*.

In addition to all these genuine toys, we cannot forget that for decades, theatrical and made-for-TV cartoons were also licensed to various home movie companies for sale in 8mm and later Super 8 formats. Like View-Master's early days, these films were sold in photo shops and department stores and were not cheaply produced. Their most glaring aspect from today's perspective is the sometimes downright sloppy artwork chosen for their box covers. When the company in question was Disney, there was no question about the quality, but such companies as Ken Films anticipated the laughable lack of quality in later public domain VHS tape covers, with their misguided attempts at depicting the beloved Warner Bros. or Terrytoons characters.

In the end, all of these products were eventually done in by the advent of home video in the late 1970s and early 1980s, leaving kids of the post–baby boomer generation to wonder why their predecessors had to get along with such crude entertainment technology. There is no doubt that being able to watch pristinely restored classic animation on DVD or Blu-Ray is a joy—but there is still something about seeing an image projected from an actual film print that digital video will never be able to replicate. That must be why so many collectors continue to seek out either the professional cartoon home movie reels or their toy equivalents; they must mean something to someone out there!

Chapter 6

FOR THE RECORD

Cartoon-related records are such a large part of the merchandising world that it is difficult to imagine a time when they did not exist. It's also difficult to imagine a time when the recording industry itself did not exist, but that's beside the point. Songs about cartoon characters go back almost as far as the toys we examined in an earlier chapter: the Yellow Kid was a character in a Broadway play (much as his descendants Li'l Abner, Little Orphan Annie, Superman, and the *Peanuts* characters would be in future decades), and Winsor McCay's artistic triumph of a strip, *Little Nemo in Slumberland*, was turned into a stage musical as a result of the circa 1903 craze for fantasy stage shows that included *The Wizard of Oz* and *Babes in Toyland*. All of these character-spawned songs were big in the sheet music business, but it would be a few years before Mr. Edison's newfangled phonograph contraption caught up with them in a big way.

Probably the first cartoon-based popular song to break out in front of the rest as a blockbuster was "Barney Google (with the Goo-Goo-Googly Eyes)," composed by Billy Rose and Con Conrad in 1923. The song was an unqualified hit, and a search on YouTube today will produce an amazing number of different recordings of it. Of course, Barney was already the star of one of the most successful comic strips of its day, which might come as a surprise to those who know his name only as the first half (and rarely seen supporting character) of today's *Barney Google and Snuffy Smith* strip. The success of Barney's Roaring Twenties hit probably inspired the Paul Whiteman Orchestra to record a "Felix the Cat" song in 1928; although primarily an instrumental, it had a simple but rousing vocal in the middle ("Felix! Felix! Felix the Cat! / Welcome! Welcome! Home to our flat!")

In 1931, an aggregation facetiously called Al Dollar and His Ten Cent Band, with vocalist Billy Murray, put out a record on the Brunswick label, "Popeye the Sailor Man." Despite what you might be thinking, this song in no way resembled the theme the one-eyed mariner would be known for singing for the next eighty years and longer. That one did not come about until two years after the Murray record, which was based solely on the comic strip. In fact, some of the lyrics present a rather different view of the character than his more familiar later image. For example: "Who can sock like dynamite? / Who can love like he can fight?" and "When he kisses Olive's cheeks / She stays black and blue for weeks."

Several of the songs from Paramount's "Popeye Song Folio" were performed by Floyd Buckley on some of the earliest Popeye records made.

As a precursor to the animated cartoons, though, "Popeye the Sailor Man" has the distinction of being the first recorded example of trying to give the old salt an appropriate voice, but only for three words: "Doesn't smile and doesn't frown / All he says is 'Blow me down.'" There is no evidence that Sammy Lerner, who composed the more famous "I'm Popeye the Sailor Man" theme for the first Popeye animated cartoon produced by the Max Fleischer studio in 1933, used this obscure tune as any sort of inspiration.

The overnight success of the Popeye cartoons ensured that the bulgy-armed gob would be called on to record again. The original animated voice of Popeye, William Costello, was already a singer prior to his cartoon work and in fact had used the gravelly tones later assigned to Popeye as a part of his act. In 1935, Costello became so difficult to work with (rumors are that his success as Popeye went straight to his head) that the Fleischers fired him and replaced him with a soundalike from their own studio ranks, aspiring animator Jack Mercer. Mercer would be the official voice of Popeye for the rest of his life, but as we shall see as we go along, that did not mean any Popeye record automatically featured his performance. In fact, at about the same time that Mercer replaced Costello, a *Popeye the Sailor* radio series premiered, with none of the cartoon voice cast represented. The radio Popeye was Floyd Buckley, who went on to record a series of the songs from the Fleischer cartoons. They were released on the Bluebird label, which was RCA's "budget brand" line. Buckley and his radio castmate Olive LaMoy (as—who else?—Olive Oyl) performed their own versions of "Brotherly Love," "A Clean Shaven Man," and other Sammy Timberg compositions for the Fleischer series. Any of these catchy tunes are more than familiar to devotees of 1930s animation, and this would not be the last time they would be heard on records.

Of less certain origin is another record made by Buckley during his radio days as Popeye. Known as "Popeye and the Pirates," it features LaMoy and the same radio actor who played Popeye's "adoptik kid," Matey. However, unlike the radio series, here the young Matey actor is referred to as Swee'Pea, who was *not* a part of the radio show. The story plays like a shortened version of one of the fifteen-minute radio episodes, with Popeye, Olive, and Swee'Pea visiting a deserted island and running afoul of a pirate crew. One of Popeye's best and most characteristic lines of his career comes when the pirate captain tries to punch him into senselessness:

PIRATE: Hey, that was my hardest punch! Why don't you fall down?
POPEYE: I doesn't falls down when I gets hit . . . I just gets MAD!

Now, remember we said that William Costello had created the Popeye voice in his precartoon days, so he was still free to use it even after the Fleischer studio gave him the heave-ho. One of the strangest relics of this period has Costello performing a 1937 novelty tune, "The Merry-Go-Round Broke Down," in what used to be Popeye's voice, minus the singular "pronunskiation." What makes this oddity so odd is that "The Merry-Go-Round Broke Down" soon became Warner Bros.'s theme for the Looney Tunes series, so to hear Popeye apparently croaking out the theme for a competing studio's cartoons is weirdly funny in its own way.

Say, what do you suppose Walt Disney was doing while his biggest rival, Max Fleischer, was getting so much mileage out of his Popeye songs? Well, to answer that, we probably need to back up a few years. As with so many other innovations, Disney had been way out in front of the rest when it came to his cartoons generating popular hit tunes. The big difference was that this time, it was somewhat unintentional. Many of the Disney cartoon shorts of the early 1930s had featured original songs written by the studio's staff composers, but the debut of "Who's Afraid of the Big Bad Wolf?" as part of Disney's *Three Little Pigs* in early 1933 truly began the company's long association with popular songs—and, simultaneously, cartoon-related records.

As Disney records historian R. Michael Murray explains,

> In 1933, Saul Bourne, then the general manager of Irving Berlin, Inc., requested a Disney license for the music of "Who's Afraid of the Big Bad Wolf" and music from other Disney short cartoons. Disney agreed and, under the arrangement with Berlin, it assigned the musical copyrights in return for a percentage of any licensing revenues produced.
>
> Berlin then licensed the music for "Who's Afraid of the Big Bad Wolf," producing immediate Depression-era hits of the song in September 1933 by the Don Bestor Orchestra on the Victor label, and Bill Scott and Orchestra on the Bluebird label.

But even that was not Disney's major contribution to the budding field of cartoon records (although it was a not inconsiderable one). Just prior to the release of his first animated feature, *Snow White and the Seven Dwarfs*, the Berlin company obtained the musical rights and licensed the songs to RCA for records. But, rather than having studio recordings made, RCA took the songs directly from the film's sound track, the first time such a thing had ever been attempted—but certainly not the last. RCA released the three-record set in January 1938, and there was no looking back. Over the next

"Who's Afraid of the Big Bad Wolf?" (1933) was the first hit song to come from a Disney cartoon. For a while, it seemed that every animated short that followed would try to make lightning strike a second time.

decade, practically every song from a Disney feature would be released on records, sometimes from the sound track but even more often recorded by the biggest musical stars of the era: Artie Shaw's orchestra working on "Whistle while You Work," Kate Smith belting out "When You Wish upon a Star," and Woody Herman's orchestra relating what "Uncle Remus Said," among countless others.

Did you notice something about all of the records discussed here so far? With the possible exception of the Floyd Buckley performances, none of them could truly be said to be "children's records." In fact, very few people were even thinking of records in those terms. A phonograph, after all, was a rather substantial piece of furniture in most households, so most parents were probably not comfortable with the idea of letting their kids play with such an instrument. Capitol Records can truly be said to have invented children's cartoon records in much the form we know them, and the person who had the idea was producer Alan Livingston.

In 1946, Livingston came up with the concept he called a "Record-Reader." Although a familiar enough concept today, at the time it was truly innovative. Each record set—usually consisting of two records, or four sides—came packaged in a heavy cardboard booklet. On the pages of this booklet, the dialogue from the record was transcribed on the left-hand pages, while accompanying illustrations could be seen on the right-hand pages. (The concept may have been inspired by the format of Whitman's Big Little Books.) On the records, a character would signal the young listener when to turn the page.

For the first Record-Reader, Livingston came up with an original character, Bozo the Clown, played by Pinto Colvig (the voice of Disney's Goofy). *Bozo at the Circus* was an immediate success, leading to a whole series of Bozo productions and a companion set starring a young boy named Sparky. Once Capitol's reputation for quality children's records was established, the company started going after the big names in the cartoon industry.

During 1947, Capitol began producing Record-Readers (as well as individual 78 rpm records) based on the Disney characters, the Warner Bros. looney crew, and Woody Woodpecker and the rest of Walter Lantz's menagerie. But Capitol went one step further, contracting with the same actors who provided the characters' voices in their

Capitol Records executive Alan Livingston created Bozo the Clown for a series of read-along book-and-record sets (Record-Readers) beginning in 1946. The big-footed buffoon soon became a star of toys and comic books and eventually moved on to television and animated cartoons.

animated productions. As we shall soon see, this was not always a prerequisite for future record producers wishing to license the appeal of these and other cartoon stars, but Capitol's records proudly advertised that they were "Made in Hollywood," and Alan Livingston wanted to be sure they sounded that way.

Most of Capitol's releases based on Disney properties stemmed from the studio's feature film output rather than its short subjects. From the first ones based on *Song of the South* (1946) and *Fun and Fancy Free* (1947) through the success of *Davy Crockett* on television in the mid-1950s, virtually every Disney release had a Record-Reader, a multirecord set, or at least a 78 rpm single in the Capitol catalog. Capitol even reached back into the approximately fifteen years before it secured a Disney license, going to considerable trouble and expense to produce remakes of some of the earlier Disney work. Capitol's Record-Reader of *The Three Little Pigs* was one of many productions narrated by the jovial voice of Don Wilson, famed for his years as Jack Benny's radio and TV announcer. *Mickey and the Beanstalk* starred the film voices of Mickey Mouse, Donald Duck, and Goofy (Jim Macdonald, Clarence Nash, and Pinto Colvig, respectively). Kids presumably were not supposed to wonder why Goofy on the Disney records sounded exactly like Bozo the Clown on Capitol's other releases.

However, one Capitol Record-Reader did not feature Macdonald as Mickey, but that record turned out to be a masterpiece anyway. In 1953, there was a big push in Disney merchandise based on the theme of Mickey's twenty-fifth birthday (usually omitting the actual number of years), and one of those items was Capitol's production *Mickey Mouse's Birthday Party*. For this time only, the celebrity mouse's falsetto was performed by Capitol's resident satirist, Stan Freberg. Freberg did a terrific job in the role and loaned his versatile voice to some of the other Disney celebrities who showed up as party guests, including the Mad Hatter and March Hare, Brer Fox, José Carioca, and several others. The female roles were handled capably by June Foray, who was appearing in virtually all of Capitol's other licensed series at the same time.

Even though Macdonald was not doing Mickey in this case, he was still on hand to re-create his original film roles of Cinderella's mice chums, Jaq and Gus. Nash was the once and future Donald Duck, of course. He got some of the biggest laughs when Mickey pressed the duck to serve as the signal for kids to turn the page in their booklets. As the story goes on, Donald becomes more and more irritated by his limited role, squawking, "Turn the page! TURN THE PAGE!" in an increasingly frustrated fit. Colvig contributed

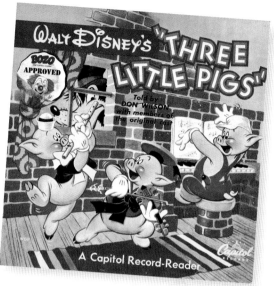

Capitol Records produced some lavish Record-Readers based on licensed Disney properties. This one re-created the 1933 story of *The Three Little Pigs*, narrated by Jack Benny's faithful announcer, Don Wilson.

Signing Mel Blanc to an exclusive recording contract enabled Capitol to use his vocal talents in records based on both the Warner Bros. characters and Woody Woodpecker, whose famous laugh Blanc had created in 1940.

not only Goofy but his long-ago film characterizations of Practical Pig and Grumpy. All in all, *Mickey's Birthday Party* was one of the most lavish Capitol productions ever and was somewhat unusual for the Disney line in that it was an original story and not an adaptation.

Capitol also reached out to the Warner Bros. studio to gain access to the many Looney Tunes/Merrie Melodies characters. As practically everyone knows, getting these characters' voices to match the cartoons pretty much involved hiring only one person, the inimitable Mel Blanc. Most of the other actors who made children's records for Capitol got a flat fee of one hundred dollars per three-hour recording session, but research by Capitol historian Walt Mitchell has shown that the company knew its association with Blanc and Warner Bros. was going to be something special. According to Mitchell,

> Mel and Warner Bros. were not required to wait until the money from record sales came in before receiving their pay. Capitol paid them in advance. . . . The advance figure was $5,000 per album. The 5% split was divided as Warner Bros. receiving 3.33% and Mel receiving 1.66%, so $3,333 of the advance went to Warner Bros. and $1,667 to Mel. Not bad for 1947!

Even though the contracts called for only Blanc's name to receive screen (and, by extension, record) credit for the cartoon voices, he had help in both genres. Foray played most of the required female roles, and both Freberg and Daws Butler filled in here and there to keep Blanc from having to talk to himself continually. Arthur Q. Bryan was the voice of Elmer Fudd both in cartoons and on Capitol records.

While most of these records were stories, in either the Record-Reader format or simply standing alone, some presented the characters singing their own "merrie melodies." Bugs, Daffy Duck, and Yosemite Sam had their own individual songs (and Blanc's roaring of Sam's performance leads one to suspect he had an awfully irritated throat for several hours thereafter), but one of them in particular took on a life of its own. "I Taut I Taw a Puddy Tat," with Blanc as both Tweety and Sylvester, was simply another single, but somehow it caught the public's attention and became a bona fide novelty hit song outside of the children's record realm. It even inspired cover versions by other record companies, including one by Danny Kaye on the Decca label that is remarkable only because it is so bad. There is no denying that Kaye was a multitalented performer and comedian, but his attempt to create totally new voices for the two well-established characters comes across as not the most shining moment in his long career.

Some of Capitol's Warner Bros. stories were loosely adapted from specific cartoons, while others were original stories. Either way, they were more faithful to their sources than many future cartoon records would be. This can be attributed in large part to Capitol's enlisting of not only the voice actors but Warner Bros.'s stable of cartoon writers and artists to moonlight on these records. The majority were scripted by Tedd Pierce and Warren Foster, two of the top gagsters in the looneyverse.

Nevertheless, as with the comic books and storybooks we saw a few chapters back, some of the cartoons' more violent impulses occasionally had to be reined in. Take, for example, the 1949 production of *Bugs Bunny in Storyland*, narrated by Elmer Fudd, which begins with the old fuddy-duddy finding Bugs helping himself to Fudd's carrot patch. "I gwabbed my wifle and woaded it," Fudd growls before taking the bite out of the situation: "Of course, I only put gumdrops in it so I wouldn't weally hurt him." The cartoon Elmer warely—er, rarely—showed such humanitarian impulses.

But all was not sweetness and candy in Capitol's version of the Warner Bros. world, either. With writers like Pierce and Foster at work, the characters could never stray too far from their roots. In the *Storyland* tale, Bugs escapes from Elmer's gumdrop-blasting shotgun by taking refuge in the magical community inhabited by all the famous nursery rhyme and fairy tale characters. After cameo appearances by Daffy Duck, Porky Pig, and Beaky Buzzard, Bugs encounters Little Red Riding Hood (June Foray) and generously offers to take her place and fix the Big Bad Wolf good and proper. But the wolf isn't as stupid as Beaky Buzzard looks, and after the obligatory "What big eyes you got, Grandma" dialogue, he pounces on Bugs:

WOLF: I knew you all the time, and I'd just as soon eat rabbit!
BUGS: Hey, just a minute, Doc! Don't you even want to look at the special crackers I brought you?
WOLF: Special crackers? Hmmm . . . let's see. Well, they're a pretty, bright red! Are they graham crackers?
BUGS: No, chum, they're FIRE-crackers! And they're all lit, Doc!
WOLF: FIRE-CRACKERS?!
BUGS: So long, Grandmaw. Happy Fourth of July!
(SOUND: BOOM, BANG, POW, ZING)

Capitol's renditions of the Warner Bros. characters continued for several years, with such titles as *Bugs Bunny and the Tortoise* (1948), *Bugs Bunny Meets Hiawatha* (1950), *Tweety's Putty Tat Twouble* (1951), *Henery Hawk's*

The unexpected pop hit status of Mel Blanc's "I Tawt I Taw a Putty Tat" song for Capitol ensured that Tweety and Sylvester would make many more appearances on that record label.

A set of Walter Lantz character songs composed by Irving Bibo was licensed to several different record producers, including Golden, Decca, and Cricket, whose cover art for a pair of them is seen here.

Chicken Hunt (1952), and *Sylvester and Hippety Hopper* (1953). The final production, *Tweety's Good Deed*, was released in 1954.

As long as Capitol had Mel Blanc under contract, company officials figured they might as well get as much usage out of him as possible. Cartoon historians know that back in 1940, Blanc was the original voice of Woody Woodpecker for the Walter Lantz Studio, and he had created the crazy laugh associated with the character. A year or two later, the Looney Tunes producers put Blanc under an exclusive contract, prohibiting him from voicing characters for other cartoon studios. This restriction did not apply to records and other media, so when Capitol began a series of Woody Woodpecker records at the same time as the Disney and Warner Bros. series, they got Blanc to re-create the role he had been forced to abandon on the screen.

It is most likely that Capitol's decision to begin a Woody Woodpecker set of Record-Readers resulted from the incredible success of "The Woody Woodpecker Song" as a single the previous year. It had been recorded by a number of different artists—including Mel Blanc—and its refrain, based on Woody's laugh, delighted many and irritated another hefty segment of the population. Its popularity inspired the creation of even more Woody merchandise, including a kazoo-like instrument that mimicked the laugh when blown.

The first in Capitol's series was *Woody Woodpecker and His Talent Show* (1949). Each installment was highlighted by the electronically sped voice of Blanc as the wacky bird, with supporting work by stalwarts Freberg, Foray, and Butler. The series outlasted Capitol's Warner Bros. productions, ending with the topical *Woody Woodpecker Meets Davy Crockett* in 1955. Just the decision to produce such a story was notable because it rode on the fringed leather coattails of Disney's success with the Davy Crockett television shows starring Fess Parker. But since Disney, Blanc, and Lantz were all so cozy with Capitol at the same time, obviously no one had any objections. (On that record, by the way, Davy Crockett was played not by Parker but by Butler.)

This might be a good place to mention that in 1958, with Capitol's rights to the Lantz characters having expired, Decca produced its own Woody Woodpecker album. By that time, Lantz's wife, Grace Stafford, was the official voice (and laugh) of Woody, so she starred in this new production. However, Blanc joined her at the microphone to play most of the supporting roles, even providing voices for characters he had never before played, including Andy Panda, Oswald the Rabbit, Wally Walrus, and Homer Pigeon.

Many of the songs on Decca's album were part of a set that was apparently licensed to several different children's record labels simultaneously;

in addition to their appearance on the Stafford/Blanc LP, they could also be found on singles and albums from Cricket Records and Golden Records. These included "The Woody Woodpecker March, "The Andy Panda Polka," "The Oswald the Rabbit Hop," and "The Woody Woodpecker Waltz," among others. The printed credits offered little information about their origins, but a search of the U.S. Copyright Office's records shows that most of their lyrics were the work of Irving Bibo, an extremely unusual choice for such work. Bibo was born in 1889 and died in 1962, making him one of the oldest participants in the 1950s children's record genre.

Identifying the performers on these songs is also somewhat of a challenge. Golden Records did not even bother to give any information at all, but Cricket at least listed the singers' names on the labels. The problem is that as far as anyone can tell, the names are just as likely as not to be fake. The woman who sang "The Woody Woodpecker Waltz," "The Andy Panda Polka," and "The Oswald the Rabbit Hop" (among others) for Cricket was listed as *Judy James*, who also appeared in a series of *Romper Room* records around the same time. The true identity of the mysterious James or what else she did in her career may never be known, but she possessed an incredible voice that could croon softly and sweetly and then one second later blast a high note that could have been heard in the back row of any theater on Broadway.

One major cartoon studio that did not license its characters to Capitol was MGM, home to Tom and Jerry, Droopy, and Barney Bear. MGM had its own record label, and from 1950 to 1952, it issued several Tom and Jerry stories whose style betrayed their debt to Capitol's pioneering efforts.

In hindsight, perhaps it was not the wisest move to build a series of records around two characters that did not speak. As we have already seen, Western Printing got around that hurdle simply by having Tom and Jerry talk up a storm in their comic book and storybook appearances. For whatever reason, MGM Records did not choose to go in that direction, so the adventures were done as lengthy narration by actor Bret Morrison. (Morrison was concurrently adopting a more sinister tone as the star of radio's classic drama *The Shadow*.) His description of what was taking place was augmented by music and sound effects. While the Tom and Jerry records preserved some of the slam-bang violence of the popular cartoons, the sound effects chosen to represent the battling cat and mouse sounded uncomfortably like the noises made by real animals in distress, cutting down on the inherent humor. MGM's Tom and Jerry records never made anywhere near the impact of Capitol's, and the series lasted for a much shorter period than did Western's work with the characters.

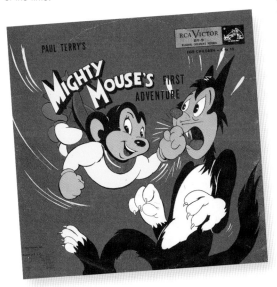

Record giant RCA obtained the rights to make Mighty Mouse records, but they bore almost no vocal resemblance to the characters as portrayed in the Terrytoons films of the time.

Meanwhile, what was going on over at RCA Victor, probably the first name most people associated with records? Well, Capitol's agreement with Disney (unlike its contracts with Warner Bros. and Walter Lantz) was not an exclusive one, because during all the years the Capitol Disney albums were being released, RCA was producing its own record versions of that studio's films—both animated and live-action—and frequently using the same actors who played the film roles. More unusual stars on RCA's label were Mighty Mouse and the other characters from the New York–based Terrytoons studio.

The Mighty Mouse records from RCA starred actor Todd Russell, who introduced himself at the beginning of each story and then proceeded to play most of the roles himself. Unlike the other studios, Terrytoons was never famous for its distinctive voice work, so it must not have bothered anyone at RCA that Russell's versions of Mighty Mouse, Dinky Duck, and the others sounded absolutely nothing like they did in the cartoons.

RCA produced many, many records starring the cast of television's *Howdy Doody* show, which is a little beyond this book's already-wide scope since they were marionettes instead of cartoon characters. From the world of children's literature, there were records based on the *Uncle Wiggily* series and, long before Disney took over the hunny pot, the adventures of Winnie-the-Pooh. The RCA cartoon catalog also had a few other oddities, including a 1948 production of *Prince Valiant and the Outlaws*, with Douglas Fairbanks Jr. as both the narrator and the voice of the medieval knight from Hal Foster's comic strip.

All of the cartoon character records we have seen up to this point were meant for children to hear but not necessarily to handle, since they were extremely fragile and even a two-record set was rather heavy for the average kid to lug around. Around the time that Capitol, RCA, MGM, and their friends were beginning these various series, another phenomenon made its first appearance, and it would come to be what most people thought of as "children's records."

You were not a child in the 1950s and 1960s if you did not have at least a few Little Golden Records, seemingly indestructible pieces of yellow plastic, usually six inches in diameter. Little Golden Records, as their name would suggest, were an outgrowth of Little Golden Books, which were still being published under the auspices of Simon and Schuster at the time. For the first few years after their 1948 debut, most Little Golden Records were

One of the more unusual choices for an RCA record was Hal Foster's masterfully illustrated *Prince Valiant* comic strip narrated by Douglas Fairbanks Jr.

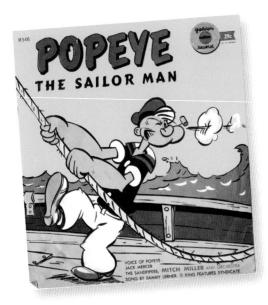

Jack Mercer performed the Popeye theme song for this Little Golden Record, but for reasons unknown, his voice was sped up until it sounded more like one of Popeye's nephews.

abbreviated audio versions of stories from the books. (Maybe it says something about a youngster's typical attention span that most of us never noticed that one side of a Little Golden Record played for approximately ninety seconds before having to be turned over.)

Little Golden Records began drawing on the animation studios around 1951, and because Western Printing had such plethora of licenses, the records incorporated characters from an astounding number of studios. One of Golden's first cartoon-related releases was a cover version of "The Woody Woodpecker Song," which had been a major hit for around three years by that time. There was also a Golden version of "I'm Popeye the Sailor Man," performed by Jack Mercer instead of some imitator. However, Mercer's Popeye voice was inexplicably sped on the finished recording, while the music and background singers remained in normal range. This 1951 rendition of the Popeye theme has been reissued over and over on 78 rpm and 45 rpm singles, long-playing albums, and even CDs over the past sixty-plus years, and every one of them sounds like Popeye just inhaled some helium rather than spinach.

Mike Stewart, who had a deep bass voice, and Anne Lloyd, who sounded like everyone's favorite singing schoolteacher, were heard on practically every Little Golden Record. Both performers were called on to simulate a wide range of styles and characterizations, and when Golden made its 1951 version of the "Casper the Friendly Ghost" theme song, each got a chance to shine, Stewart as the spooky-sounding singer for the chorus, and Lloyd singing Casper's lines. ("I always say hello, and I'm really glad to meet'cha / Wherever I may go, I'm kind to every living creature.")

Capitol and RCA were still producing Disney records when Golden joined with them in the wonderful world of Walt as well. The Golden versions of songs from the animated features usually starred Lloyd, Stewart, and their fellow singers, but to Golden's credit, when Mickey, Donald, and Goofy appeared, the authentic trio of Jimmy Macdonald, Clarence Nash, and Pinto Colvig were brought in to do the honors. (Apparently that flat one hundred dollars per session at Capitol was not enough to give that company exclusive rights to their talents.)

Several of the early 1950s Disney Little Golden Records were simple, ninety-second stories that still managed to squeeze in some clever dialogue and humor. *Donald Duck, Fire Chief* tells of the unfortunate day when the feathered first responder had to answer a call about a fire at Goofy's house. The result can be summed up in Goofy's closing remark: "Oh well . . . ahyuk . . . I never liked that house very much anyway." Another, *Pluto and his Phonograph*, was almost a commercial for the record company. Unable to speak like most other Disney animals, Pluto buys a toy record player and uses various nursery rhyme records to let Mickey know what he wants—"Jack and Jill" to ask for water, "Little Tommy Tucker" for a meal, and so on. The hound finally overdoes it by playing "Rub-a-Dub-Dub," leading Mickey to think he is asking for a bath. As narrator Peter Donald concludes, "Pluto learned a lesson then and there / You have to choose the records you play with the greatest of care!"

Little Golden Records spared no effort when it came to another of its mid-1950s releases, a magnificent version of the theme song from CBS-TV's *Mighty Mouse Playhouse*, widely considered the first Saturday morning cartoon in the medium's history. Unlike Paramount's Casper series, the Terrytoons theatrical shorts had never had a theme song, but that was rectified for Mighty Mouse's television debut. Golden Records' rendition, though, was such a showstopper that it put the TV version to shame; done in the style of a marching band, it makes the listener want to stand up and cheer, especially

Little Golden Records produced this rendition of Paramount's *Casper the Friendly Ghost* theme several years before Harvey Comics purchased the character.

The early Disney titles made by Little Golden Records had a somewhat generic cover design, with only a spot or two to customize them for whatever was contained on the record.

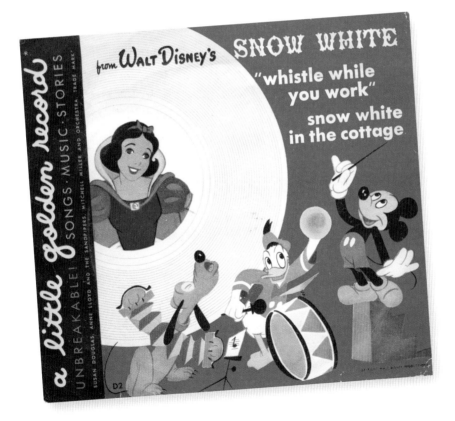

with Mighty Mouse's repeated refrain, "Here I come to save the day!" (Mighty sounded much more like himself on this record than in any of RCA's depictions of his adventures.)

The Golden Records "Mighty Mouse" song has become an icon of cartoon music, usually replacing the original CBS version in any compilations of such themes. It even became the basis for a legendary routine by comedian Andy Kaufman. Getting lesser attention was the B side of the record, which gave a similar lavish treatment to another Terrytoons TV theme, this time from *The Farmer Al Falfa Show*. While lacking the Mighty Mouse magnificence, Golden's "Farmer Al Falfa" made liberal use of fiddles and cowbells to give the proper bucolic atmosphere.

Once Capitol's exclusive license with Warner Bros. ran out after 1954, Golden made haste to begin its own series of Looney Tunes tunes. There was only one little problem—as we saw, Mel Blanc was still under contract with Capitol for another couple of years, so most of Golden's output had to be done without him. That would seem to be a rather major hurdle to jump, but Golden simply did what it could and hoped kids would not notice. They did.

Actually, while the unidentified actor(s) Golden hired to substitute for Blanc's many voices rarely came close to matching him, there are occasions where sheer versatility has to be recognized anyway. In a staggering two-sided record based on the tune of the Merrie Melodies theme, "Merrily We Roll Along," a single actor (in what sounds like a single take) simulates Bugs Bunny, Sylvester, Henery Hawk, Pepé le Pew, Porky Pig, Elmer Fudd, Foghorn Leghorn, Tweety, Daffy Duck, and Yosemite Sam. Listening closely, one can occasionally hear this exhausted thespian trying to gasp for breath between voices.

Some of Golden's other Warner Bros. singles are even more bizarre. In one of them, it sounds for all the world like they got the real Elmer Fudd, Arthur Q. Bryan (who was apparently not under an exclusive contract with Capitol), performing opposite a patently bogus Bugs. One can only imagine how odd Bryan must have felt in the recording studio while that song was being cut. In a couple of other instances, the voices of Sylvester and Daffy Duck sound so much like Blanc's inflections that collectors still debate whether he could have slipped in a performance or two without Capitol's knowledge.

Meanwhile, back in Disney's world, Little Golden Records was about to take part in what would be an important development for the studio, television, and merchandising all at once. As we saw many pages ago, the Disney merchandise machine learned early on

As long as Mel Blanc was still under contract to Capitol, Little Golden Records had to use impersonators on its Warner Bros. productions. A number of these singles were later collected for this LP.

Free! A MICKEY MOUSE CLUB RECORD* will be given for a limited time with each subscription to WALT DISNEY'S MAGAZINE. The combination makes a perfect Christmas gift. Use the order blank bound inside the back cover of this issue.

*45 rpm

the value of having tie-in merchandise on store shelves in advance of a film's actual release. That went for television as well, and when *The Mickey Mouse Club* was scheduled to hit the ABC-TV airwaves in October 1955, Golden and Disney teamed up to be sure that records of the forthcoming show's music were on store shelves weeks or even months ahead of time. But there was a difference—although the records were virtually identical in appearance to the usual Little Golden Records line, they instead bore the imprint of "A Mickey Mouse Club Record," and were pressed in orange plastic rather than yellow.

A number of the Golden/Mickey Mouse Club Records were produced before the final casting of the TV show had been completed, so other than adult Mouseketeer Jimmie Dodd, most of them featured the voices of adults pretending to be the kids who would eventually be the stars. Record buyers did not seem to care, and the success of the Mickey Mouse Club Records line caused the Disney Studio to seriously begin considering going into the record business for itself. It did so in 1956, and the resulting label was known as Disneyland Records.

Now, one of the biggest hits of the late 1950s was—wait, what was that you said? What about Disneyland Records? Well, folks, there is something that should be explained here. Back in 2006, there was a book by Greg Ehrbar and Yours Truly, from this same publisher, known as *Mouse Tracks: The Story of Walt Disney Records*. Since it took some two hundred pages to relate that history, there seems to be little point in rehashing it here. If you want to go order a copy of it now, while it is fresh on your mind, we'll be glad to wait for you here until you get back.

The all new *Walt Disney* RECORD LIBRARY

15 ALBUMS TO AUDITION FREE IN YOUR OWN HOME!

RECORDS THAT TEACH!

RECORDS THAT TELL STORIES!

RECORDS TO INTRODUCE YOUR CHILD TO MUSIC!

SONGS FROM THE ELECTRIC COMPANY TV SHOW
Eight contemporary favorites from the popular television show that teach and entertain!

THREE LITTLE PIGS
A favorite classic narrated for you by Sterling Holloway with music. Fun for all.

WINNIE THE POOH
All the delightful music from Winnie the Pooh and the Honey Tree. Six songs in all.

ACTING OUT THE A, B, C'S
Learning can be lots of fun. Counting and Acting Out Songs. Sure to make a lasting and memorable impression.

CHILD'S INTRODUCTION TO MELODY
& Instruments of the Orchestra. A primer of music—how it's made and played. All basic instruments of the orchestra are introduced.

ADDITION AND SUBTRACTION
Songs with numbers and cheery explanations have the kiddies adding and subtracting and enjoying it!

LEARNING TO TELL TIME IS FUN
And this wonderful album proves just that! Its step-by-step instructions in song and verse make learning easy. The back of the album becomes a toy clock, too!

MICKEY and the BEANSTALK
The complete story with all the songs and the original cast . . . Mickey, Donald Duck and Pluto. A fun fantasy.

101 DALMATIANS
Story and songs from Walt Disney's fun-filled feature cartoon film. Characters come to life to create hours of happy entertainment.

THE LITTLE ENGINE THAT COULD
A delightful fantasy that will entertain and amuse for hours on end. The album also includes The Submarine Streetcar, Casey Jones and John Henry.

PETER AND THE WOLF
Here is an all-time favorite Disney classic told in an exciting fashion. The other side of the album — The Sorcerer's Apprentice from Fantasia.

HANSEL AND GRETEL
Music from the world-famous opera by Humperdinck. Orchestra conducted by Camarata. An eternal favorite.

CINDERELLA
All the songs and music from the original motion picture sound track. A truly memorable musical experience for any child.

SWISS FAMILY ROBINSON
The greatest adventure story of them all. Fully narrated by Kevin Corcoran with musical background and sound effects to enhance the excitement.

SONGS FOR BEDTIME
Favorite lullabies from classic Disney films like Cinderella, Lady and The Tramp and Peter Pan along with songs from other countries such as Brahms' Lullaby, the most famous of them all!

© 1974 Walt Disney Productions

In 1956, the Disneyland Records label was launched, and many of the most fondly remembered LPs, 45s, and 78s of our baby boomer childhoods ensued.

Okay, that didn't take long. Putting it into a single paragraph, Disneyland Records suffered through some initial hard times in the late 1950s before becoming a major moneymaker for the parent company in the 1960s. Its most popular series was its "Storyteller" LPs, with the plots of famous (and not-so-famous) Disney movies re-created for the audio format. Because the contracts with the film performers frequently prevented the use of their voices on records, Disneyland Records developed its own stable of regularly heard performers—primarily Robie Lester, Sam Edwards, Ginny Tyler, and Dallas McKennon—to re-create these roles. Under the musical direction of Tutti Camarata, Disneyland Records more often than not overcame its limited budgets to become first-rate entertainment that holds up well to this day.

Have you finished ordering *Mouse Tracks* yet? Good! Now, as we were saying . . . One of the biggest hits of the late 1950s was an act created by songwriter Ross Bagdasarian, who quite understandably used the stage name David Seville. The invention of magnetic recording tape had done wonders for the music industry, making it much easier to edit performances and use any manner of tricks to get the final product to sound better. (In a way, tape did for music what Photoshop would do for photography a half century later.) Bagdasarian was playing around with a reel-to-reel tape recorder and found that if he recorded his voice at half the usual speed and then played it back normally, the result was a squeaky voice that had great potential as a gimmick.

After testing out his new attention-grabber in a novelty tune he called "Witch Doctor," Bagdasarian took it to a new level. He sang harmony with himself by overdubbing his voice three times, and the new high-pitched musical group made its debut during the 1958 Christmas season with "The Chipmunk Song." Bagdasarian's genius lay in the fact that he not only made sure the sped-up voices were intelligible but also imparted personality to his singing rodents. The star was Alvin, the incorrigible brat who seemed determined to louse up every recording session.

Bagdasarian/Seville, Alvin, and the Chipmunks turned out hit singles and then long-playing albums one after another for the next ten years. Alvin merchandise began appearing in stores, licensed by the Chipmunks' record label, Liberty, almost as soon as "The Chipmunk Song" started climbing the charts like a chipmunk after an acorn. That early merchandise did not have a consistent appearance for the audio-only characters, sometimes making them look like real rodents and at other times taking a more cartoony approach. In 1961, the Chipmunks became stars of their own animated prime-time series, and the look designed for them became the official model from then on. Along with Capitol's Bozo the Clown, the Chipmunks were the most merchandised characters originating on records instead of comic strips or animation.

As we already know, by the time the Chipmunks emerged from wherever singing rodents emerge from, Hanna-Barbera was on its way to becoming the

When Ross Bagdasarian (alias David Seville) began his long-running series of Chipmunks records in 1958, Alvin, Simon, and Theodore were usually depicted as fairly realistic—though humanized—rodents.

Along with Bozo the Clown, Alvin and the Chipmunks were the most merchandised cartoon characters to originate on records rather than in animation or comic strips.

QUICK DRAW McGRAW

ORIGINAL TV SOUNDTRACK VOICES

COLPIX
CP 203

STARRING
DAWS BUTLER
&
DON MESSICK···DOUG YOUNG

PRODUCED BY
WILLIAM HANNA–JOSEPH BARBERA
DISTRIBUTED BY
SCREEN GEMS, INC.

Since Hanna-Barbera's initial TV productions were distributed by Columbia Pictures, that company's Colpix record label had the first rights to adapt the characters for LPs.

biggest thing in TV animation. Since the shows were produced under the auspices of Columbia Studios, it was natural that Columbia's record division, Colpix (short for Columbia Pictures, for those who are slow on the uptake) would gain the exclusive right to use them and their voices on vinyl. The Colpix label released a number of sound track LPs from the *Huckleberry Hound* and *Quick Draw McGraw* programs, usually with voice whiz Daws Butler providing new narration to explain the visual gags that were lost in an audio-only format.

However, as with the Warner Bros. characters, just because Butler was not available did not mean the show could not go on without him—painful though it might be. In 1960, an obscure New York–based toy company came up with a device it called a Movie-Wheel—basically a large cardboard disk containing a series of comic strip–like photos that could be viewed through a perforated window while an accompanying record played. This invention could just as easily have been covered in our chapter on optical toys, but the record is most important to this discussion. Because Butler was unavailable—and even if he had been, these recordings were done on the opposite coast from where he lived and worked—an impersonator was brought in to be Yogi Bear and Huckleberry Hound. And who was the natural person for the job? Well, actually there was no natural person, so Movie-Wheels used . . . Jack Mercer, the voice of Popeye. Mercer was a talented actor and comedian, and even though his versions of these characters would have fooled no one, they have their own twisted charm, such as when Mercer's version of Huck as an astronaut drawls, "Ah would like to report that the moon is NOT made o' green cheese—it looks more like frozen oatmeal."

Little Golden Records also jumped onto Hanna-Barbera's bandwagon, again having to find suitable substitutes for Butler and his usual cartoon voice cohort, Don Messick. From the records that include credits on the labels, it seems that two longtime radio actors, Gilbert Mack and Frank Milano, were the one-stop (or maybe two-stop) shop for most of Golden's Hanna-Barbera voice needs. Several of Golden's singles put new lyrics to the television theme songs, while others were made up of completely new compositions. Among the latter, Ranger Smith could be heard crooning "Before Yogi" ("Jellystone Park was dismal and dark before Yogi / Tourists were bored and bears were ignored before Yogi"), and Quick Draw McGraw demonstrated "What I say almost every day" in a song titled "Ooch, Ouch, Ooch." At times it appears that different performers were used for the characters' speaking and singing voices, as with a record starring Yogi's sweet intended, Cindy Bear, or another that introduced a couple of new additions to the Huckleberry Hound series, Hokey Wolf and Ding-A-Ling.

Golden was certainly on a constant watch for the next big thing in television, and the live-action *Dennis the Menace* TV sitcom starring Jay North seemed a likely candidate. Golden released a number of Dennis-related songs performed by young Philip Fox; among the most memorable was his rendition of the TV show's theme song, which had not previously been graced with lyrics ("Dennnnnn-issss, that's my name / But some call me the mennnnnn-ace").

Somehow, when Hanna-Barbera's much-publicized initial prime-time series, *The Flintstones*, was set to make its debut in September 1960, Golden managed to snatch the "original cast album" rights out from under Colpix's lady with the torch. Golden's *Flintstones* LP featured those old pros Alan Reed

The record accompanying the lower-than-low-tech Movie Wheel had Popeye voice artist Jack Mercer trying to impersonate Daws Butler's Yogi Bear and Huckleberry Hound.

As with Mel Blanc, Little Golden Records had to work around Daws Butler's exclusive contract to perform most of his Hanna-Barbera voices for Colpix. Veteran radio actors Gil Mack and Frank Milano were brought in to substitute, with highly variable results.

(Fred), Jean VanderPyl (Wilma), Mel Blanc (Barney), and Bea Benaderet (Betty) in top form. New lyrics were composed to go along with the many pieces of background music that were used on the series as well as the instrumental theme song, "Rise and Shine." The most intriguing thing about this album is that one of the snippets of background scoring received lyrics that turned it into "Meet the Flintstones"—a couple of years before it became the theme for the TV series. Other than the opening line, all of the other lyrics were different from the eventual TV version, however ("Dino is our little dinosaur / He's good, but nobody knows what for"). Besides having the melody carried at one point by a kettle drum—surely a first in the music industry—it had a second verse based on the concept of "Meet the Rubbles."

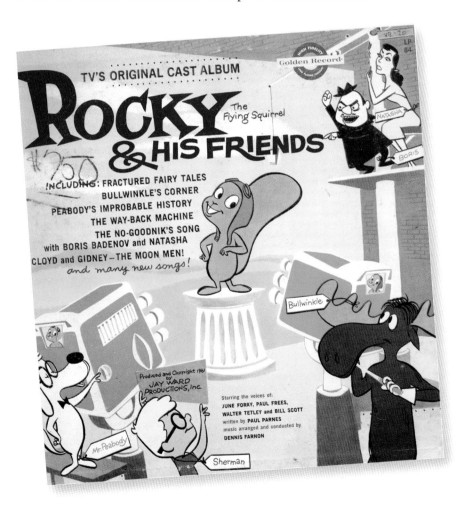

In early 1961, the cast members of Jay Ward's *Rocky and His Friends* assembled to give their all for Golden Records' version of the show.

Colpix refused to get caught napping in front of the TV set a second time, so when the Flintstones' mirror image, *The Jetsons*, premiered in 1962, Golden once again had to make do with New York–based voice impersonators. The resulting LP was nowhere near as impressive as the Flintstones songs, but Herb Duncan did a more than capable job of channeling George O'Hanlon's George Jetson voice, with support from Ann Thomas, Rose Marie Jun, Gene Steck, and Gene Lowell. Colpix's penchant for having the "real" Hanna-Barbera character voices under exclusive contract would soon come back to bite like Yogi chomping on a tourist's sandwich, but we will get to that story a bit later.

It should have been no surprise that Herb Duncan pulled off this album as well as he did, because he seemed to have an innate ability to closely duplicate a wide range of character voices. When King Features Syndicate produced a series of short cartoons based on the *Beetle Bailey, Krazy Kat*, and *Barney Google and Snuffy Smith* comic strips, Golden took the opportunity to make a short album (not as long as an LP but longer than one of its ninety-second singles) with original songs from all of these characters, and Duncan performed a nearly carbon copy of every cartoon voice. It is a little-known but extremely impressive production.

Fortunately, Golden managed to pull a squirrel out of its hat and did not have to depend on impersonators when it came time to produce a *Rocky and His Friends* album. The entire cast of the wickedly satirical cartoon was enlisted to re-create their roles in short skits that connected longer segments taken directly from the television sound tracks. As always, June Foray was Rocky and Natasha, and Bill Scott was Bullwinkle and Mr. Peabody, with Paul Frees as that crumb of crumbs, Boris Badenov, and Walter Tetley as Peabody's pet boy, Sherman. The new dialogue was tailored especially to fit the audio medium:

ROCKY: Well, now that we're here, what'll we do on our record?
BULLWINKLE: We'll *stand* on our record, is what!
ROCKY: You know what I mean.
BULLWINKLE: Yeah, heh heh . . . how 'bout if I do my famous juggling act, like this?
ROCKY: No, no, it's gotta be something people can *hear*!
BULLWINKLE: Believe me, when I juggle, you can hear it!
(SOUND: Crash, bang, bam, clatter, rattle)

Jay Ward studio historian Keith Scott reports that production on the *Rocky and His Friends* album was done at an accelerated pace, with barely one

As Disneyland Records became more and more successful, Little Golden Records seemed to lose interest in trying to keep up. This release made no attempt to duplicate Paul Frees's hilarious delivery as Ludwig Von Drake.

The last Disney production to have its songs recorded by Little Golden Records was *The Sword in the Stone* (1963). By that time, Golden was no longer using Disney artwork for the sleeves.

month passing between the signing of Golden Records' initial contact with Ward and the end of the recording sessions. Fortunately, the audio tracks of the master recording sessions for this album have survived, and they give a marvelous view into its creation. All of the actors were such professionals that they were able to start a song or routine, stop at the director's signal, and pick it up and do it again without once sounding tired of the job. Perhaps the funniest moment of the whole LP comes at the very end. After the big closing number is finished and the record is seemingly done, Bullwinkle's voice solemnly intones, "And now . . . ten seconds of needle scratch," before the stylus slides into the dead space on the record's interior circle.

Even with all of the new cartoon studios and characters coming on the scene in the late 1950s and early 1960s, Golden continued its output of Disney titles, but not for much longer. Not surprisingly, the Disney studio reserved its best material for the Disneyland label, and once that label began issuing a series of six-inch 78 rpm and seven-inch 45 rpm disks that were virtually identical in format and pricing with the Golden product line, the two began to seem redundant. By the early 1960s, it sounded like Golden was barely trying any more; an odd choice was a rendition of "Professor Ludwig von Drake," the theme from a Disneyland Records LP of the same title. Although Paul Frees put his own unique style into performing Ludwig's voice for the Disney label, Golden's cover version made no attempt to make the voice sound anything like Frees. The final Golden/Disney releases were a few songs from the animated feature *The Sword in the Stone* (1963).

Before moving along, we need to take a quick look at a few albums that could be considered "one-shots"—that is, they did not fit in as part of any other group. We have already seen that Walt Kelly's *Pogo* was among the least-merchandised of all newspaper comic strips, largely because Kelly was personally opposed to having other artists mass-reproduce his characters. The strip might have seemed like the least viable candidate for a record, but a number of nonsense verses had appeared in the strip from the beginning, and even more had been penned for the various strip reprint books, so with that as a basis, 1956 saw the release of the LP *Songs of the Pogo*. Most of the selections were Kelly's text set to music by Norman Monath, although a few credited Kelly with both the words and music.

For all practical purposes, *Songs of the Pogo* was a Golden Record, although it was not released under that name because it was marketed for adults. Simon and Schuster was the publisher of the Pogo books, so with Golden still as its record division, the two fit together well. (In fact, Simon and Schuster simultaneously published a *Songs of the Pogo* book of sheet music.) Golden Records regular Mike Stewart was heard on several of the album's eighteen tracks, with Fia Karin handling the female solos. The biggest surprise was that Kelly himself performed three of the songs, including the rousing lead tune "Go Go Pogo." Kelly was a born showman, and only he could have pulled off this conglomeration of gobbledygook that was meant to reflect the vacuousness of a typical campaign speech.

Not all of the songs were intended as such hilarious nonsense; for example, "A Song Not for Now" was a moving poem Kelly wrote in 1953 after the death of his infant daughter. The liner notes on the back of the jacket, however, proved that the album's creators did not take it too seriously: "Suitable for many occasions—birthdays, clandestine trysts, medical checkups, elevator rides, evenings at the public library, noons when the kettle boils over, music-to-pay-last-year's-bills-by, etc."

With Mister Magoo's distinctive voice by Jim Backus, one would think he might have been a natural for the audio medium, but such was not the case.

Although Walt Kelly's *Pogo* would seem an unlikely candidate for a record album, several of Kelly's poems from the strip and its reprint books were set to music for this Simon and Schuster release.

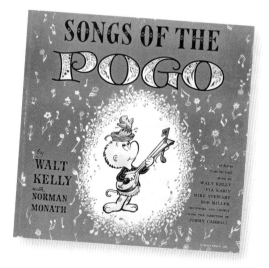

In this humorous demonstration of high fidelity, Mister Magoo fumbled with his new stereo system and managed to enrage most of his neighbors.

Perhaps Magoo's standard mistaken-identity gags would have required too much explanation; at any rate, one of the character's very few ventures into records was RCA's *Magoo in Hi-Fi* (1956). More than anything, the album attempted to demonstrate the wide range of high fidelity, from musical selections to sound effects. The very slight story has Magoo trying to assemble his own hi-fi stereo system (initially hooking it up to the washing machine), with Backus doing his own inimitable brand of ad-libbing around the script. It ends with Magoo in jail for disturbing the peace with his loud music.

As mentioned earlier, after from Golden Records and Disneyland Records, probably the next two most-prolific children's labels from the 1950s through the early 1970s were Peter Pan and Cricket. We will get to the second of those in a minute, but first let's examine some of Peter Pan's more notable entries in the cartoon derby.

Like Golden and RCA before it, Peter Pan aligned itself with the Terrytoons studio for a wide variety of releases. One in particular stands out simply because its concept was so odd. Famed film and animation historian Leonard Maltin has correctly pointed out that Mighty Mouse spent less actual time on-screen during his cartoons than any other major animated star, primarily because he was so invincible that the plot would have ended as soon as he entered the picture. Peter Pan Records took this to an extreme, producing a two-sided disk, *Mighty Mouse in Toyland*, in which the miniature superguy did not even appear at all.

The entire story is taken up with narration and songs—some recycled from earlier, more generic Peter Pan releases—as the inhabitants of Toyland prepare to welcome Mighty Mouse as a guest of honor. Mr. Mouse is talked about a lot, but he never actually appears. Perhaps that is just as well, because one of the songs about him just might have made him gag if he had been there to hear it; it contains the immortal couplet, "He flies, he dips, he does a somersault / He stops and winks and drinks a chocolate malt." At the end, Mighty ostensibly leads a parade of all the toys, but since we can't see what's happening, we have to take the playthings' word for it.

Peter Pan also enjoyed a long association with the characters owned by Harvey Comics. A huge, brassy rendition of the "Casper the Friendly Ghost" theme song ("the friendliest ghost you know") was recycled endlessly on a string of Peter Pan 45s, 78s, and LPs—sometimes in stereo, making the big band sound even more impressive. Peter Pan also produced a series of Casper stories in both album and single format; the voice performances were among some of the best ever heard on that company's recordings, probably because they took advantage of the New York–based voice casts responsible for the Casper television cartoons of the era.

If anything, Cricket Records was an even lower-budget company than Peter Pan. We have already seen how one of its earlier ventures into cartoon territory involved the 1956 Walter Lantz character songs, and Cricket only occasionally went near that neighborhood in the future. The company did manage to snatch up the theme song for the *Felix the Cat* TV series ("Whenever he gets in a fix he reaches into his bag of tricks"). Cricket also continued licensing and producing its own renditions of Disney songs for some time after Golden had already thrown in the Mickey Mouse towel; Cricket, for example, was still in the Disney biz in 1964, when the songs from *Mary Poppins* became immediate sensations.

With the obvious exception of Disneyland Records, all of these labels (and then some) sought to capitalize on one of the most phenomenal successes in TV cartoons beginning in the late 1950s. The entire series of 256

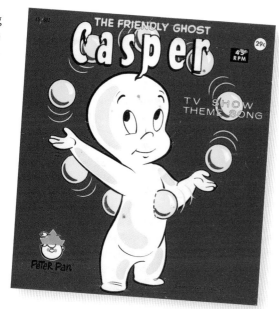

Although Peter Pan Records kept this brassy arrangement of the Casper theme available for many years, it was not technically the "TV theme song," as the cover indicated; instead, it was the same Paramount theme Golden Records had recorded years earlier.

Years after his origin in silent films, Felix the Cat ("the wonderful, wonderful cat") made a triumphant debut in his own TV series, and Peter Pan Records released this version of his new theme.

theatrical Popeye cartoons had been released to television by Associated Artists Productions (AAP) in September 1956; actually, at the same time AAP also released the bulk of the pre-1948 Warner Bros. cartoons, bringing Bugs and his buddies to the small screen for the first time. But Popeye quickly became the ratings leader, as local stations across the country booked the shorts and assigned a staggering array of sea captains, cowboys, clowns, and other types of hosts to introduce them. While Popeye records had been made off and on since 1931, nothing could compare with the number and variety of them produced beginning in 1957.

Certainly one of the earliest was produced by AAP and released on its own label. It starred Allen Swift, a busy cartoon voice actor who was also hosting the Popeye cartoons on New York City television at the time. Swift was widely known as "the man of a thousand voices" (a title also given to Mel Blanc), but his performance on this 45 rpm single proved that Popeye was not one of that thousand. With Mae Questel re-creating her roles as Olive Oyl and Swee'Pea, most of the record is taken up with Popeye playing *another* record consisting of "Captain" Allen Swift performing public domain tunes. Occasional comments from Popeye break up the routine; after Swift sings "Down in the Valley," Popeye malaprops, "I just love mountain songs. They makes me feel neuralgic."

Another "captain" handled the Popeye duties for Cricket Records. Unfortunately, in keeping with Cricket's usual policy of not providing reliable credits, all we know is that he was "Captain Paul and the Seafaring Band." His output for Cricket consisted primarily of the same 1930s compositions that Floyd Buckley had recorded for Bluebird a couple of decades earlier. Unlike Swift, Captain Paul made no attempt to even sound like Popeye, and this approach caused some of the lyrics written in "Popeye-speak" to come out rather oddly when sung in a relatively "straight" voice. As an example, try to imagine how "I'm strong to the finich 'coz I eats me spinach" sounds if *not* delivered in Popeye's unique way of speaking.

Peter Pan Records, at least in the late 1950s, might have seemed to be at a disadvantage because it did not have the rights to that famous Popeye theme song. Did that stop the company from issuing a line of Popeye records? Blow me down, I sez it didn't! Peter Pan simply put its uncredited composers to work and came up with a new Popeye theme that did not resemble the original in the least. The chorus

Associated Artists Productions, which syndicated the Popeye cartoons to local TV stations nationwide, produced a Popeye record with New York City kids' show host Allen Swift trying his best to imitate the mariner's unique voice.

repeatedly pointed out, "Popeye the Sailor Man / Eats his spinach by the can," and one verse aptly summed up what casual viewers might have surmised to be the standard Popeye cartoon plot:

If someone comes along and tries to bully Olive Oyl,
Old Popeye gets so fightin' mad his blood begins to boil;
He springs right into action with the strength of fifteen men,
Now the bully isn't apt to make the same mistake again.

While Peter Pan's new Popeye theme mentioned Bluto in the lyrics, it was also used for an LP that took scripts from four of King Features' made-for-TV cartoons and turned them into audio productions featuring the newly named Brutus. Actor Harry Foster Welch performed all the roles, including Popeye, Bluto, Olive, Swee'Pea, the narrator, and incidental characters.

Welch is an interesting footnote in Popeye history, and years after his death, he remains something of an enigma to cartoon voice historians. During the late World War II years, while Jack Mercer was serving in the military, Welch performed Popeye's voice for a small batch of the theatrical cartoons and made personal appearances in costume as Popeye. However, by the time of his death in 1973, Welch claimed to have done *all* the voices in *all* the Popeye cartoons dating back to 1933. Padding his résumé even further, he claimed to have done all the voices in Disney's miniseries of cartoon shorts starring the Three Little Pigs and the Big Bad Wolf. Of course, all of these claims were eventually proven false, but for Peter Pan Records' rendition of the TV cartoon scripts, at least Welch finally got to do all the roles—just as he had been telling people he had done.

Golden Records got the rights not only to the Popeye theme but also to Jack Mercer's vocal talents along with it. As we saw earlier, a Popeye Little Golden Record had been released as far back as 1951, but once the cartoons found their new popularity, Golden decided to make the old salt their newest star. Mercer did a fine job as Popeye (and Wimpy), supported by Questel as Olive (and Swee'Pea) on a number of singles and LPs for Golden. One of them obviously dates from the period between Bluto and Brutus, as it includes repeated generic statements such as "Olive's in the villain's clutches," and "Just wait'll I eats me spinach! I'll takes care of that villain for ya!" An entire LP was devoted to "Popeye's Songs of Health," in which kids were expected to take advice on—among other subjects—brushing their teeth from a mariner who had no teeth.

At some point around this same time, Mercer made one album for the

During the late 1940s, Harry Foster Welch had performed as Popeye in a handful of cartoons while Jack Mercer was in the military. Welch continued making personal appearances as Popeye long thereafter and in the 1960s performed as the old salt for Peter Pan Records.

Vocalion label. "Popeye's Zoo" was surprising in a number of ways, not the least of which was that it did not sound cheap. Full orchestrations and creative arrangements make the music alone a joy to hear. Each track involved Popeye describing one of the animals in the zoo, leading into a song either with a story of how he captured the beast in question or with a natural history lesson about the animal's biology and habits. True to the cartoon tradition, Popeye does not eat spinach until the final story, when a grizzly bear in the north woods is trying to squeeze him to death. Even at that, the record avoids the expected violence: "Brutus threw me a rope, and I tied up that grouchy grizzly and led him straight to the zoo." Probably the strangest thing about the whole album is that Popeye refers to "Olive Oyl, Wimpy, Brutus, and all of me other comic book pals," tying them to their Dell/Gold Key/King/Whitman careers rather than newspaper comics or animated cartoons.

By the late 1970s, Mercer apparently had become a free agent again, because Peter Pan Records got him (and the traditional theme) for a series of "read-along" titles. Some of these took the form of LPs with bound-in comic books to look at as the dialogue unfolded (more on this a little later), but there were also the standard seven-inch records with accompanying read-along books. Titles such as *Pollution Solution* and *Oyl on Troubled Waters* remained available for years.

In the mid-1960s, the Hanna-Barbera record output was still being handled by Colpix (for TV sound tracks) and Golden (for other singles and LPs). Probably inspired by Disneyland Records, the studio announced the 1965 formation of Hanna-Barbera Records (HBR), which would balance children's albums based on its traditional cartoon characters with what was intended to be cutting-edge rock music. Neither series lasted long, but for a couple of years, some interesting productions resulted.

We really do not have the space here to delve into HBR's attempts to conquer the "garage band" market. However, since the studio executives had less than zero experience with such things, they hired a young musician, Dan Hutton, to oversee that part of the company. Hutton would later go on to bigger things with his band, Three Dog Night. He presumably had nothing to do with HBR's cartoon-related releases.

Listening to a selection of these LPs, one fact becomes immediately obvious. Even though Hanna-Barbera was now controlling its own records, some of the pesky contracts with other labels were still in effect, meaning that Daws Butler and Don Messick could not vocally portray any of their characters covered by those contracts. Instead, the roles were recast with other performers who were also toiling in the Hanna-Barbera salt mines, giving the

YOGI BEAR AND FRIENDS

Bill Hanna and Joe Barbera, two of the most creative men in the entertainment world, have now entered the field of recording with their own recording company, "Hanna-Barbera Records."

Besides producing hundreds of cartoon shows for television each year, the team of Hanna-Barbera is now busy bringing such top favorite T.V. personalities as the Flintstones, Yogi Bear, Huckleberry Hound, The Jetsons, Topcat, Quick Draw McGraw and others to their millions of fans throughout the world on highest quality records.

From their new ultra-modern recording studios in Hollywood, they are presenting the greatest classics of the ages as well as new stories featuring the actual T.V. stars of the Hanna-Barbera Studios.

START YOUR LIBRARY OF THESE GREAT ALBUMS OF TV'S MOST POPULAR STARS...
HANNA-BARBERA RECORDS / HOLLYWOOD, CALIFORNIA

TREASURE ISLAND / SINBAD — HLP 2039
ON THE GOOD SHIP LOLLIPOP — HLP 2040
ATOM ANT AND MUSCLE MAGIC — HLP 2041
WINSOME WITCH — HLP 2042
SQUIDDLY DIDDLY'S — HLP 2043
THE HILLBILLY BEARS — HLP 2044
PRECIOUS PUPP / HOT ROD GRANNY — HLP 2045
SECRET SQUIRREL and MOROCCO MOLE — HLP 2046

DOGGIE DADDY TELLS AUGIE DOGGIE The Story of Pinocchio — HLP 2028
THE RELUCTANT DRAGON / Touche Turtle — HLP 2029
JONNY QUEST 20,000 LEAGUES UNDER THE SEA — HLP 2030
ROBIN HOOD / TOP CAT — HLP 2031
FRED FLINTSTONE and BARNEY RUBBLE / Mary Poppins — HLP 2035
James BOMB SUPER SNOOPER and BLABBERMOUSE — HLP 2036
THE JETSONS — HLP 2037
HANSEL & GRETEL The Flintstones — HLP 2038

MONSTER SHINDIG SUPER SNOOPER and BLABBER MOUSE — HLP 2020
THE FLINTSTONES GOLDILOCKS AND THE THREE BEARASAURUSES — HLP 2021
HUCKLEBERRY HOUND Tells Stories of UNCLE REMUS — HLP 2022
YOGI BEAR AND BOO BOO — HLP 2023
MAGILLA GORILLA TELLS OGEE THE STORY Alice in Wonderland — HLP 2024
PIXIE and DIXIE with MR. JINKS TELL THE STORY OF Cinderella — HLP 2025
SNAGGLEPUSS Wizard of Oz — HLP 2026
THE FLINTSTONE Tell the story of Bambi — HLP 2027

impression that all the characters' names were put into a hat and then the regular voice artists pulled them out randomly to decide who was going to play which part.

Since Butler and Messick were normally Yogi Bear and Boo Boo, on HBR's output those roles were assumed by Allan "Magilla Gorilla" Melvin and June Foray. Butler's Huckleberry Hound voice was also under contract to Colpix, so HBR used Paul Frees's version of Huck's drawl. Pixie, Dixie, and Mr. Jinks were also contracted out, so they were played on records by Foray, Dick "Speedy Alka-Seltzer" Beals, and Frees. For most of the Flintstones' records, Alan Reed and Mel Blanc were on hand as Fred and Barney, although on at

Probably as an answer to Disneyland Records, Hanna-Barbera formed its own record label in 1965. Pictured here are a number of its LPs based on its famous characters, but Hanna-Barbera Records also tried hard (and failed) to make it big in the rock-and-roll music market.

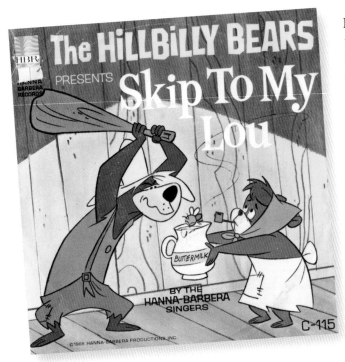

Many Hanna-Barbera Records, including this 45, featured generic singers performing generic children's songs but included some of the well-known TV characters on the sleeves as hosts of sorts.

least one occasion, they were replaced by Henry Corden (who would take over the role of Fred after Reed's death) and Daws Butler (whose Barney sounded a lot like the Yogi Bear voice he could not perform on HBR's releases).

However, Colpix was not releasing any Snagglepuss material, so for that beloved character, Butler was free to give one of his greatest performances, narrating the story of *The Wizard of Oz* as the hammy lion. Other than Janet Waldo pulling double duty as both Dorothy and the Wicked Witch, Butler essayed all the roles in the story, impersonating Frank Fontaine (as the Scarecrow), Jimmy Stewart (as the Tin Woodman), Ed Wynn (as the Cowardly Lion), Shelley Berman (as the Wizard), and several others.

Regardless of the strange voice casting, HBR's big strength was in its scripts. The majority of the albums took the form of the characters telling modernized versions of famous fairy tales (or the opposite in the case of the Flintstones, with Fred narrating the story of "Goldirocks and the Three Bearosauruses"). Sometimes, rather than a strict retelling of a classic tale, the script would use it merely as a jumping-off point, such as when Top Cat and his gang read about Robin Hood and then decide to emulate the legendary hero by robbing the rich and giving to the poor (namely, themselves). One of the most consistently funny is the story of "The Reluctant Dragon," starring Touché Turtle, with Bill Thompson and Daws Butler providing all the voices.

One of the most unusual has Atom Ant starring in "Muscle Magic." Side A is a fairly typical story, with the mighty mite—perhaps the only superhero smaller than Mighty Mouse—battling some outsized ants threatening a rural Texas town, and Side B taking the form of a physical education class, as Mr. Ant explains to kids how to develop their own powerful muscles through diet and exercise. The most notable thing is that Atom freely expresses the opinion that his tips on strength and health are equally valid for both boys and girls. In those days long before Title IX school programs, the idea that girls, too, could be strong was years ahead of its time.

Some releases were guaranteed to disappoint the kids who bought them based on the eye-catching cover art. Some were simply renditions of nursery songs and other public domain tunes performed by an anonymous group of singers, but the sleeves featured the familiar characters. For example, the "Children's Marching Song" (aka "This Old Man") showed Secret Squirrel leading a marching band down the street, even though he had nothing to do with the record. The French standard "Alouette" showed Winsome Witch flying over the Eiffel Tower on her broomstick—again, even though she didn't actually appear on the record.

Even the character-related songs on the story LPs were a bit odd in that none of the familiar Hanna-Barbera TV themes were used but the stock background music cues from the cartoons were utilized extensively. Instead, completely new themes for Huck, Yogi, the Flintstones, and the rest were performed by a group of busy studio singers Al Capps (not to be confused with Li'l Abner creator Al Capp), Carol Lombard (not to be confused with Mrs. Clark Gable), and Ron Hicklin. Most of the new songs had heavy traces of HBR's desire to be a rock music label, although they were not nearly as gritty as the singles put out under Dan Hutton's supervision.

The reason for HBR's quick demise in 1967 is obscure after so many years, but it most likely had something to do with the Hanna-Barbera studio being purchased by Taft Broadcasting. Taft had big plans for its new acquisition, including theme parks intended to resemble Disney's, but records apparently were considered an expendable division. The license to produce records with H-B's properties soon shifted to Peter Pan Records, and the results were generally not pretty (and almost unlistenable).

Record historian Kliph Nesteroff's assessment is a bit harsh but not entirely inaccurate: "By the 1970s, most Hanna-Barbera recordings seemed to feature nameless sound engineers or delivery boys filling in for the voices of Yogi Bear and Wilma Flintstone." There is no doubt that Peter Pan's cartoon albums and contemporary book-and-record sets fairly scream "cheap." The albums at least occasionally used professional voice talent; on one early 1970s Flintstones LP, for example, Fred and Barney were played by Allen Swift, who certainly came closer to matching those voices than he did Popeye. But most of the "read-along" sets did not even have that luxury. Whoever was chosen to be the narrator—and more often than not did not receive credit for the performance—also had to perform any voices called for by the written dialogue. Hearing an anonymous story reader try to impersonate Huckleberry Hound makes one fervently wish to hear Paul Frees's rendition of that character again. The stories were written by the mysterious Horace J. Elias, whom we encountered taking over most of Hanna-Barbera's print work back in the chapter on books.

Peter Pan also produced "read-along" sets and albums for many of its other licensed properties. The ones involving the Warner Bros. characters at least used part of their budgets to pay for Mel Blanc to do his traditional

The Archies were probably the most successful cartoon characters to enjoy a record career, churning out bubblegum rock hits including "Sugar, Sugar" and "Jingle Jangle."

Hi! Girls and Boys.

LAUGH, SING, HAVE FUN WITH THE CHARACTORS FROM YOUR FAVORITE TV SHOWS. ... JOIN IN WITH THEIR SILLY SONGS, PLAYFUL ANTICS AND DARING EXPLOITS. HAVE A GOOD TIME. HERE ARE SOMEMORE OF YOUR CARTOON FUN FAVORITES ON PETER PAN RECORDS.

Peter Pan Industries: Newark, N.J. 07105

It is easy to tell that Peter Pan Records was not very consistent in its depiction of well-known animated stars. Perhaps the answer lies in this promotional text: these distorted faces were "charactors"—actors playing the roles of Popeye, Bugs Bunny, and others.

roles; however, by that point in his career, age and smoking had caused Blanc's voice to coarsen to the point of hoarseness, giving all but the lower-pitched characters (Sylvester, Yosemite Sam, and so on) a very different sound. The thriftiness the Peter Pan producers extended to the background music sometimes got in the way of the story the writers were trying to tell; *Maestro Bugs* is supposed to involve the wascally wabbit's misadventures in a concert hall, but since the orchestra is represented by a single electric organ, the effect is less than convincing.

Earlier we mentioned that Peter Pan also had a successful (in financial terms) set of Popeye stories done in this format. There were also entries from Bozo the Clown—long divorced from Capitol and now played by Larry Harmon— and occasional other one-shot characters. For Peter Pan's version of *Mister Magoo's Christmas Carol*, a strange choice was made when it came to the title character's voice. Rather than hiring Jim Backus or an impersonator, it sounds as if a sound technician simply held a microphone up to a TV set to capture snippets of the dialogue from a broadcast of the much-loved 1962 animated special. While all the other characters sound clear, Magoo sounds as if he is locked in a closet.

Most of the artwork in these "read-along" sets was furnished by our old friend from earlier in this book, George Peed. Long after his days of illustrating Disney merchandise had ended, Peed freelanced for Peter Pan Records, turning out illustration after illustration for covers and interior art. While his talent was obvious, it is also clear that he was more comfortable with some licensees' properties than with others: he never could seem to get the Popeye cast right somehow. His work on the Warner Bros. characters certainly gives them more animation than Blanc's somewhat tired reading of the scripts, but Peed sometimes made odd choices about how to picture the looney stars. He seemed bent on keeping Bugs Bunny in the jacket and straw hat he wore for the opening theme and connecting segments of the network TV *Bugs Bunny Show*, even when that attire was not dictated by or even appropriate for the story. For some reason, Peed never seemed to be called on to illustrate the Hanna-Barbera material; it would indeed have been interesting to see his approach to those characters.

Now we turn to another subject, and that is the history of the *Peanuts*

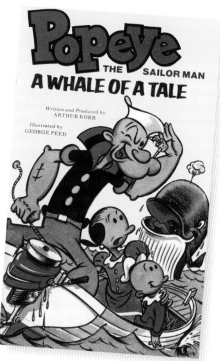

George Peed's days as a Disney artist were over by the time he hooked up with Peter Pan Records, but these examples show that he was better at depicting some characters than others. Hanging around with Bugs apparently had a negative influence on both Tweety and Porky Pig, who had taken on the wabbit's thieving ways.

characters in the record industry. As phenomenally popular as the strip and its merchandise were, it seemed rather difficult to translate into an audio-only medium. The first *Peanuts* album was released by Columbia in 1962, and it was definitely meant to take its place alongside such popular spoken-word comedy LPs as those ringing up big sales for Bob Newhart and Vaughn Meader, among others. Titled simply *Good Grief, Charlie Brown! Peanuts*, it featured comedy writer Arthur Siegel and Broadway comedian Kaye Ballard simply reciting dialogue from the comic strips. With its cast of only two, no characters other than Charlie Brown and Lucy were used; Ballard made repeated use of her cackling stage laugh in conveying Lucy's well-honed putdowns of Charlie Brown.

A few albums preserved the wonderful jazz scores composed by Vince Guaraldi for the animated specials but contained no dialogue or lyrics. The next *Peanuts* record attempt that did include vocals would have long-lasting consequences. Songwriter Clark Gesner had been penning tunes based on the comic strip for a couple of years before MGM Records released the songs on an album, *You're a Good Man, Charlie Brown*. It starred Orson Bean as Good Ol' You-Know-Who, with Barbara Minkus as Lucy, Bill Hinnant as Snoopy, and Gesner filling in for some other roles. Not long after its release, plans began swirling to turn the songs into the basis for a Broadway show, and MGM Records put up half the initial cost to get *You're a Good Man, Charlie Brown*, the stage musical, up and running. The play debuted in March 1967 and was yet another example of how Schulz's strip was turning into something much bigger than its four daily panels on the newspaper page.

Peanuts grew even more when a group of musically inclined college-age lads from Ocala, Florida, formed the Royal Guardsmen. They were just beginning to attract attention around Tampa when record producer Phil Gernhard brought them the lyrics to "Snoopy vs. the Red Baron," a song he was hoping to release as a novelty record. The group was not overly enthused about it, but they gave it their all, and it was released as a single by Laurie Records.

Neither Gernhard nor the Royal Guardsmen had bothered to ask Charles Schulz or United Feature Syndicate before releasing the record, but as Guardsman Barry Winslow later related to historian Ed Tucker,

Phil sent a copy of the record and a letter to Charles Schulz. Charles looked at it but never sent a response on whether we could do this or not. His lawyers smelled money and whether Charles cared or not, the lawyers put a ding in us! Schulz eventually gave his consent, they got a pretty healthy chunk of money, and we moved right on down the road.

The off-Broadway musical *You're a Good Man, Charlie Brown* actually began as an album of *Peanuts* songs by Clark Gesner. (Greg Ehrbar collection)

LES-900

sounds great in STEREO

An Original MGM Album Musical based on Charles Schulz' *Peanuts*
You're a good man, Charlie Brown
Starring ORSON BEAN as Charlie Brown

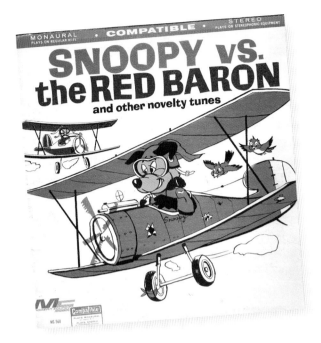

Once the Royal Guardsmen were official *Peanuts* licensees, they parlayed their first Snoopy record's success into a whole string of sequels, beginning with "The Return of the Red Baron" and continuing with "Snoopy's Christmas" and "Snoopy for President," by which time the novelty had worn off for both the performers and the record-buying public.

The Royal Guardsmen songs and the *You're a Good Man, Charlie Brown* tunes faced the same intriguing fate. In the late 1960s and early 1970s, both sets of songs were licensed for "cover versions" by a number of children's record labels, most notably Pickwick/Cricket and Peter Pan Records. These companies found themselves in a quandary: they had the rights to make their own recordings of the songs but not to use artwork of any of the Schulz characters. For the "Red Baron" series, most of them chose to illustrate the public domain villain and only hint at the presence of his copyrighted canine adversary, but at least one of them chose to illustrate a Snoopy who did not look like Schulz's Snoopy in the least. The *You're a Good Man, Charlie Brown* albums were illustrated with everything from generic-looking artwork of kids to photographs of actual children.

So, just what was a company to do when it had the rights to produce records of songs based on the *Peanuts* characters but not the rights to depict those characters on the covers? These two approaches show how that could be handled: not well.

In the late 1970s, Disneyland Records began an offshoot, Charlie Brown Records, to release audio re-creations of some of the animated TV specials.

Finally, in 1977 came the biggest *Peanuts* record push to date. Disneyland Records, in a most unusual move for the company, formed a subsidiary label, Charlie Brown Records, for the sole purpose of marketing LPs and "read-along" book-and-record sets based on the animated *Peanuts* TV specials. Most of them were composed primarily of sections taken from the television sound tracks, but some had to incorporate new narration to further the stories. Since the young performers who voiced Charlie Brown and company in the 1960s had long matured and gone on to other pursuits, the narration (when necessary) was recorded by the new generation of child actors working in the TV shows, with little regard for whether Charlie Brown or Linus sounded the same narrating as they did in their dialogue.

A more lavish Disneyland/Charlie Brown Records production was *Flashbeagle*, released in 1984. It was tied to an animated special, *It's Flashbeagle, Charlie Brown*, but contained longer and more numerous songs than could be squeezed into a half-hour cartoon. They were composed by Ed Bogas and Desiree Goyette (at that time, married to producer Lee Mendelson), and were certainly the best *Peanuts*-related songs to come along since Gesner's *You're a Good Man* suite. Goyette's naturally bubbly personality came through in her vocal performances on the album, particularly on her inspiring "Someday, Charlie Brown," which uses most of the comic strip's standard elements and turns them into an uplifting ballad guaranteed to give the listener moist eyes.

In 1972, yet another famed comic book/cartoon company made a little-remembered attempt to start its own record label. Issues of the various Harvey Comics titles announced, "The first red-hot disc on the Harvey label is headed your way!" Yes, Harvey decided to produce and market its own records based on its characters, beginning with a 45 containing "Casper, Casper (Whatcha Doin' on the Moon)" and "Richie Rich" as the first two songs.

The first of the two was nothing if not timely. In April 1972, the Apollo 16 mission had nicknamed its command module *Casper* (following the lead of the May 1969 Apollo 10 mission and its *Charlie Brown* and *Snoopy* spacecraft). Naturally, Harvey was more than willing to use Casper's space voyage for publicity purposes, licensing other forms of merchandise featuring the theme, including a set of bed sheets.

To write the lyrics for its new records, the company did not even have to search outside its own ranks. Sid Jacobson had been the editor of Harvey's comic book line since the early 1950s and had been the lyricist for a number of hit tunes (Frankie Avalon's "Boy without a Girl" and Jimmie Rodgers's "Wonderful You," among others), so when the company needed original

Longtime Harvey Comics editor Sid Jacobson composed the lyrics for a series of singles based on the company's star characters. Casper and Richie Rich were the first two to be immortalized in this manner. (Donnie Pitchford collection)

Casper's role as mascot for the Apollo 16 moon mission inspired not only the first release from Harvey Records but also other pieces of merchandise such as these sheets and pillowcases. (Donnie Pitchford collection)

Two years after Harvey Records' beginning, the line had increased to include songs about nearly every major Harvey character. Since they were available only by mail order and not in retail stores, they are more difficult to locate today than most other types of children's records. (Donnie Pitchford collection)

songs for its characters, Jacobson was a natural choice. And, since he had already been editing the comics for approximately twenty years by that time, he certainly needed no crash course in becoming familiar with them.

Jacobson's lyrics were set to music by Jimmy Krondes, who used an amazingly varied range of styles for them. That initial release with Casper on the moon paired with Richie Rich "in a house with a thousand rooms" was credited to "the grooviest, ginchiest rock 'n' roll group EVER, namely, THE COMIX!" in its ads, but some of the singles that followed went for a different sound. "The Magic Wand of Wendy," for example, was performed by an unidentified female soloist in a dreamy style that, true to its subject matter, can practically induce hypnosis. "Baby Huey," on the other hand, was sung by a children's choir with a saxophone providing the requisite quacking noises. "Here Comes Little Audrey" had a British-accented group for its vocals, while "Hiding from Spooky" and "Hot Stuff, the Little Devil" had more traditional rock sounds.

The Harvey Records releases were marketed strictly through ads in the comic books, not on store shelves. This probably accounts for their relative rarity today, although their original selling price of one dollar per record, compared to Golden, Disneyland, Peter Pan, and Cricket's usual retail of twenty-nine cents, does make them seem a bit costly. However, each Harvey Record release came with two free issues of its title characters' comic books. In the end, the Harvey Records were great melodies that deserved to find a wider audience.

From 1975 to 1977, Peter Pan Records made a concentrated effort to push new recorded adventures for characters that had rarely been heard in that form: the superhero stars of DC Comics. The *Wonder Woman* TV movies (and subsequent series) starring Lynda Carter had become a hit in 1975, so that is no doubt what inspired that character's debut on vinyl. She was quickly followed by her cohorts Superman and Batman; all of these records came with a comic book bound into the sleeve, taking the old Record-Reader concept to a new level. The vocal performances were surprisingly good, perhaps because Superman, Batman, and Wonder Woman had never been defined by their voices in the same way as, say, Bugs Bunny or Yogi Bear. Low budgets showed through in some of the sound effects; the same footsteps would be used whether they were supposed to represent Wonder Woman's boots or a teenager's sneakers. They were successful enough for several of the Marvel superheroes (Spider-Man, the Incredible Hulk, the Fantastic Four) to receive record productions of their own. Peter Pan Records added to its noncartoon line with similar releases based on *Star Trek*, *Kojak*, *The Six Million Dollar Man*, and several of the famed Universal movie monsters.

About the time the DC superheroes were becoming record stars, the disco phenomenon hit the music industry. A small label, Happy Time Records, proved it was in the groove with *Kartoon Disko*, a mostly instrumental album of rearranged cartoon themes ranging from *Popeye*, *Woody Woodpecker*, and *Batman* to several Disney songs. Its success is what partly led Disneyland Records to hire most of the same creative and production personnel to bring to life *Mickey Mouse Disco* (1979), which went on to become the first children's album in history to be certified double platinum (two million copies sold).

Peter Pan Records got away from its usual lighter fare with the sometimes grim adventures in its LPs based on the DC Comics superheroes.

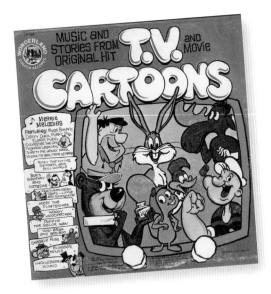

In 1973, selections from many of Little Golden Records' cartoon releases were compiled into this album. Even the cover art was a montage taken from past Golden sleeves. (Greg Ehrbar collection)

Columbia Records re-released many of the 1965–66 Hanna-Barbera Records in 1977. New, inferior artwork was created for the covers, and the recordings were "artificially enhanced to simulate stereo."

The last topic to touch on briefly in this protracted discussion concerns the mid- to late 1970s, when many of the cartoon records from as much as thirty years earlier were reissued for a new generation. Golden Records put out an album with the prosaic title *Songs from Movie and TV Cartoons*, which was a hodgepodge of its 1950s and 1960s productions. Included were the impersonated all-star version of the Merrie Melodies theme, several selections from *Rocky and His Friends* and the Gilbert Mack/Frank Milano Hanna-Barbera records, individual tracks from the Flintstones and Woody Woodpecker releases, and the always sped-up Popeye theme from 1951. Columbia Records reissued many of the albums from the defunct Hanna-Barbera Records label, clumsily reprocessing them to simulate stereo and replacing the original painted cover art with much cheaper designs.

Capitol Records, for its part, had preserved its rights to its many Disney, Warner Bros., and Woody Woodpecker Record-Readers, reissuing them in the 1970s on LPs after editing out any references to "turning the page." The Warner Bros. Capitol Records even became the basis for a traveling arena show, *The Bugs Bunny Follies*, which was similar in concept to the long-running *Disney on Parade*. Although Mel Blanc recorded some new dialogue, most of the show's sound track was taken from Capitol's stories and songs of the late 1940s. Capitol, Golden, and other companies thus ensured that these classic recordings would continue to entertain the children of those former children who had originally heard them.

BUY DIRECT AND SAVE!

CHILDRENS 12" LP RECORD CLASSICS

Order 1 · $4.95
Order 3 · $9.95 (Save $5.10)
Order all 12 · $36.95 (Save $22.45)

1 L6956 — WALT DISNEY'S THREE LITTLE PIGS — from the Disney film with members of original cast — SPARKY'S MAGIC PIANO — the original classic favorite. It makes music appreciation fun.

2 L6957 — BUGS BUNNY AND HIS FRIENDS — three stories featuring BUGS, ELMER FUDD, DAFFY DUCK, PORKY PIG and others—BOZO AT THE CIRCUS — the original all time classic of children's records.

3 L6958 — TWEETY PIE — two stories with TWEETY and SYLVESTER THE CAT — TEENA THE LAUGHING HYENA and HOW THE FIRE ENGINE GOT ITS SIREN — two original fun stories.

4 L6959 — BOZO ON THE FARM — the original BOZO takes children to meet farm animals — HENERY HAWK — two stories featuring HENERY, the famous Warner Bros. Cartoon Chicken Hawk.

5 L6960 — WALT DISNEY'S THE GRASSHOPPER AND THE ANTS — adapted from the motion picture with original cast — RUSTY IN ORCHESTRAVILLE — the original classic music appreciation story in which instruments talk.

6 L6961 — WOODY WOODPECKER'S PICNIC — famous Walter Lantz cartoon character takes animal friends on a picnic — SPARKY AND THE TALKING TRAIN — a little boy's love for trains leads to an exciting adventure.

7 L6962 — BUGS BUNNY AND THE TORTOISE — BUGS has a race with a tortoise with a surprise ending — BOZO AND HIS ROCKET SHIP — the original BOZO goes on a trip to foreign lands.

8 L6963 — I TAUT I TAW A PUDDY TAT AND OTHER SONGS with TWEETY, DAFFY DUCK, YOSEMITE SAM, PORKY PIG, and BOZO.

9 L6986 — WALT DISNEY'S TALES OF UNCLE REMUS — from the motion picture, "Song Of The South," with original cast — TICKETY TOCK — an alarm clock learns how to tell time.

10 L6987 — WALT DISNEY'S LITTLE TOOT — from the motion picture, "Melody Time." Also includes Disney's THREE ORPHAN KITTENS — BOZO AND THE BIRDS — the original BOZO goes up in the air to meet the various birds.

11 L6988 — BUGS BUNNY IN STORYLAND — BUGS visits famous fairy tale characters — BOZO AT THE DOG SHOW — the original BOZO talks to dogs in a humorous and educational way.

12 L6989 — WOODY WOODPECKER AND HIS TALENT SHOW — famous Walter Lantz cartoon character invites animal friends to a talent show — BOZO HAS A PARTY — the original BOZO has a party for all of his friends.

ORDER DIRECT AND SAVE!
UNITED MAIL MART P.O. BOX 1482 BEVERLY HILLS, CALIFORNIA 90213

Please make Check or Money Order payable to:

UNITED MAIL MART
P.O. BOX 1482
BEVERLY HILLS, CA 90213

Please print

Name _____
Address _____
City _____ State _____ Zip _____

Price includes shipping and handling California residents add 6% Sales Tax. Allow 4-6 weeks delivery

Enclosed ☐ Cash ☐ Check ☐ Money Order
☐ Charge to my MASTERCHARGE
☐ Charge to my BANKAMERICARD/VISA

for $ _____
Account No. _____
Expiration Date _____
Signature _____ Age _____
All Charge orders must be signed

PLEASE CHECK ALBUMS DESIRED AND QUANTITY

Price per album	Any three albums	All twelve albums
$4.95	$9.95	$36.95

1 ☐   2 ☐   3 ☐   4 ☐
5 ☐   6 ☐   7 ☐   8 ☐
9 ☐   10 ☐   11 ☐   12 ☐

TOTAL _____

The craze for reissuing classic cartoon records hit Capitol as well, as indicated by this 1980 ad promoting the new availability of many of what had originally been the 1940s–50s Disney, Bozo, Warner Bros., and Woody Woodpecker Record-Readers. (Donnie Pitchford collection)

Capitol Records' Warner Bros. releases of the late 1940s and early 1950s provided the bulk of the soundtrack for *The Bugs Bunny Follies*, a traveling stage show of the late 1970s.

LIVE ON STAGE!

RODGER HESS presents

BUGS BUNNY FOLLIES

Souvenir Book

In 1953, kids could obtain Halloween masks (plus other loot) relating to Popeye, Olive Oyl, Dick Tracy, and Little Orphan Annie simply by dragging their parents to the nearest Motorola TV dealer.

Ben Cooper became one of the primary licensees for cartoon character costumes. By the time of these Snow White and Hong Kong Phooey editions, even the boxes featured the stars available in Cooper's universe.

Chapter 7

HAPPY HOLIDAYS

For youngsters, holidays are always a big deal. Well, that is not to say that adults don't enjoy them too, but when one is a kid, holidays are often the only break from the daily monotony of school and homework. (Surely someone knew what he or she was doing when the Fourth of July turned out to be the only major holiday that fell while school was closed for the summer.) Fortunately, we could keep our favorite cartoon characters close at hand to help celebrate those special days.

Although Christmas was obviously the holiday for which kids were likely to receive the most toys, cartoon or otherwise, most merchandise was not geared specifically toward it. We will shortly take a look at some that was, but first we should deal with the holiday that produced the most specific cartoon-related merchandise—in fact, none of it was of any real use before or after its one special day: Halloween.

Like most of the other types, cartoon Halloween costumes had their origins in the early 1930s. Not surprisingly, Disney was way out in front when it came to licensing them. What is a bit more intriguing is how different they were, in both style and appearance, from the ones most of us grew up with from the 1950s to the 1970s. According to pioneering cartoon

collectors Robert Heide and John Gilman, in the 1930s, Disney Halloween

masks were not made of plastic, as they would be today, but of a stiffened net fabric of a cheesecloth consistency, molded into the shape of Mickey or one of the other creatures. These face masks could have an almost eerie look; they were not intended just to be cute, but to frighten and bedevil.

Actually, when you stop to think about it, many of our most beloved cartoon stars would have been pretty frightening to meet. Popeye was a lot of fun to watch on the screen, but just imagine how you would react to seeing a real person who looked like him. So it was with the early cartoon Halloween costumes; as Heide and Gilman point out, they were as scary as they were funny-looking.

The masks were only one component of those first costumes; unlike later costumes, the bodysuits tried as hard as possible to duplicate the look of the character in question. In the mid-1930s, Sears sold Mickey and Minnie Mouse costumes that came with white felt gloves (the illustration showed only three fingers and a thumb, in best animated tradition), plus either

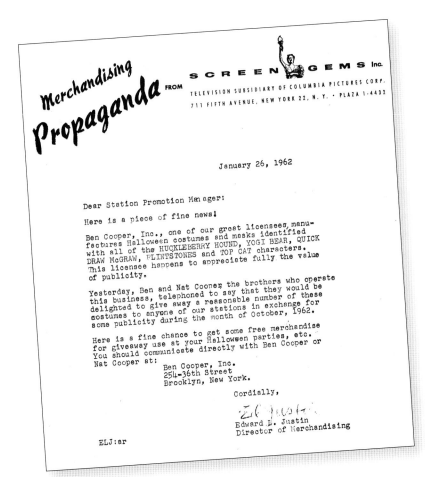

Merchandising Propaganda FROM **SCREEN GEMS Inc.**

TELEVISION SUBSIDIARY OF COLUMBIA PICTURES CORP.

711 FIFTH AVENUE, NEW YORK 22, N. Y. · PLAZA 1-4432

January 26, 1962

Dear Station Promotion Manager:

Here is a piece of fine news!

Ben Cooper, Inc., one of our great licensees, manu-
factures Halloween costumes and masks identified
with all of the HUCKLEBERRY HOUND, YOGI BEAR, QUICK
DRAW McGRAW, FLINTSTONES and TOP CAT characters.
This licensee happens to appreciate fully the value
of publicity.

Yesterday, Ben and Nat Cooper, the brothers who operate
this business, telephoned to say that they would be
delighted to give away a reasonable number of these
costumes to anyone of our stations in exchange for
some publicity during the month of October, 1962.

Here is a fine chance to get some free merchandise
for giveaway use at your Halloween parties, etc.
You should communicate directly with Ben Cooper or
Nat Cooper at:

        Ben Cooper, Inc.
        254-36th Street
        Brooklyn, New York.

        Cordially,

        Edward D. Justin
        Director of Merchandising

ELJ:ar

In January 1962, Hanna-Barbera licensing king Ed Justin was already sending out letters offering local TV stations Ben Cooper's costumes in exchange for publicity.

Mickey's famous red two-button shorts or Minnie's skirt, both of which had black rubber tails protruding from the appropriate spot. The first Popeye costumes followed much the same pattern, with the addition of rayon appendages pinned to the sleeves to duplicate the sailor's trademark bulging forearms.

Other pre-1940s costumes included Mammy and Pappy Yokum (Mammy's cloth mask came complete with a hole in the mouth for inserting a corncob pipe). Little Orphan Annie came packaged in a box showing a crowd of Annies dancing around Daddy Warbucks, who is apparently confused about which one is the real thing. Perhaps he should have been tipped off to look for the Annie with no pupils in her eyes . . . but since he, too, lacked pupils, that clue might not have done him any good.

As the costume industry matured into its familiar post–World War II form, three companies became the leaders, and even one of those was a poor relation. The biggies were Ben Cooper, based in Brooklyn, New York; and Collegeville, based in the Pennsylvania town of the same name. Their weak sister was Halco, based in Nashville, Tennessee. Like other manufacturers, these three costume tycoons waged a constant battle to see which one could score the most desirable cartoon licenses—and Halco was invariably left to eat off the floor.

Ben Cooper got lucky early on, sewing up the Disney and Hanna-Barbera licenses. The number of characters those two studios produced kept the designers at Cooper busy churning out costume versions. By this time, the standard outfit was a thin plastic mask that was extremely susceptible to crushing or splitting and that was held on by a rubber band that was prone to breaking—but then again, meant to be used for only a few hours on one night of the year. The bodysuits, made from an equally insubstantial nylon-like material, gradually moved away from trying to look like the character's actual body and instead featured artwork to help identify just who the mask was supposed to be.

That was a good thing, because a number of costumes from all three companies made some drastic departures from their subjects' usual appearances. Ben Cooper manufactured a Bullwinkle costume for more than a decade, using the same mold for the mask but somehow failing each time to get the color scheme anywhere near correct. One year, Bullwinkle's face was blue, with yellow antlers and a peach-colored muzzle; another season, his face was black and his antlers were lavender. By 1973, Bullwinkle had red hair and nostrils and green eyes to go with his black face and peach muzzle.

Ben Cooper also seemed to be stretching a bit when it made a Pogo Possum costume in 1969. The only possible catalyst for such a move would seem to be the animated *Pogo* TV special that had aired on NBC earlier that year, as Pogo's brand of political satire was not the usual stuff of kids' dreams. As with Bullwinkle, Cooper made a boo-boo with Pogo's mask, which was peach-colored with yellow hair and looked more like a deformed human than an opossum. The bodysuit was decorated with a six-panel comic strip that was definitely *not* Walt Kelly's work; in fact, it could have been created by one of those authors we met a few chapters back who seemed to have never seen the characters about whom they were writing. The Ben Cooper Pogo strip tried to be true to its source by having the characters discuss Pogo's chances of being elected president, but the dialogue made little sense. The best line came from Albert Alligator in the final panel: "Being President could be a real head start program."

Pogo Possum was one of the least likely characters to be adapted for a children's costume. The mask barely resembled him, and the artwork on the bodysuit hardly conveyed the wit and satire of Walt Kelly's strip. (Steve Thompson/ Pogo Fan Club collection)

Collegeville's heavy hitters were the Warner Bros. characters, plus Casper and the other Harvey Comics stars. During the 1970s, Casper even hosted Collegeville ads in issues of the company's comic books, tempting readers with not only his own costume but also those of the Road Runner and Popeye. As with Ben Cooper's constantly morphing version of Bullwinkle, Collegeville felt the need to redesign its Popeye costume every few years. He evolved from a 1950s-design face bearing a permanent case of five o'clock shadow to the made-for-TV version with a huge white eye and oversized pipe. Collegeville also manufactured some companion costumes, including Olive Oyl and the Sea Hag. The company's relationship with King Features Syndicate was cozy if not exclusive; while Collegeville had Snuffy Smith and the Phantom represented in its catalog, Ben Cooper was working the other side of the street with fellow KFS characters Beetle Bailey and Blondie. Collegeville also kept an Underdog costume on the market for years, with the superhound's face mask evolving from peach to glow-in-the-dark yellow.

(Perhaps it is prudent to pause here and mention that virtually all of the costumes from all three companies used loud Day-Glo fluorescent colors in their masks. Presumably these colors made the wearers more visible on dark Halloween nights, but their true glory can only be appreciated by viewing them under ultraviolet black light, something that would have been a rare fixture at most kiddie parties.)

During the 1970s, Casper shilled not only for Collegeville Costumes but also for the long-standing tradition of trick-or-treating for UNICEF. The amiable poltergeist urged his faithful readers to get one of the special UNICEF boxes from that agency's local office and wear one of nine different buttons picturing Harvey's stars doing their bit for the children's charity.

Halco had to make do with whatever characters were left over after Cooper and Collegeville got finished with their licensing antics. Not that all of them were born losers: Halco somehow got the rights to Li'l Abner, Alvin and the Chipmunks (in their pre-animated days), Felix the Cat, Linus the Lionhearted, and Mister Magoo—not exactly cartoon lowlights but hardly in the same league as Mickey Mouse, Bugs Bunny, and Yogi Bear.

Character costumes remained mainstays of variety store counters into the early 1980s. Of course, after several product-tampering scares, traditional trick-or-treating had taken a hit, and increased concerns about safety soon relegated the old plastic masks, with their eye holes and snappy rubber bands,

Collegeville Costumes took out advertising in Harvey Comics for years, using the space to plug not only its Casper costume but those of Popeye and the Warner Bros. characters, too. (Donnie Pitchford collection)

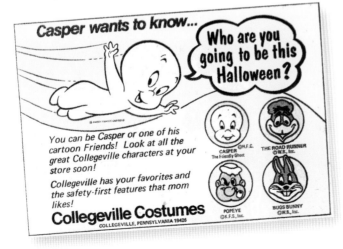

to the trash heap (or to the antique store). "Trick-or-treat for UNICEF" went in the same direction, leaving Casper without a charitable cause to promote. Fortunately, Halloween was not the only holiday for which one could buy specially made cartoon character items, so we now turn the pages of the calendar to see what others we can celebrate.

For a kid, Valentine's Day could be every bit as weird as Halloween—maybe even more so. Let's face it: you were expected to give a valentine card to every other student in your classroom, completely disregarding such important factors as gender and whether they had bullied you out of your PB&J sandwich the day before. Card manufacturers did a big business by selling children's valentines in boxed sets meant to mirror the average size of a class; invariably, there was an additional design especially for the teacher, which if you stop to think about it only increases the potential creepiness factor. Be that as it may, if those little cards could increase their appeal by licensing famous characters to deliver their messages, all the better.

During the 1930s and 1940s, valentine cards were more likely to be sold individually than in boxes, and many comic strip stars of the era moonlighted in the greeting card business. Some of the cards were known as "mechanical," meaning that certain pieces of them could be manipulated puppet-style. For example, one early 1940s card showed Wonder Woman lifting a globe up and down and declaring, "I'd move heaven and earth for you!"

As usual, Disney made it into big business when Kay Kamen put the studio together with Hall Brothers of Kansas City—later known as Hallmark—to produce Mickey Mouse cards for any occasion, be it Valentine's Day, birthdays, Christmas, or any of the others. When the baby-boomer-era boxed sets came along, Disney was right there, too. One group that sold for years featured a mixture of characters from short subjects and animated features, each with its own simple wordplay. A few samples:

The Harvey characters could also be found doing their bit to promote UNICEF, a popular Halloween fund-raising effort. (Donnie Pitchford collection)

These Disney valentines from the 1960s and 1970s are but a few of the many, many designs that have been made available from the depression up to the present.

Kids could also give each other Hanna-Barbera valentines during the early 1960s. The style of artwork differed according to the manufacturer.

Donald Duck (on the telephone): "Nothing 'phoney' about it—I'm your valentine"

Bambi: "Deer-me, valentine, I like you!"

Lady and the Tramp: "Putting on the dog to say be mine!"

Goofy (eating popcorn): "Corny, but be my valentine!"

Practical Pig (with bricks and mortar): "Just a build-up to say be mine!"

Had enough yet? We thought so.

But while Disney's valentines were the most common, there were others. Around 1961, some very handsome Hanna-Barbera boxed sets featured artwork that surpassed even the Disney designs. Yogi Bear, Boo Boo, Ranger Smith, Hokey Wolf, and Yakky Doodle all put their own spin on the usual slogans, and a Flintstones set did likewise. (Fred, stirring a pot with a giant bone: "My heart's in a stew over you!")

Unlike plastic Halloween masks and trick-or-treating for UNICEF, boxed cartoon valentines have never gone away. Step into any corner drugstore during early February, and you can find the tradition continuing with cards based on any number of modern-day characters plus occasional appearances by old standbys such as Mickey Mouse or the *Peanuts* crowd. And even with all the well-intentioned attempts to change things, some poor kid is probably still getting beaten up on the playground because he inadvertently gave the class tough guy a valentine with a mushy sentiment on it. Some holiday traditions will always be with us, good or bad.

Now, let's hop on down the bunny trail and pay our brief respects to Easter—brief not because the holiday is unimportant but because when it came to merchandise, about the only two things to consider were candy and egg decorating kits. In the late 1930s, the venerable Paas Dye Company (surely no other brand name was ever as associated with Easter) began marketing Disney egg decorations in the form of both tattoo-like food coloring transfers and paper accessories to make your colored eggs look like Mickey, Pluto, et al. It should come as no surprise that Donald Duck was the star of the Paas line, being the nearest thing to an Easter animal in the Disney menagerie; the traditional rabbits pretty much only appeared in an obscure 1934 theatrical short, *Funny Little Bunnies*. In the late 1940s, after the release of *Song of the South*, Brer Rabbit occasionally took his place among the other holiday hares.

In the late 1970s, a new form of egg decoration was introduced, again using Disney scenes. Plastic wrappers would be immersed in boiling water, causing them to cling to the surface of an egg to create the impression of "handpainted European porcelain"—at least if you believe the ads. Perhaps the masterpiece scene was an infuriated Donald Duck being forced to wear a bunny suit as his nephews, Mickey, and Goofy guffawed at his plight.

By its very perishable nature, any cartoon-related Easter candy would be difficult to document, but in the 1950s, Brach's did hire Bugs Bunny to promote its Easter line in magazine ads that were luscious enough to make the reader drool all over the paper. Inexpensive cartoon toys would also sometimes be mixed in with the candy in prepared Easter baskets, paving the way

Although the box is definitely showing its age, it is somewhat remarkable that this late 1940s set of Disney Easter egg decorations has survived at all.

Donald Duck here shows his usual enthusiasm in promoting Egg Art, a set of plastic wrappers that adhered to boiled Easter eggs like a second shell.

If one were going to get a chocolate bunny for Easter, why not go
all out and make it the most famous
bunny of them all?

Take our advice and do not gaze
at this 1950s Bugs Bunny ad for
Brach's Easter candy for too long:
your drool will ruin the pages of
this book.

for today's market. Most prearranged Easter baskets now consist solely of
toys, frequently themed to a particular character license—Disney's princesses or the Teenage Mutant Ninja Turtles, for example. In recent years,
the companies that normally make hollow chocolate bunnies and eggs have
gone a bit further and made chocolate versions of Garfield, Fred Flintstone,
and Bugs Bunny, but for one reason or another, these novelties have never
seemed to last for more than one or two seasons.

Now, about that busy season for retailers, Christmas. Back in the early
twentieth century, the companies that manufactured tree ornaments out of
various materials—among them blown glass—began working popular comic
strip and later animated cartoon characters into their designs. Like the chalk

carnival prize figures we will examine in chapter 9, many of these characters might have been making unauthorized appearances, but semireasonable facsimiles of Popeye, Little Orphan Annie, and of course Mickey Mouse could be found dangling from tree branches from coast to coast.

Even more unusual was actual screw-in light bulbs that were shaped in the images of these characters. These are exceedingly rare finds today, as most people saw no need to keep the bulb once it burned out. There was a very well-done set of Disney characters in this format, and the tradition continued into the 1950s with bulbs shaped like the cast of *Howdy Doody*. More common, especially during the depression, were lights with shades made of "Beetleware" (an early form of plastic) covered in decals depicting favorite characters in holiday scenes. The NOMA Corporation, manufacturers of nearly every type of Christmas light one could imagine, made several different varieties of these; its Disney line included both a Mickey Mouse set and a Silly Symphonies set, giving exposure to the characters that appeared in only one or two cartoons. (The box for NOMA's Silly Symphonies lights was a masterpiece, showing the Big Bad Wolf delivering Christmas presents to the Three Little Pigs, apparently without malice aforethought.) There was also a Barney Google/Snuffy Smith set of lights, which perhaps stands alone as the only Christmas tree decorations to depict a character blasting another with a shotgun.

Even after figural and decal cartoon lights fell from favor, cartoon ornaments never hung up and quit entirely. They did become rare for a while; in the late 1960s and into the 1970s, Sears sold Winnie-the-Pooh ornament sets consisting of lightweight Styrofoam figures covered in felt and flocking, as well as a set of "beagles" that bore an uncanny resemblance to a dog of that breed who belonged to a kid named Charlie Brown. In the late 1970s, Sears even sold a five-foot-tall lighted version of Pooh wearing a Santa hat that was suitable for adorning a porch or front lawn.

Not until the 1980s did Hallmark (and its competitors such as Carlton Cards) begin marketing high-quality molded cartoon ornaments in exclusive yearly lines. In the decades that followed, Hallmark would immortalize a staggering number of cartoon characters in this form, and its line, combined with those of the other manufacturers, finally enabled one to decorate one's entire tree in cartoon figures.

Since Sears made such good use of its Winnie-the-Pooh license in every other way, it was only natural for the Hundred Acre Wood delegation to move into the Christmas decoration department as well.

Thanks to such companies as Hallmark, Carlton Cards, and Christopher Radko, by the 1990s it was possible to decorate an entire Christmas tree with cartoon character ornaments.

One of those other manufacturers who came along in the late years of the twentieth century was Christopher Radko, whose delicate glass creations were sold through upscale department stores, not the traditional five-and-dime. According to Radko,

As a way of reaching a wider audience for my glass ornament collection, I started working with Disney in the mid-1990s. I licensed their classic pie-eyed Mickey & Co. characters. At first the execs at Disney were unable to understand that my ornaments were hand made and not stamped out from machines. But once the higher-ups saw the success record of my sales, and the big royalty checks they were getting, it grew to include more modern versions of Mickey. Then we added Pooh, other Disney classic characters like Snow White and the Seven Dwarfs, and newer properties like Little Mermaid and Hercules.

In time, my ideas and concepts got immediate approval, because I clearly knew what worked. In all, I probably created about 250 Disney ornament designs, and probably about 100 more that were sold exclusively at L'Ornament Magique, my own ornament store in New Orleans Square at Disneyland. I enjoyed working with Disney, despite their reputation for being "ruthless." I had a great product and a huge following. At the prestigious Disneyana Conventions, people would wait over three hours to meet me and have their ornaments signed.

I enjoyed my relationship with Warner Bros. as well. My ornaments were in over 100 of their better stores, and the execs and store managers were very enthusiastic. They'd take full-page ads in the New York Times to promote my personal appearances in their Fifth Avenue store. They had me create Superman, Batman (the movie characters), the Wizard of Oz, and of course a host of their Looney Tunes characters.

I found that people enjoyed cartoons, old films, and retro TV shows. American culture (and our own childhoods) have been enriched by characters from books, toys, movies, radio, and television. These personalities take us back to our own childhoods, a time that we've seemingly lost, but can connect with again, at Christmastime. The Christmas tree became a canvas to display their heartfelt memories and relive the joys of the past. For fans, young and old, my ornaments were a sparkling feast for the eyes, and a colorful treat for the kid in all of us.

A number of pages ago we discussed the many different types of licensed cartoon character storybooks, but Christmas was a major topic for those as

well. Legendary among Disney collectors is a pair of Big Little Book–sized volumes produced exclusively for Macy's renowned Santa Claus to hand out to his young visitors. Both *Mickey Mouse and Minnie at Macy's* (1934) and *Mickey Mouse and Minnie March to Macy's* (1935) dealt with the debut of the first Disney character balloons in the store's famous Thanksgiving Day Parade, another tradition that has lasted well into the next century.

The 1950s and 1960s were the golden age for Christmas-themed cartoon stories, though. Those two decades brought such future collectibles as *Donald Duck and Santa Claus* (Little Golden Books, 1952), *Donald Duck and the Christmas Carol* (Little Golden Books, 1960, with illustrations by comic book legend Carl Barks), *Mighty Mouse: Santa's Helper* (Wonder Books, 1955), *Tom and Jerry's Merry Christmas* (Little Golden Books, 1954), and *Dennis the Menace Waits for Santa Claus* (Little Golden Books, 1961). Once the Hanna-Barbera cast joined in the fun, additional adventures included the Little Golden Books *Huckleberry Hound and the Christmas Sleigh* (1960) and *Yogi Bear: A Christmas Visit* (1961), plus Whitman's *Yogi Bear Helps Santa* (1962).

In a seeming fit of generosity, Uncle Scrooge appears to be enjoying his role as Santa Claus on the cover of this Dell coloring book.

This combination coloring and activity book from Whitman depicts Yogi Bear's preparations to throw a Christmas party for his costars on *The Huckleberry Hound Show*.

These are but a few examples of the several King Features Syndicates Christmas card designs available for mailing to friends and family.

Yes, even superheroes have to have a holiday every now and then, and DC Comics used this oversized volume to reprint Yuletide adventures starring its most famous figures.

As for the other holidays throughout the year, most would be represented at least by cartoon greeting cards, usually from Hallmark. The Disney and *Peanuts* gangs could be found celebrating St. Patrick's Day, Mother's Day, Father's Day, Thanksgiving, and it sometimes seemed everything else but Guy Fawkes Day. Hallmark realized it had a cartoon-laden gold mine, so one can only imagine the goggle-eyed terror that shot through the company in the early 1980s when Disney made overtures about purchasing one of Hallmark's principal competitors, Gibson Greetings, to operate it as a branch of the Walt Disney Company. Fortunately for Hallmark, that deal fell through, and Mickey and his cheerful chums continue to beam from Hallmark card counters nationwide, just as they have since the 1930s.

Now, for most kids, another holiday was not pre-printed on any calendar yet was probably second only to Christmas as a highlight of the year: birthdays. (Somehow, the more birthdays one accumulates, the less appealing they get to be, but that's another topic for another day.) Fortunately, thanks to the profusion of party products produced primarily by a paltry pack of producers, a birthday party could be completely themed around any number of characters, from the tableware to the cake decorations and even the gift wrap.

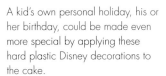

A kid's own personal holiday, his or her birthday, could be made even more special by applying these hard plastic Disney decorations to the cake.

In the late 1950s and early 1960s, at least two different styles of Huckleberry Hound/Yogi Bear birthday tableware were available. You may notice that one of these is the same as that shown in one of the photos in this book's introduction.

A large number of these cartoon designs were the work of a single company, C. A. Reed of Williamsport, Pennsylvania. Sometimes marketed under the Reed banner and sometimes under the brand name Futura, Reed's party products were always brilliantly colored and nicely illustrated. At some times, two completely different designs of the same characters were marketed simultaneously under both brands.

Take, for example, the company's Huckleberry Hound party supplies from 1959. One design was sold as Futura, the other as Reed, but both featured the primary cast of *The Huckleberry Hound Show* (Huck, Yogi Bear, Jinks the cat, and Pixie and Dixie) surrounded by a plethora of their lesser-known, sometimes one-cartoon-only supporting players: Yowp the hunting dog, Iggy and Ziggy the crows, the meeces' aggressive Cousin Tex, and Itty Bitty Buddy the duck, who would be reincarnated a couple of years later as Yakky Doodle. On the Futura version, Yogi was seen trying on a sweater a size or three too large for him—which was odd, since the illustrated birthday cake had Huck's name on it. Why was Yogi getting a birthday present at Huck's party?

Futura made a similar line of party products a decade later, but by that time Yogi was the star and Huck merely an onlooker. In the 1969 illustrations, Yogi played the piano, but he was uncharacteristically overdressed in a white shirt and red pants with suspenders. Huck, leaning on the piano, was yellow instead of his usual blue color, while a red Jinks chased a yellow and white Pixie and Dixie around the scene. Sometimes it appeared the Reed company's color choices were geared more toward being bright than being accurate.

The colors became almost fluorescent on Futura's 1964 Magilla Gorilla line. Day-Glo oranges, blues, and greens abounded in the scene showing Magilla receiving a birthday cake made from a stalk of bananas from his friends Mushmouse, Ricochet Rabbit, and Droop-a-Long Coyote. Futura made a Flintstones line as far back as 1962—significant because Pebbles and Bamm-Bamm had not yet been born—but the company's 1969 Flintstone design was the most eye-popping. Against a hot pink background—pinker than the pinkest Pepto-Bismol—Fred and the two youngsters held a birthday cake in

Yes, that is your beloved author at his eighth birthday party, where once again Huck and Yogi were putting in an appearance on the napkins and paper tablecloth.

front of them as they raced along in their car, with a terrified Barney running for his life barely ahead of the bumper. Nothing like a little implied vehicular homicide to brighten up a birthday party, right, kids?

Among the other cartoon characters represented in equally colorful party designs was the Walter Lantz cast. Their 1959 artwork resembled the Huck Hound set of that year in that it crammed a number of relatively obscure characters into a small space. As an unusually short Woody Woodpecker and Andy Panda shook hands in the center, they were surrounded by Oswald the Rabbit, Chilly Willy, Homer Pigeon, Charlie Chicken, Miranda Panda, and Cuddles the dog. A later Woody set eliminated the bit players and presented a fluorescently colored Woody with girlfriend Winnie and nephew and niece Knothead and Splinter.

Perpetually popular Popeye was the subject of a rather unusual ad campaign in the early 1960s. Conducted through the countless TV stations that were showing the Popeye cartoons on their locally hosted kids' shows, the campaign was built around a song composed by Paul Tripp (most famous for portraying "Mr. I. Magination" on 1950s network television and writing the

Magilla Gorilla got to be the top banana on these 1964 birthday napkins. Ricochet Rabbit, Droop-a-Long Coyote, and Mushmouse were also on hand for the simian's celebration.

The Flintstones were always good for a birthday party appearance, but a few parents might have been concerned about Fred's apparent glee at running down good buddy Barney with his car.

ubiquitous song "Tubby the Tuba"). Tripp's song for Popeye began with the lyrics, "If fishes were wishes / We'd catch us a whale / We'd tie a blue ribbon / Around its big tail," and progressed from there to wishing Popeye a happy birthday. TV stations were furnished with slides depicting the members of the Popeye cast as they appeared in the made-for-TV cartoons, acting out the lyrics. In both the illustrations and real life, the Popeye birthday party supplies showed the squinty sailor balancing atop the spouting water from a whale with a giant ribbon tied around its tail, just as the song said.

As we saw earlier, Hallmark made the most of its long-established license with Disney, but by the 1970s, Hallmark's *Peanuts* line threatened to overshadow even Mickey and company. Even more than the other party products companies, Hallmark provided the complete package—the invitations, the birthday cards, the plates, cups, napkins, tablecloth and centerpiece. There was more than one Hallmark *Peanuts* party design over the years, but one of the most interesting accoutrements was a booklet of "Peanuts Party Games" from the mid-1970s.

The pages, which were meant to be torn out and distributed among party guests, consisted of poses of the various characters lifted from Schulz's strips of that era, put together collage-style to form scenes that had never before appeared in the strip. There was a maze that challenged the player to get flying ace Snoopy back to his doghouse, a page on which one had to identify the most objects beginning with the letter B (including Linus's blanket and Lucy's psychiatric booth), and another in which kids had to pick out of the crowd the two character drawings that were exactly alike. Once the booklet drifted away from licensed art, however, it got a little cheesy.

Among the suggestions for "other *Peanuts* games" was one called "Pass Charlie Brown's Baseball Cap." An old ball cap was to be lettered "Charlie Brown" and passed from hand to hand as music played, musical chairs style, and the youngster holding the cap when the tune stopped was out of the game. (Yes, even

This late 1950s Woody Woodpecker birthday party paper cup surrounded Woody and Andy Panda with a crowd of their lesser-seen Walter Lantz castmates.

Somewhat unusually, Hallmark decided to illustrate the cover of this book of party games not with a Charles Schulz drawing but with artwork from the 1971 feature film *Snoopy Come Home*.

This Mickey Mouse paper tablecloth made the scene at the author's fifth birthday party. Look closely, and you will notice that I am wearing a souvenir T-shirt from Georgia's Stone Mountain Park—not coincidentally, the subject of yet another of my books.

when Charlie Brown was not present in person, just holding his cap was bad luck.) Another game was "Follow Snoopy," in which "one child is chosen to be Snoopy and the others follow him in whatever he does. After a short time, another child becomes Snoopy." Strangest of all was the suggestion of placing a prize inside a box with multiple layers of wrapping paper—likely a Hallmark ploy to sell even more gift wrap—and having kids take turns unwrapping it until the final one received the prize. This is where it got rather cheap: the suggested grand prize was a package of peanuts. (With Schulz's well-known dislike for the name of his strip, this suggestion was probably not submitted for his approval ahead of time.)

So, whether we were celebrating a birthday with peanuts or *Peanuts* to go with our cake, decorating our Christmas tree with cartoon ornaments or lights, turning our Easter eggs into Brer Rabbit or choosing whether to be Casper, Underdog, or Pogo Possum for Halloween, holidays were always welcome opportunities to see our favorite characters outside their normal activities. Perhaps hearing about some of these and seeing them illustrated has reminded you of a fond memory from decades past. While the manufacturers never intended for people to still be collecting them more than fifty years after they were first made, the sheer power of their graphics and nostalgic appeal continue to make them highly desirable acquisitions.

Chapter 8

EAT, DRINK, AND BE FUNNY

Unlike toys, records, or most of the other categories we have dissected so far, there seems to be no particular reason that cartoon character licensing should have become such a powerful and competitive force in the food market. Perhaps it is simply that every human being who has ever lived has had to eat, and if applying a famous cartoon star to a product that was already intended to be consumed could help move it from the grocery shelf to the kitchen at home, so much the better.

Another big difference is that unlike most other pieces of cartoon memorabilia that are bought and sold today, cartoon food products were by nature perishable. Many times, the value of a collectible toy is increased exponentially if its original box or other packaging is present; well, when it comes to cartoon character food, it should go without saying that the package is the *only* component that could reasonably be expected to survive. (There have been exceedingly rare occasions when an abandoned store or warehouse has yielded unopened packages of food products, but a person would probably need oatmeal for brains to think about opening them and examining what horrors might lie inside.)

So, since these product containers usually ended up being saved by accident, as it were—used to store postage stamps or buttons or tax receipts or other things for which they were never intended—documentation of the earliest cartoon grocery products is very spotty. It is known that Oswald the Rabbit was licensed for a candy bar during the first burst of his popularity in the 1920s, and there are ads for a Betty Boop candy bar from a few years later. Cookies seem to have been an especially popular outlet for cartoon licenses, perhaps because it was relatively easy to imprint the characters' faces onto them. There are expensive surviving examples of packaging for cookies using Mickey Mouse, Popeye, and Joe Palooka, so there were undoubtedly many others. (Noncartoon licensed characters including Rootie Kazootie, Hopalong Cassidy, and Rudolph the Red-Nosed Reindeer also were conscripted for cookie duty.)

Besides cookies, Mickey and the rest of the Disney cast became some of the first cartoon characters to appear on cereal packages, their cheerful countenances brightening Post Toasties boxes during the worst

We wonder if someone could get punch-drunk from eating too many of these Joe Palooka cookies. (Ira Gallen collection)

Many different local mills produced flour that was sold in these bags, but oddly, nowhere on them is there any Disney copyright notice.

years of the Great Depression. There was a bottled chocolate drink branded as Kayo, using the derby-wearing little tough of the same name from the *Moon Mullins* comic strip as its mascot. Tiny candy boxes featuring famous characters and containing a Cracker Jack–type prize were popular and inexpensive treats from the 1930s all the way into the early 1970s. But no 1930s cartoon food product was as long lasting and generated as much controversy as Skippy Peanut Butter.

Today, very few people outside the most devoted cartoon historians even remember the *Skippy* comic strip, which was the brainchild of Percy Crosby and began in 1923. The strip has sometimes been cited as a distant ancestor of *Peanuts* in the way it assigned adult dialogue and emotions to its cast of youngsters. In 1933, the Rosefield Packing Company of Alameda, California, began using "Skippy" (in red, dripping-paint letters on a white picket fence, the comic strip's logo) as the brand name for its peanut butter, although the Skippy character did not appear on the label. The company claimed that Crosby had issued a license for this use; Crosby strongly disagreed. As a matter of fact, with the dozens of licensed products officially bearing the Skippy image and copyright, it seems the peanut butter was the only one that did *not* have a license.

This disagreement would plague Crosby until his death in 1964, and his heirs mince no words when it comes to their hatred for the product. Crosby's daughter's account of the fiasco on her website, www.skippy.com, shows just how deeply this seemingly minor irritant affected Crosby's health and his family unit. (Her remarks will not be quoted here, as many of them might fall under the heading of libel.) Of course, the end result is that Skippy Peanut Butter is still on the market and ironically was pitched in a long series of TV commercials by none other than America's (and Disney's) sweetheart, Annette Funicello.

Speaking of Disney, you know very well that company would have brooked no infringement on its trademarks, for food products or anything else. There was a brand of Snow White Flour that was milled by various companies across the country; even though it used Disney's rendition of the princess on the packaging, no Disney copyright notice appears, so the exact arrangement (or lack thereof) remains unclear.

Of the many internationally famous Disney stars, however, there was absolutely no good reason that the one with the greatest presence in the grocery aisles was Donald Duck. This phenomenon resulted entirely from the sales acumen of Kay Kamen, as Disney merchandising historians Robert Heide and John Gilman document:

> The Kay Kamen campaigns found receptive consumers for Donald Duck, who had major success with food products that included Donald Duck Bread, Donald Duck Chocolate Syrup, Donald Duck Coffee, Donald Duck Mayonnaise, Donald Duck Sandwich Spread, Donald Duck Peanut Butter, Donald Duck Apple Sauce, Donald Duck Mustard, Donald Duck Chili Sauce, Donald Duck Catsup, Donald Duck Rice, Donald Duck Popcorn, and his most popular, Donald Duck Grapefruit or Orange Juice. Canned vegetables like corn, peas, lima beans, succotash and others also utilized Donald Duck on their food labels.

By far the most successful Disney character when it came to food licensing was Donald Duck, who had his own brands of bread, fruit juice, soft drinks, and dozens of other products.

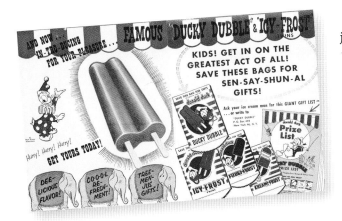

Among the more unlikely products bearing Donald Duck's name and image were these frozen Popsicle-like treats.

There was no logical connection between Popeye and popcorn, but that tenuous relationship was enough to keep this product on shelves from the 1940s into the 1980s.

One can still find Pop-Ice in stores, but it no longer has this Bill Zaboly–style version of Popeye's mug gracing the packages. (Donnie Pitchford collection)

The hometown of the abovementioned orange and grapefruit juice products, Lake Wales, Florida, even had its own tourist attraction long before Walt Disney World set up shop nearby. Known as Donald Duck's Citrus World, the packing and canning plant offered tours to those who might be wondering just how a duck managed to get that juice out of the fruit and into the can. Donald's orange and grapefruit juice can still be found in grocery stores to this day. And if one wanted a carbonated beverage instead of a natural one, there was a Donald Duck Cola, bottled in regional plants around the country.

Disney's primary rival for cartoon popularity, Popeye, also loaned some muscle to grocery stores. Beginning in 1935, a *Popeye the Sailor* radio show was sponsored by Wheatena, a hot cereal product. Besides a handful of premiums and store displays produced to tie in with the series, the most notable thing about this venture was that in the course of an adventure, Popeye relied not on spinach for that extra burst of strength but on bowls of Wheatena. Somehow, no matter where he happened to be when the necessity hit, Popeye would manage to procure a sufficient amount of the stuff, usually carried by Olive or Wimpy.

Around 1949, Purity Mills of Dixon, Illinois, introduced a line of Popeye products, including popcorn (available into the 1980s) and puffed wheat, among others. After television renewed Popeye's star status, Buitoni marketed Popeye macaroni. (Somehow, "I'm strong as a pony 'coz I eats macaroni" just doesn't have the same ring, does it?) Another company introduced Pop-Ice, a frozen popsicle-type treat that had no real connection to the sailor other than the name and his picture on the box. Even the former was tenuous, as today Pop-Ice is still sold, though Popeye's one-eyed mug no longer graces its packages.

Of all these food products promoted or endorsed outright by Popeye, does it not seem strange that spinach was not among them? (Buitoni's Popeye macaroni contained spinach bits as flavoring, a move that probably did not do much to help sales.) Amazingly, not until 1965 was a Popeye brand of spinach was licensed, and when it was, it did not involve some national food conglomerate. King Features Syndicate somehow became convinced that the tiny—at least by national standards—Steele Canning Company of Springdale, Arkansas, deserved to produce Popeye Spinach, and the most logical cartoon/grocery product tie-in of all time was born.

Popeye Spinach has proven as durable as its namesake. The license eventually was taken over by Allen's, but until 1998, the original 1965 artwork of Popeye, arms folded, decorated the labels. Then, when official King Features Popeye artist Stephen Destefano produced new art for the label, instead of being modern and up-to-date, it followed Destefano's preferred style of the 1930s Fleischer Popeye cartoons. Naturally, over the years Popeye Spinach offered a staggering number of premiums—spoons (the better to eat the stuff with, my dear), T-shirts, and pretty much anything else you can think of. It might also have produced a few black eyes among gullible kids who ate it and then tried to administer some junior justice to the neighborhood bully, but that is beside the point.

While cartoons and television were enjoying their first honeymoon in the latter half of the 1950s, Hanna-Barbera had the good fortune to hook up with Kellogg's as the sponsor of its initial syndicated series. Kellogg's was no stranger to offering cartoon character premiums, and the sheer star power of Huckleberry Hound, Quick Draw McGraw, Yogi Bear, and the rest was enough to give the cereal makers giggling fits. In 1961, Kellogg's took the unprecedented step of ditching practically all of its established mascot characters (Tony the Tiger and those noisy elves Snap! Crackle! and Pop! escaped the purge somehow) and replacing them with a different Hanna-Barbera character for each brand. Much more could be said about this mutually

It is a mystery why it took until 1965 for a company to begin marketing a Popeye brand of spinach, but Steele's was the lucky recipient of that license. As you can see, the company also applied the name to less likely canned products. (Donnie Pitchford collection)

Steele's offered a number of different premiums on its Popeye Spinach labels, including an 8mm film (complete with soundtrack record) and a set of Popeye spoons. (Donnie Pitchford collection)

This May 23, 1965, ad ran in Sunday comics sections nationwide, announcing the introduction of pre-sweetened Kool-Aid with multicolored Bugs Bunnies on the packages. (Donnie Pitchford collection)

beneficial association, but since our space is limited here, we suggest you consult yours truly's *Part of a Complete Breakfast: Cereal Characters of the Baby Boom Era* (University Press of Florida, 2012) to get two scoops on that saga.

Seeing the success Kellogg's was having with Hanna-Barbera's output, General Mills quickly aligned itself with Jay Ward, while Post and its parent company, General Foods, enlisted the Warner Bros. gang for its cause. Post sponsored the prime-time *Bugs Bunny Show* on ABC-TV beginning in the fall of 1960, but even after the show moved into Saturday morning reruns, General Foods was not weady to wid itself of the wascally wabbit.

Beginning in late spring 1965, General Foods assigned Bugs to plug Kool-Aid. The hook was that Kool-Aid had finally developed a "presweetened" recipe, making it easier for kids to whip up a batch of it without having to add sugar. Unfortunately, this was accomplished by the use of cyclamates, later identified as a health hazard, but in the mid-1960s, presweetened was considered just ducky, Daffy. Each of the presweetened powdered drink's six flavors featured a different color Bugs on the packaging (it was admittedly unusual to see him rendered as green, pink, or purple), and ads in the Sunday comics sections of newspapers nationwide announced the Warner Bros. crew's new obsession with Kool-Aid. Packages of the regular old "you add the sugar yourself" Kool-Aid continued to star the smiling, frosty pitcher.

The one-two punch of the grocery aisle and Sunday comics campaign was aided by clever animated TV commercials produced by legendary director Tex Avery. Ironically, the final Bugs Bunny cartoon had been released only the previous year, and these commercials were arguably funnier and more entertaining than the theatrical shorts being produced by Warner Bros. at the time. Although Bugs's appearance and personality evolved over several shorts in the late 1930s and early 1940s, Avery usually gets credit for bringing Bugs into his best-known form. This was something of a point of pride for Avery, who in the early 1970s told historian Joe Adamson,

We've been doing Bugs Bunny Kool-Aids for six or seven years, and when they started doing those the agency people said, "Wonder if Avery knows how to draw Bugs Bunny." I think that's when I started making it clear just who created Bugs Bunny.

We talked with them all day—how the rabbit acts, and what he does, and what he doesn't do. And we told them what was wrong with their storyboards, that the rabbit wouldn't do that. They would have him running from the people. If he ever runs from anyone, he has a trick in mind, but they had him scared to death.

Kool-Aid's connection with Bugs produced a number of collectibles, one of the most common of which is a plastic mug shaped like Bugs's mug. The Warner Bros. characters were also used to promote General Foods' version of Pop-Ice, Kool-Pops, with games and puzzles printed on the packages and a set of Hasbro's Rub-Ons (available by mail) designed specifically to be used with backgrounds included in the Kool-Pops boxes. The ad campaign also spawned some unexpected collectibles, as Avery also related to Adamson:

> After we had done a bunch of Bugs Bunny commercials on Kool-Aid, I remember I had some old cels and drawings in the back of the car, gotten from camera. So little kids find out, they say, "Mr. Avery, got any Bugs Bunnies?" So I reach in there, dust them off and throw them a little batch. Next night, they're waiting for me at the mailbox! "You got any more Bugs Bunnies?" And I said to myself, "Well, if this is gonna be a habit, hell with them." I said, "No, I don't have any more."
>
> So then the third time, just one little girl was there. She said, "You got any Bugs Bunnies?" And I said, "Oh, I gave you a whole batch of them!" And she said, "But my brother takes them to school and sells them for fifty cents apiece!"

Kool-Aid was certainly proud of its Bugs Bunny license, offering premiums ranging from plastic mugs to drinking bottles to a specialized set of Hasbro Rub-Ons.

We can only assume that the schoolboy in that story grew up to become an eBay dealer and that some of the kids who bought original Bugs/Kool-Aid cels from him still have them framed and hanging in their living rooms.

Meanwhile, the Sunday comics campaign got even bigger for the summer 1966 season. During May, June, and July, every other week produced a "Kool-Aid Funday News" column, once again starring the whole Warner Bros. cast. One change was that instead of his face of many colors appearing on the presweetened Kool-Aid envelopes, now Bugs was involved in a different action scene on each of them, still color-coded to the flavor contained therein, of course. After the Food and

In the summer of 1966, Kool-Aid revived its Sunday comics ad campaign with these gag-laden installments of the "Kool-Aid Funday News." (Donnie Pitchford collection)

In 1979, Nabisco picked up a license to manufacture Bugs Bunny Graham Cookies, sold in this clubhouse-shaped box.

Just in time for Bugs's fiftieth birthday in 1990, Tyson came up with a line of Looney Tunes frozen dinners, each with its own mascot character.

Drug Administration banned cyclamates from the U.S. market in 1969, only the original Kool-Aid with the smiling pitcher was left, and Bugs had to move on to other commercial endeavors.

In 1982, Nabisco introduced Bugs Bunny Graham Cookies. The advertising for this product is notable mainly for its wildly inaccurate depiction of some of the characters; for example, Elmer Fudd was the size of an elf. Later in the decade, someone at the Borden company must have been reminiscing about the long-ago Kool-Aid campaign, because the famous milk makers brought out a line of Bugs Bunny and Pals drink mixes. Unlike Kool-Aid, Bugs shared star billing with other members of his cast, with a different character appearing on each flavor. But like its predecessor, Bugs Bunny and Pals was presweetened, this time with Nutrasweet.

Just in time for the big celebration of Bugs's fiftieth birthday in 1990, Tyson launched a series of Looney Tunes frozen dinners. As with Borden's flavored drink mixes, a different Warner Bros. character represented each variety of the dinners. Some of the pairings made more sense than others: Bugs Bunny's entrée was chicken nuggets, but the dinner also included carrot sticks, so that made it a bit more credible. It was also natural that Sylvester would go with fish sticks, Yosemite Sam would endorse barbecued chicken wings, and Speedy Gonzales would recommend beef enchiladas. Some of the other choices seemed to stretch logic a bit. The only connection between Tweety and macaroni and cheese seemed to be that both were yellow, while the only similarity between Daffy Duck and spaghetti and meatballs was that both were mixed up.

General Foods also had a hit when its Post division introduced Pebbles cereal in 1969, with Fred, Barney, and the gang covering the packaging and the TV commercials. Shortly thereafter, the original flavor of Pebbles was renamed Fruity Pebbles and a companion Cocoa Pebbles variety joined it on grocery shelves. For a brief time in the early 1970s, diners could wash down their Pebbles cereal with several different flavors of Yabba Dabba Dew soft drinks, giving the Flintstone family yet another product to plug on TV.

Speaking of the world of soft drinks, Pepsi-Cola had started a new fad in 1964 when it acquired the formerly regional Mountain Dew brand and began distributing it nationally. Its success made Mountain Dew's hillbilly-themed advertising ("Ya-HOO! Mountain Dew!") an easy target, and soon the market boasted Hillbilly Brew and White Lightnin', among others. One of those that thumbed a ride on the Mountain Dew jalopy was Kickapoo Joy Juice, a longtime favorite feature of the *Li'l Abner* comic strip.

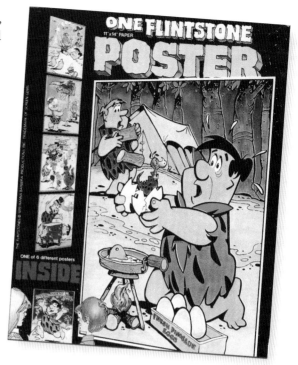

Perhaps the most durable cartoon-related food product was Post's Pebbles cereals, introduced in 1969. These pin-up posters are among the dozens of Flintstones premiums offered in the decades since. (Donnie Pitchford collection)

At some point in the late 1940s or early 1950s, Orange Crush was designated the "official drink of Dogpatch." Whoever drew this promotional piece did not even do a good job of forging Al Capp's signature on it.

In 1965, the NuGrape Corporation of Atlanta introduced a Mountain Dew–like soft drink version of Dogpatch's Kickapoo Joy Juice sold in these character-laden cartons.

Dudley C. Ruttenberg bought Atlanta's National NuGrape Company in 1964, with one new product in mind. "I've always been an admirer of Capp and his satire," Ruttenberg told *Newsweek*. "I thought how funny—and possibly how profitable—it would be to bring out Kickapoo Joy Juice." Capp concurred, not surprisingly securing an agreement whereby he would receive a royalty on every bottle of the concoction that was sold. In return, he designed the label and carrying cartons, which of course featured all the Dogpatch residents.

Both Capp and Ruttenberg took pains to point out that the bottled Kickapoo Joy Juice was not the same explosive drink that had long been portrayed in the strip. The newsprint Kickapoo Joy Juice consisted of any number of ingredients that might be found lying about the poverty-stricken community; for example, "If it needs more body, throw another body in," its inventors Lonesome Polecat and Hairless Joe were fond of explaining. NuGrape's version was bright yellow and said to be tangy with a touch of orange in its taste.

While Kickapoo Joy Juice did not exactly make everyone forget about Mountain Dew, neither was it a rapid failure. The name was eventually acquired by the Moxie soft drink company, and the beverage seems to have lasted at least until the comic strip's demise in 1977.

Most of the association of cartoon characters with soft drinks came in the form of various series of drinking glasses, as detailed a bit later in this chapter. However, by 1972, Casper the Friendly Ghost had been recruited to cheer (instead of boo) for Hi-C fruit drinks. At some unknown date, Producers Dairy marketed a Superman fruit punch in a colorful pink and green container. It inspires one to speculate about an appropriate slogan: "Superman's punch is a knockout," maybe?

What was probably the most successful cartoon/grocery connection came about in 1969. It is possible that the name Interstate Brands might not be immediately familiar to many people, but the products it controlled certainly are. Interstate's national brand name for its line of snacks was Dolly Madison ("Neat to Eat Treats"), but the company also owned bread bakeries across the country that operated under such long-established local names as Butternut, Weber's, Millbrook, Hart's, and Mrs. Karl's, among others.

Through Dolly Madison, Interstate had become one of the sponsors of the animated *Peanuts* specials, and in early 1969, the company went a step further and made arrangements with Schulz and United Feature Syndicate to incorporate Charlie Brown and his winning team of losers into its advertising. The characters would appear in the packaging and advertising for

We all know that Superman packed a punch, but with this product he was able to literally pack it in pink and green paper cartons.

The many different local varieties of bread owned by Interstate Brands issued premiums featuring the *Peanuts* characters beginning in 1969. (Donnie Pitchford collection)

HELP SNOOPY SPOT THE RED BARON WITH...

The Bristol F2-B

Sopwith Camel

Fokker D VII

Spad XIII

Fokker DR-1

FREE SNOOPY WORLD WAR I AIRPLANE STICKERS

That cursed Red Baron is coming! And he's up to nothing but trouble.

This time, even our famous World War I Flying Ace can't stop him. You've got to help!

Keep the Red Baron from stealing the secret of how we make our Mrs. Karl's bread so good!

There's one in every specially-marked loaf. Collect all 8. And help stop the Red Baron.

INTERSTATE BRANDS CORPORATION

Kids. Get your own Peanuts Cartoons

15 different cartoons. Look for them on loaves of Hart's Bread.

It's Charlie Brown and the Peanuts gang with funny things to say about going to school.

They're bright, colorful... and lots of fun.

You'll want all 15 Peanuts back-to-school cartoons. What a combination. Your favorite cartoon characters on Hart's, your favorite school-lunch bread.

Hart's BREAD

CAN SNOOPY STOP THE RED BARON FROM SHOOTING HOLES IN MILLBROOK BREAD?

We don't know.

The cursed Red Baron is flying here to shoot holes in MIRACLE-MIX Bread, baked by the bakers of MILLBROOK. (MIRACLE-MIX is the bread with no holes. That's why it's more fresh, more tender, more nice!)

We've recruited Snoopy, the famous World War I Flying Ace, to foil the Baron's evil designs. It's our only hope!

While Snoopy works out his battle plan, use this coupon to try MIRACLE-MIX Bread for yourself. So you can understand what's at stake.

This is serious.

STORE COUPON

8¢ OFF

8¢

8¢

(This coupon worth 8¢ toward the purchase of MILLBROOK Bread.)

Dolly Madison snacks nationally; locally, they would push Interstate's various brands of bread.

In a December 1969 interview with *Business Week*, Interstate Brands president Ernest Hueter, who had arranged the *Peanuts* deal, expressed a fear that seems rather naive in hindsight: "Our main concern is that the property is terribly vulnerable to depreciation. Overexposure could make *Peanuts* too commonplace." But even treading carefully, Hueter remained confident: he told the reporter that while the original agreement to use the *Peanuts* characters ran through 1973, they had just extended it to last through 1985—a time that must have seemed very far-off indeed in 1969.

So, just what did Interstate Brands get for its investment? Well, one or another of the *Peanuts* characters could be found on the packaging of practically any product the company produced. Dolly Madison fruit pies came in so many different flavors that a different character represented each one. Snoopy added a new persona to his repertoire of alter egos: the "Prince of Sandwiches," in which guise he appeared on bread wrappers, premiums, and animated TV commercials produced by Bill Melendez. Among the most frequent premium offerings from Interstate were decals picturing the characters in some activity or another, with a blank space left for the owner to fill in his or her name in the dialogue. There were embroidered patches, wall posters, and a pair of Charlie Brown and Snoopy inflatable beach-toy-type figures.

In this early ad campaign for Interstate Brands, kids could become members of Snoopy's Spotters Club and prevent the Red Baron from shooting holes in the bread.

Dolly Madison was the national brand for Interstate, and most former kids will remember chowing down on these fruit pies, each with its own *Peanuts* representative. (Dan Goodsell collection)

Not to be outdone by Dolly Madison's *Peanuts* blitz, rival snack maker Hostess took out dozens of comic book ads with its tasty treats endorsed by the Marvel Comics superheroes, the Harvey Comics cast, and other famous funnybook stars. (Donnie Pitchford collection)

Watching Interstate Brands' success, its biggest competitor, Hostess, could only grit its Twinkies and try to study up a counterattack. Instead of choosing only one character or cast of characters, Hostess joined forces with a number of different properties from the world of comic books. Crossing all ownership lines, Hostess's products were pitched by the Harvey Comics cast (Casper, Wendy, Richie Rich, Hot Stuff, and the rest), the Archie Comics crowd, and the Marvel Comics superheroes. The single-page adventures of these characters in support of Hostess products looked exactly like any other page of their comics, with a necessarily quick resolution to the predicament at hand. In one short story, Richie Rich faces the difficulty of what to get his gazillionaire father for his birthday, inasmuch as "he already has several thousand ties and we gave him another golf course last year." Finally, for the man who literally has everything, Hostess fruit pies prove to be the perfect gift. In another, miniature demon Hot Stuff uses devil's-food Hostess cupcakes (what else?) to calm down the "blankety blank blank" swearing of hot-tempered Grandpa Blaze.

An Andy Capp brand of snack foods has been around since 1971; this cellophane bag dates from several years later, after the indolent Brit had given up the cigarette that formerly dangled from his lower lip.

No, this was apparently not a licensed product, but a Glendale, Arizona, produce company decided to redesign Hanna-Barbera's Top Cat into a vegetative emblem for its carrots.

One unusual thing about these ministries is that they did not always appear in their own characters' comic books. A Casper or Wendy story, for example, might appear in a Marvel comic book, while Captain America and Spider-Man were shilling for Hostess in *Walt Disney's Comics and Stories*. (Apparently the Disney characters were off-limits to Hostess, as no examples of them being used in a similar fashion have surfaced.)

Now let's talk about some other types of snack foods. In 1971, Goodmark Foods introduced a line of chips using perhaps the most unlikely of cartoon mascots: Andy Capp, the cigarette-smoking, indolent lout of Reg Smythe's imported British comic strip. Andy Capp snacks came in many different forms but stayed true to their source by reprinting selected Smythe strips on their cellophane bags. After many different mutations over the years, the products remain on the market today, branded as Andy Capp's Fries and manufactured by ConAgra Foods.

A few obscure tie-ins can only be described as just plain strange. A Glendale, Arizona, company, Navajo Marketing, packaged vegetables under the name "Top Carrot," with the plastic bags decorated with an obviously unauthorized version of Hanna-Barbera's Top Cat redrawn as a carrot. (At least

the Three J's Packing Company of Los Angeles stayed within the realm of credibility by naming its carrot line Bugs Bunny and officially licensing the logo from Warner Bros. in 1966.) The Good Humor ice cream company made Bullwinkle Pudding Stix, which did not look a whole lot like him but gave new meaning to the phrase "chocolate moose."

Miles Laboratories, long the home of Alka-Seltzer and One-A-Day Vitamins, decided in 1960 to create a market for chewable children's vitamins, and its first such attempt was known as Chocks. (Surely you remember the commercials featuring astronaut Charlie Chocks, whose facial expression never changed, no matter what.) Okay, so vitamins are not exactly the same as food, but they must be taken via the same opening in one's face, so they belong here. In 1969, Miles jettisoned Charlie Chocks and signed up the Flintstones for a new brand of chewable vitamins; whereas Chocks were somewhat boring in shape, Flintstones Vitamins came in the forms of the famous cartoon cast—with the notable exception of Betty Rubble, whom it was believed would look too much like Wilma. Her place was taken by the shape of the Flintstone car until a mid-1990s publicity campaign ended with the long-absent Betty vitamin being added to the group. Typically for the era, Flintstone Vitamins were advertised via animated commercials in which Fred sang, "Yabba-dabba-doo! Flintstone Vitamins are good to chew!" Premiums included an inflatable Fred with that slogan printed on the front of his tunic, and plastic mugs in the shape of Fred, Dino, Pebbles, and Bamm-Bamm. (What? No Barney mug? He must have been on strike in support of his wife.)

Good Humor's Bullwinkle Pudding Stix did not resemble Rocky's pal very closely, but where else could one help Boris Badenov achieve one of his goals by biting off the moose's head?

Flintstones Vitamins, introduced in 1969, offered many premiums, including these plastic mugs. A Pebbles and Bamm-Bamm pair was also available. (Donnie Pitchford collection)

Just why Miles thought it needed a second line of chewable vitamins has never been made clear, but in 1971, the Flintstone brand was joined by Bugs Bunny Vitamins. Except for the six character shapes (Bugs, Daffy, Elmer, Porky, Petunia, and Yosemite Sam), they were virtually indistinguishable from Flintstones. Bugs Bunny Vitamins were also featured in animated commercials, with Porky's tag line, "They're de-de-deli-de-de—taste great!" After regulations banned the advertising of drug products directly to children, Fred and Bugs remained on the job, but the new commercials made it clear that they were addressing parents instead of their offspring.

Other companies thought they could siphon off some of the Miles market with their own character-based vitamins, but to Miles's glee, none of them made a dent in Flintstones and Bugs Bunny. Miles even produced a slick sales flyer in 1989 that dared to show some of these failures (Popeye Vitamins, Pac-Man Vitamins, Smurf Vitamins, and Spider-Man Vitamins, among others) relegated to the dumpster while the Flintstones and Bugs Bunny brands continued to dominate the market.

People could even manufacture their own cartoon food products if they so chose. During the 1970s, the Wilton company began making a wide variety of aluminum cake pans in the shapes of various characters, complete with instructions on how to use the icing to get the desired professional result. Doing so took a bit of artistic skill not available to everyone, so in the case of Wilton's Wonder Woman cake design, her face came included as a plastic mask, leaving the rest of her torso at the mercy of the decorator. Mickey Mouse, Donald Duck, and Winnie-the-Pooh also had their pans immortalized in Wilton pans, but perhaps the greatest moment came with Wilton's Popeye design. The enclosed paper liner depicted the whole Popeye cast of characters commenting on the cake's uncanny likeness, with the best line going to Bluto/Brutus: "I'd like to decorate Popeye's face." Wilton continues to offer these pans today, with such classics as Batman, Pooh, Scooby-Doo, and the Disney characters joined by many newcomers, among them Dora the Explorer, Thomas the Tank Engine, and such noncartoon characters as Elmo and his friends from *Sesame Street* and Barbie.

In the 1980s, Miles Laboratories issued this promotional timeline depicting the early package designs for Flintstones and Bugs Bunny Vitamins.

1960	Miles introduces Chocks®, the first Children's Chewable Vitamin.
1969	Flintstones Vitamins and Flintstones Plus Iron were introduced.
1971	Bugs Bunny Vitamins and Bugs Bunny Plus Iron were introduced.
1980	Flintstones with Extra C and Bugs Bunny with Extra C were introduced.
1982	Flintstones Complete with Iron, Calcium and Minerals was introduced.
1984	Bugs Bunny Vitamins were reformulated to Sugar Free and Natural Formulation. Bugs Bunny Vitamins Plus Minerals was introduced.

The Wilton company is known for its seemingly endless line of licensed character cake pans. In these examples, Superman and Batman could be made from the same mold, with only their icing and plastic faces to distinguish them.

Wonder Woman was another of Wilton's cake pan creations. Although her face was plastic, the rest of her anatomy was at the mercy of the decorator's talent. (Julie Ellingsen collection)

Now, with all these different edible food products and their cartoon connections, people certainly had to have something to eat or drink them out of, and that brings us to our next lengthy discussion. It must begin in the early 1930s, when Disney merchandise genius Kay Kamen developed a promotion that would require the cooperation of local dairies nationwide. In 1990, glass collectors Carol and Gene Markowski explained,

> The idea was to develop a proven campaign and sell the national quality promotional program to one company in each city. The dairy campaign featured Mickey and his friends on glasses and milk bottles. Early character glasses were containers for cottage cheese or sour cream. A new glass was featured each week, and often customers could purchase missing glasses at the end of the promotion.

According to the Markowskis, nearly three hundred different local dairies eventually subscribed to the Disney promotion. From glasses depicting Mickey, Donald, and the other characters from Disney's short subjects, to an eight-glass set tied to *Snow White and the Seven Dwarfs* (1938), to the largest promotion of all, a *Pinocchio* set (1940) that featured a new glass each week for three months, the Disney dairy glasses were a definite success and showed clearly (as glass should) that the idea could be expanded further.

During the 1930s, local dairies offered different Disney glasses each week. The characters from the short subjects were joined by the *Snow White* cast in 1938 and a huge twelve-glass *Pinocchio* set in 1940.

Welch's jelly sponsored *Howdy Doody* in the 1950s and *The Flintstones* in the 1960s, using both shows' casts of characters on the glasses in which the product was sold.

By the 1950s, home delivery of dairy products was on the way out, thanks to postwar suburbs and those newfangled supermarkets that sprang up everywhere, so it fell to other grocery manufacturers to take up the slack. Welch's Jelly was the purple prince of cartoon glasses, as they were the perfect size to hold its products. In two different series during 1952–53, Welch's decorated its glass containers with the characters from TV's *Howdy Doody*. Of all the series Welch's would produce in the coming years, the 1953 *Howdy Doody* set was the only one that featured advertising for the company's products.

In the early 1960s, Welch's became one of the rotating sponsors for *The Flintstones* in prime time, and that seemed as good a reason as any to revive the glasses promotion. One set was produced in 1962, and another continued from 1963 into 1964 to commemorate the birth of Pebbles. Some collectors go absolutely prehysterical trying to collect the three Flintstones series, because each individual design ("Fred in his Sports Car," "Bedrock Pet Show," and so on) was available in eight different colors. Add to that Welch's innovation, beginning with the Howdy Doody set, of embossing the bottom of each glass with a different character's face, and you begin to see how many combinations of color, artwork, and embossed bottom could result.

Welch's next venture involved two separate series of glasses depicting the Archie Comics cast, one in 1971 and the other in 1973; it is difficult to say whether the glasses were based on the comic books or on the highly successful Saturday morning cartoon show from Filmation, as they included elements of both. In 1974, Welch's issued a set of eight glasses with scenes of the Warner Bros. characters; at about the same time, that cast of loonies was responsible for launching a whole new fad in the drinking glass world.

Whereas previous glass promotions had involved dairy or grocery products, with the glass serving as the container for the product, in 1973 Pepsi-Cola teamed up with fast-food restaurants nationwide for one of the most successful cartoon glass promotions in history. Each week for an incredible eighteen weeks, customers could obtain a different glass picturing a member of the Warner Bros. crew. With so many glasses, it was natural that the series included not only the superstars but several of the lesser-known figures that might have made the casual buyer say "Who?" (It is difficult to think of people rushing

A Warner Bros. set of jelly glasses joined the Welch's parade in 1974, and some were sold in special promotional four-packs such as this one.

Pepsi started the practice of restaurants offering cartoon glasses with this 1973 Looney Tunes set. They would be offered again in coming years, and today they may be the most common glasses on the collectors' market.

In 1976, Pepsi took the unusual step of offering Bicentennial-themed glasses that included characters from Jay Ward, Total TeleVision, Walter Lantz, and Harvey Comics.

Coca-Cola, for its part, largely stayed out of the cartoon glasses business, but this mid-1970s Popeye set was an exception. The designs were based on the characters as they appeared in the early 1960s made-for-TV cartoons.

out to get their glass the week it was Slowpoke Rodriguez or Cool Cat, for example.) These glasses are among the most common in antique stores today, testifying to how many must have been distributed.

Pepsi could see when it had a good thing going. Throughout the rest of the 1970s, the company produced one series after another, all following the same pattern of one per week but using any imaginable group of characters. There were series devoted to Tom and Jerry and their MGM cohorts, the Jay Ward characters and their often-mistaken look-alikes the Total TeleVision crowd (Peter Piech at work again), Woody Woodpecker and friends, the DC Comics superheroes, and a Disney series in honor of Mickey Mouse's fiftieth birthday in 1978. Sets were also devoted to the Disney animated features *The Rescuers* and *The Jungle Book*. At the height of the inexplicable CB radio craze, one set depicted characters from both the Ward and TTV shows spouting trucker lingo, as truck drivers Bullwinkle and Boris Badenov mixed it up with airborne law enforcers Dudley Do-Right and Underdog. A similar series mixing all of Peter Piech's properties appeared in time for the U.S. Bicentennial in 1976, with the various characters acting out scenes from colonial days; Pepsi even expanded the licensing scope by throwing Woody Woodpecker and members of the Harvey Comics cast into the patriotic punchbowl.

It has been theorized that Coca-Cola preferred to stay above Pepsi's fray in the belief that the famous Coke logo had more selling power than any cartoon character. The "Real Thing" succumbed to temptation at least once, though, issuing a 1975 Popeye set that used the 1961 made-for-TV versions of the characters. Although not as plentiful today as the various Pepsi series, there are enough survivors to indicate that a lot of people chose Coke to wash down their spinach during the promotion's run.

It is no accident that we referred to the glasses above as "survivors." It should be obvious that by their very nature, cartoon glasses were fragile and a slip during dishwashing or childhood carelessness could make Donald Duck go to pieces even worse than he ever did in his cartoons. The advent of automatic dish-washers meant the glasses faced additional perils in the form of hot water and harsh detergents that could reduce a colorful images to faded shadows. Another type of cartoon dishware was virtually impervious to breakage, although the dishwasher was no better friend to it.

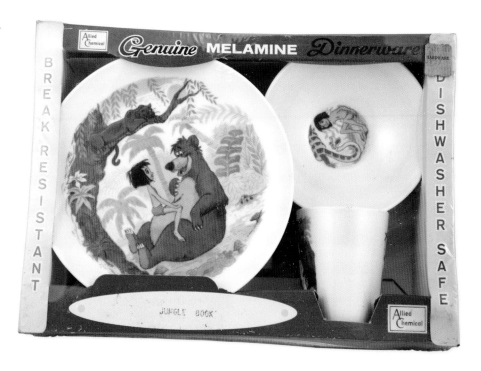

Melamine, a virtually unbreakable plastic, was the ideal substance for children's dishes. Most of them were sold in boxed sets such as this *Jungle Book* grouping from 1967.

Beginning in the 1940s, various companies began making dinnerware out of melamine, a form of Superman-tough plastic. The most famous brand name was Melmac, but the same product was manufactured under by Arrowhead, NHP, Allied Chemical, Sun Valley, Lenox Ware, and other imprints. Many different types of adult dishes were sold in this format, but it was particularly valuable for the children's market, since kids are remarkably proficient at shattering both nerves and dinnerware. The melamine dishes not only could take whatever abuse kids might dish out but also featured smooth plastic surfaces that offered terrific canvases for colorful cartoon artwork (which would hold its lustrous appearance for decades unless submitted to the tortures of automatic dishwashers).

Melamine dinnerware was a staple for practically all major cartoon licensing firms. As might be expected, Disney was a most popular subject. One *Mickey Mouse Club* set depicted Mickey leading Huey, Dewey, and Louie in a

Allied Chemical was only one of several companies producing melamine dinnerware for kids, but it was lucky enough to have the Disney license. *Mary Poppins* and *The Mickey Mouse Club* are among the designs shown in this ad.

This "unspillable" Donald Duck cup was a bit unusual in that it was decorated with scenes of Donald and his nephews actually using the product on which they were pictured.

self-congratulatory parade; in a famous break from tradition, Donald Duck was portrayed wearing a mouse-eared hat, quite a contrast from his TV persona, who was constantly interrupting the theme song to demand equal billing. The *Mary Poppins* set followed the lead of most of the other merchandise tied to that 1964 blockbuster by bearing renditions of the characters that did not resemble the live actors in the least. Zorro, *The Jungle Book*, and Winnie-the-Pooh were also featured in melamine, usually sold in boxed sets that contained a plate, a bowl, and a cup.

Other characters forming a wide swath from Alvin and the Chipmunks to Bullwinkle to Magilla Gorilla to the Flintstones (both before and after Pebbles's debut) to Huckleberry Hound helped make mealtime into fun time. Another interesting Hanna-Barbera plate showed the complete casts of *Huckleberry Hound*, *Quick Draw McGraw*, and *Yogi Bear* gathered for a picnic in Jellystone Park; well into the 1970s, the plate was still being sold as a souvenir at the chain of Jellystone Park Campgrounds (about which more in our next chapter).

Melamine having made dishes unbreakable, there was also a desire to make cups unspillable. A company identified only as Eagle (through its stamped logo) marketed a line of plastic cups with tight-fitting lids. A straw could be inserted, but the cups otherwise held their liquid contents inside. A couple of different Donald Duck designs were notable because they showed Donald's nephews using the cups on which they were appearing, doing their best to hold their cups upside down to graphically demonstrate their secure nature. Other Disney designs, including the casts of *Pinocchio* and *Snow White and the Seven Dwarfs*, avoided such product placements but were just as visually appealing.

And now we come down to what was probably the most ubiquitous food container in any baby boomer's life: the lunch box for lugging one's peanut butter and jelly sandwich and milk to school. Although the first post–World War II generation was responsible for the lunch box in its best-known form, metal food containers had been marketed with cartoon images at least as far back as the 1930s, when Disney designs (what else?) were used. Other characters, including Joe Palooka, were also part of the lunch box vanguard, but some of them resembled pails and others looked like small baskets with handles—not the famous rectangular boxes that more than once have been compared to miniature TV sets.

The two giant competitors in the lunch box derby were Aladdin, based in Nashville, Tennessee, and American Thermos, based in Connecticut. (The company later changed its name to King Seeley Thermos, so to make things simple, we will refer to it simply as Thermos from here on.) Aladdin started the whole thing in 1950 by taking its metal lunch boxes and simply slapping on a decal of movie/TV cowpoke Hopalong Cassidy. Thermos responded in 1953 with a Roy Rogers box, which did Hoppy and Aladdin one better by having colorful lithography all over the surface instead of a mere decal. From that point, Aladdin and Thermos would be at each other's throats, with other minor players occasionally joining in but quickly knocked out of the ring.

Fussy kids could not possibly overturn their cups if they were anchored by Wonder Woman's mighty muscles. (Julie Ellingsen collection)

Aladdin and Thermos were the two huge rivals when it came to school lunch boxes. Each company was constantly trying to put one over on the competition by grabbing potentially valuable licenses.

Vintage lunch boxes became hot collectibles in the late 1980s, largely as a consequence of the promotional abilities of Boston resident Scott Bruce, who dubbed himself "Mr. Lunch Box" and set out to make the country aware of the subject. (In the 1990s, Bruce got out of the lunch box market and tried to start a similar craze for collecting cereal boxes, but the available surviving supply was woefully inadequate to meet the demand.) It may never be known whether the public would have discovered the nostalgia inherent in lunch boxes if not for Bruce's tireless efforts, but his research unquestionably uncovered many stories and individuals related to the topic, some of whom would not be around just a few years later.

Representatives of both Aladdin and Thermos told Bruce stories of the level of seriousness they brought to their competition: "They hated our guts and we hated theirs," one Thermos old-timer frankly admitted. An Aladdin veteran elaborated on the two companies' Cold War balance of power:

> It all depended on the hot properties, the licensed characters from TV. Getting those properties, at $10,000 down and five percent royalties, was a lot of fun because the TV networks controlled the shows and they'd rent a New York City hotel floor and preview them all. We'd try to sew up the first refusal rights on as many properties as we could.

Since neither company could afford to snap up everything, choices had to be made, and sometimes they were not the wisest ones in hindsight. In the mid-1960s, with the popularity of *Peanuts* just beginning to approach its peak, the strip was offered to Aladdin. The Nashville guys decided *Peanuts* was more appealing to adults than to kids and passed on it, giving Thermos one of its biggest hits. Bruce cites the 1966 *Peanuts* kit as the first piece of merchandise to carry Nick LoBianco's close copying of Schulz's art; although the clues are subtle, close study of the box reveals that the drawings are based on Schulz's work but not actually by him. To even the score, Aladdin grabbed Batman from under Thermos's insulated nose just as the satirical prime-time series was making its debut.

As stated earlier, Disney lunch pails had been around since the depression, but their revival in

Aladdin's ads trumpeted its lunch boxes' "3-D" appearance, in which some of the figures were embossed to stand out from the background.

Aladdin's Disney School Bus was the biggest selling lunch box in history, moving some nine million units during a dozen years of production. Here we see the box's creator, Disney merchandising guru Al Konetzni, autographing one of the hundreds of examples of his beloved box he was asked to sign over the years.

the 1950s began with one of the smaller companies of that era, ADCO Liberty. By the middle of the decade, Aladdin had grabbed the Disney license, and the company maintained its iron grip on Mickey et al. for decades to come. Some Disney properties appeared in multiple designs over the years. At least three different *Mickey Mouse Club* boxes were manufactured, including one in the 1960s that included Ludwig von Drake among Mickey's entourage even though he had not yet been created when the show originally aired. Others were based on re-releases of the animated classics such as *Snow White and the Seven Dwarfs*, *Peter Pan*, and *Pinocchio* or more contemporary productions including *The Rescuers* and *Pete's Dragon*. Aladdin even had several boxes that starred Disneyland (and later, Walt Disney World), some with the famous characters and others solely depicting park attractions.

But no matter how many designs Aladdin came up with, the Disney box that outsold all the others—outsold any other lunch box from Aladdin, Thermos, or anyone else, for that matter—was the venerable Disney School Bus. Back in chapter 1, we met Al Konetzni of Disney's New York licensing office, and this lunch box was the biggest idea of his long career. It was really pretty

Thermos's Have Lunch with Snoopy doghouse-shaped box seemed almost as ubiquitous in the 1970s as the Disney School Bus had been in the 1960s.

simple: take a lunch box with a rounded top and print it to look like a school bus with Goofy as the driver. (Most kids in Disney films lacked parents to oversee their actions, a situation that probably made it much easier for Goofy to retain the job year after year.) Whatever school this bus traveled to each day, the classrooms must have been a hoot, because peering from the bus windows could be seen Huey, Dewey, and Louie; Mickey's nephews, Morty and Ferdy; Dumbo; Alice in Wonderland; Dopey; Thumper; and Pinocchio. Standing in the school bus door was Jiminy Cricket, looking larger and more humanoid than usual and apparently in the role of adult supervisor/teacher of this unpredictable crew.

The Disney School Bus lunch box remained in production from 1961 to 1973, and over those dozen years, an astounding nine million were sold. Thermos could not even hope to make a dent in that much metal but made a hearty effort to fight back with *Peanuts*. Thermos's Have Lunch with Snoopy used a box with a rounded lid to mimic the pointed roof of Snoopy's doghouse. This box seemed almost as ubiquitous in the 1970s as Aladdin's bus had been a decade earlier, but the sales never approached quite the same level.

Other cartoon studios would sell their latest creations to the highest bid-
der. With the many Hanna-Barbera shows airing simultaneously, both Aladdin and Thermos grabbed some of the offerings. Aladdin got *Quick Draw Mc-
Graw*, *Huckleberry Hound*, *Yogi Bear*, *The Flintstones*, and *The Jetsons*; Thermos
had to be content with some of the studio's rather entertaining yet definitely
lower-echelon creations: *Secret Squirrel*, *Atom Ant*, *Help! It's the Hair Bear
Bunch*, *Goober and the Ghost Chasers*, and *Inch High Private Eye*.

With the many characters available from other studios, Aladdin made
deals for *Archie*, *Woody Woodpecker*, *Dick Tracy*, *Bozo the Clown*, *Steve Canyon*,
and others, while Thermos got the Warner Bros. properties, *Blondie*, *Fat Albert*, *Superman*, and many more. Sometimes characters would shift allegiance
from one company to the other; Thermos made a Popeye lunch box in 1964,
with the character designs mixing their original look with that of the made-
for-TV cartoons, but Aladdin took up the old salt's banner in 1980, no doubt
anticipating the release of the live-action feature starring Robin Williams.
The Aladdin Popeye box, however, featured artwork based on the comic strip.

The 1964 Popeye lunch box chose
to mix the comic strip designs of
most of the characters with the
version of Brutus developed for the
made-for-TV cartoons a few years
earlier.

Speaking of artwork, it was obvious that at times the artists who illustrated these boxes had little or no instruction about what sort of scenes they were to depict. The 1964 Popeye box, for example, showed truant officer Popeye and assistant Wimpy delivering an unconscious Brutus to Olive Oyl's schoolhouse. Why was a middle-aged brute like Brutus expected to be in school, and when did Olive get a teaching degree, anyway? Aladdin's 1974 Yogi Bear box came with one side depicting the unusual view of Yogi and girlfriend Cindy Bear cavorting with their gang of look-alike children. Perhaps someone at Hanna-Barbera belatedly caught on to what was being hinted at, because the more common version of this box has the weird scene replaced with a simple school blackboard held by Yogi and Boo Boo. Thermos's Secret Squirrel box was obviously produced using publicity art of the characters, with no clue to the artist as to the roles they would play in the show. Otherwise, how can one explain Secret Squirrel holding a gun on good guys Squiddly Diddly and Chief Winchley, who appear to be guarding a stolen treasure chest?

The Secret Squirrel lunch box was apparently designed before the show ever got on the air, as it depicted some totally out-of-character situations.

Although these metal lunch boxes are the best remembered, another variety proved far less durable. Vinyl kits, as they were known, were substantially less substantial. One Thermos veteran told Bruce, "They were just a piece of shower curtain plastic, heat sealed over cardboard. You'd get it out in the rain, and that was about it . . . plus, the decoration was stinko."

While it is true that the vinyl kits required a different sort of artwork—inasmuch as it had to be stamped onto the plastic rather than lithographed on metal—some major licensed characters got their only lunch box exposure in that format. Alvin and the Chipmunks, Beany and Cecil, the Banana Splits, Rocky and Bullwinkle, Deputy Dawg, and Linus the Lionhearted were but a few who were limited to vinyl box exposure, as were such noncartoon superstars as Captain Kangaroo and Barbie.

Metal lunch boxes were phased out in the mid-1980s after parents began to voice fears about kids bashing each other over the head with them, and the end of their production no doubt inspired the beginning of their career as collectibles and museum pieces. While only some former children would have had parents who bought Donald Duck bread or Andy Capp snacks, practically everyone had a lunch box at some point in their lives, so the little metal containers seem to push all the right buttons in folks' memory banks when they are encountered today. If we really were what we ate, as school tried to teach us, it is surprising we do not all have yellow bills; round, bald heads with round black ears; and bulgy arms with anchor tattoos and go around saying, "What's up, Doc?"

Although Felix Chevrolet was originally named for its owner, it adopted the famous magical cat as its mascot in the 1920s and has kept him around ever since. (Jerry Beck collection)

Chapter 9

CAR TOONS

Naturally, kids (both current and former) could expect to see their favorite cartoon characters on TV or at the movie theater as well as in the toy room and sometimes even in the kitchen. But surely they could escape the constant barrage of Mickey, Yogi, Popeye, and their chums by getting out of the house and going for a drive—maybe even on a long vacation. Nope. The Great American Roadside was full of those friends, making gas goofier, food funnier, and lodging loonier.

One of the earliest and certainly longest-lasting automotive-related cartoon licenses came about in Los Angeles in the early 1920s. Winslow Felix opened his Felix Chevrolet dealership in 1921, at the same time the silent cartoons with Felix the Cat were enjoying the first of several bursts of popularity. The connection could not have been a difficult one to make. The story goes that in 1923, Felix the Dealer made a deal with Felix the Cat producer Pat Sullivan to use the famous feline in advertising; in return, Sullivan received a new Chevy.

The most notable architectural feature of the Felix Chevrolet building is its neon sign, which by most reports did not exist until the late 1950s. Surprisingly from a nostalgia standpoint but not so much from a business one, Felix Chevrolet has strongly opposed all efforts to have its building and sign designated as historic sites—mainly because that designation would mean they could not be demolished in the name of modernizing the business.

Almost forty years after Felix began purring for Chevrolet, rival automaker Ford became the first corporation to license the *Peanuts* characters for an ad campaign. The date of this event has been given variously as anywhere from 1959 to 1961, but what does seem to be established is that Schulz agreed to the deal because he was personally a "Ford man all the way," as the saying went. Ironic as it seemed for little kids to be pontificating about the finer points of Ford automobile ownership, the campaign generated the first *Peanuts* animation in the form of TV commercials as well as a number of promotional items that are not cheap when encountered today. The same 1969 *Business Week* article we have seen referenced elsewhere in this book pointed out that, up until that time, Ford was the only *Peanuts* licensee voluntarily to drop the characters.

Plymouth's Road Runner automobile model was introduced in 1968, surely making it the most expensive piece of licensed character merchandise.

When Gulf Oil began sponsoring the weekly Disney TV show, much promotion ensued. These eight beautiful placemats were available at Gulf service stations, as was a slickly produced *Wonderful World of Disney* magazine. (Donnie Pitchford collection)

There was never a strong connection between cartoon characters and car culture, but a few notable pairings deserve mention. During the late 1930s, V. T. Hamlin's Alley Oop appeared in advertisements for Pan-Am gasoline and motor oil; Pan-Am service stations offered booklets reprinting selected Oop newspaper strips. (Ironically, competitor Sinclair was also using dinosaurs to emphasize the age of its crude oils.) In the 1970s, service stations occasionally offered cartoon drinking glasses, similar to the ones we saw in the previous chapter, but such promotions were not nearly as frequent as those by fast-food restaurants.

Probably the most expensive car and toon tie-in was Plymouth's "Road Runner" car line, rolled out in 1968. Plymouth reportedly paid Warner Bros. fifty thousand dollars for the licensing rights, a figure that sounds like birdseed today. Plymouth even developed a "beep beep" horn as a distinguishing feature. The animated commercials, naturally, showed Wile E. Coyote fruitlessly extending his pursuit of the beeping bird through an automobile showroom, and those who purchased cars could get inflatable figures of the two characters that dangled from suction cups. The Road Runner model remained in production, in one form or another, until 1980. Obviously, with vintage

muscle cars selling for huge amounts, a genuine Road Runner from Plymouth is a rare sight among cartoon memorabilia collections.

One of the most fondly remembered associations between cartoons and gas stations involved Disney and the Gulf Oil Company. In the fall of 1967, Gulf began sponsoring the Sunday night Disney TV show, offering customers a record album of songs taken from past Disneyland Records releases. By March 1968, a new promotion was in progress: a set of eight plastic placemats, each picturing a different Disney scene, available for fifteen cents each along with a fill-up.

The artwork on these placemats ranged from stunning to puzzling. In the former category was Tinker Bell, with everyone's favorite pin-up pixie causing the Disneyland castle to materialize against a hot pink background. Chief among the latter was one that, for possibly the only time in Disney history, pictured Donald Duck and Mickey Mouse in what would have been their true relative sizes in the natural world, with the feathered fowl pushing mini-Mickey in a diminutive toy locomotive. Others featured Pinocchio, Pluto, Snow White, Merlin the Magician, and two with Ludwig Von Drake. (Examples of some of these placemats exist printed with the RCA logo, indicating that at least a few might have originally been issued as an early 1960s promotion for that TV sponsor.)

In the fall of 1968, an even longer-lasting promotion began, with Gulf offering the first issue of a *Wonderful World of Disney* magazine—produced, of course, by those creative geniuses at Western Printing. That premiere issue set the pattern for the ones that would follow: articles about natural history combined with travelogues and stories about beloved Disney characters old and new. There was a "How to Draw Donald Duck" feature and a "Swingin' Fairy Tale" version of "Rapunzel" that was strongly reminiscent of Jay Ward's "Fractured Fairy Tales" of a decade earlier. Kids could learn how to make Winnie-the-Pooh puppets out of brown paper grocery bags, and there were previews of the upcoming episodes of the TV series. Succeeding issues contained continuing versions of many of these sections.

The public response to the first issue was sufficiently positive to warrant a second in the spring of 1969. This one came with a special insert geared toward teachers who might be inclined to use the magazine as a learning aid in their classrooms. The pages that had the best artwork of the Disney characters were noted so that teachers could cut them out to use as bulletin board decorations. The magazine then quaintly suggested,

Walt Disney Productions

Go with Gulf...the <u>service</u> station

Disney and Gulf had a cozy relationship for several years, but would you really trust Mickey, Donald, and Goofy to take care of your automobile?

If you need larger figures, put the pages in an opaque projector. Project on butcher paper or tag board. Copy the outline and all important characteristics. Cut out and color. Then watch how other teachers will want to borrow your Disney bulletin board materials.

The Disney company of today would frown on the idea of encouraging people to make bootleg decorations using its copyrighted characters.

Actual advertising for Gulf Oil was confined to the inside back cover of each issue, but sneak attacks occasionally took place. A photo feature about historic American lighthouses, for example, contained a terrific aerial view of the one on the beach at Biloxi, Mississippi—as well as the Gulf station at the U.S. 90 intersection behind the lighthouse.

Six Gulf issues of the magazine appeared, with the last one released in the summer of 1970. A number of the features were recycled from the *Mickey Mouse Club Magazine* (aka *Walt Disney's Magazine*) of the late 1950s. They would be recycled once again when the concept resurfaced in September 1976. Now titled simply *Disney Magazine*, it was offered as a Procter and Gamble premium in supermarkets, reaching those who had not yet been born when Gulf had taken the plunge.

At the end of a long day of burning gasoline (whether it be Gulf, Pan-Am, or one of the others), many travelers needed comfortable motels in which to bed down for the night. With the exception of one grand plan for a chain (discussed later in this chapter), most cartoon-themed motels were small, mom-and-pop affairs, and finding evidence of their existence can be difficult at best.

Thanks to the Internet, one of the best known is the Bugs Bunny Motel in Lakewood, Colorado. This business enlivened its neon sign with a more-than-slightly off-model rendition of the wascally wabbit in 1952; just why the owners chose good old Bugs as their mascot and namesake may never be known, but the establishment served travelers under that name until 1997, when Warner Bros. learned of its existence and insisted that trademark infringement was afoot. The owners responded by having the sign repainted to read Big Bunny Motel but made no change in the rabbit image since it did not look much like the "real" Bugs.

The Bambi Motel in Perry, Florida, and the Snow White Motel in Richmond, Virginia, could probably have gotten away with using those names, but they chose to flaunt themselves with the Disney versions of their respective characters on their signage. The Snow White was especially elaborate; in postcards, it is difficult to tell whether the sign was neon or painted (or

Ample evidence still shows that this Lakewood, Colorado, establishment was originally known as the Bugs Bunny Motel.

a combination of both), but it clearly depicted young Miss White and her seven famous guardians in their animated feature designs. The Snow White Motel is reportedly still in business, but it now has a generic neon sign with no traces of the cartoon characters. In Cherokee, North Carolina, the Pink Motel had no apparent cartoon connection in its name, yet its colorful neon sign featured a not-even-thinly-disguised version of Tinker Bell.

In between stopping for gas and turning in for the night, hungry tourists needed places to eat, and fortunately for our discussion here, cartoon-themed restaurants have had a long and illustrious career. Historian Mark Newgarden has discovered evidence of a 1930s Oswald's restaurant in San Jose, California. It seems to have followed the Felix Chevrolet tradition of starting with an owner whose first or last name was Oswald and then incorporating the mid-1930s version of Oswald the Rabbit into its logo.

There were few cartoon/food associations any stronger than that of Popeye's pal Wimpy and

Both Bambi and Snow White took on extra work, without Disney's consent, lending their names and images to motels in Perry, Florida, and Richmond, Virginia, respectively. (Al Coleman collection)

In Cherokee, North Carolina, the Pink Motel did not reference Tinker Bell by name, but her figure was unmistakable on the neon sign.

Hundreds of diners and cafés specializing in hamburgers used Wimpy's as their name, whether or not they had a license from King Features Syndicate to do so. One such eatery in Memphis, Tennessee, decorated its exterior wall with a reproduction of this Bud Sagendorf illustration from *Popeye Goes on a Picnic* (Wonder Books, 1958).

hamburgers, so scores of diners and hole-in-the-wall beaneries chose to name themselves after the meddlesome moocher without bothering to get a license from King Features Syndicate before doing so. They frequently hired local sign painters to craft some version of Wimpy to decorate their buildings but just about as often depended on the name alone to make the connection in customers' minds. Among the latter was the chain known as Wimpy Grills, founded by Ed Gold in Bloomington, Indiana, in 1934. The Segar/King Features character was present in name only, but that was enough to spread the chain coast to coast. According to hamburger chronicler Jeffrey Tennyson, by 1977 fifteen hundred Wimpy Grills operated in thirty-nine countries. Gold's will stipulated that all North American Wimpy Grills would close forever at the time of his death, which occurred in 1978. Since he had long ago sold the rights to the international market, however, people apparently are still paying on Tuesday for hamburgers today at Wimpy Grills in Europe and other non–North American locales.

When a nonchain Wimpy's in Cape Girardeau, Missouri, closed in 1997, the owner, Bill Lewis, told newspapers that according to his research, more than 140 U.S. restaurants were still using some variant of the Wimpy name. Some even attempted to skirt any possible legal entanglements by coming up with creative alternative spellings: one neon sign proudly welcomed diners to Wympee's,

By the 1960s, small, locally owned restaurants were fading fast, and the era of franchising had begun. It suddenly seemed that anyone could start a restaurant franchise, and licensing the name of a celebrity made selling franchises that much easier—at least in theory. In November 1968, *Editor and Publisher* magazine opined, "A Sunday drive in the country might soon resemble a tour through the Sunday funnies." And the writer was right.

We now come to the amazing story of Roy Abell, who had been paralyzed while an architecture student at Auburn University in Alabama. Abell would remain a quadriplegic for the rest of his life, but his injury made him more determined than ever to make his own way in the world. "The doctors had told me I would be a ward of the state in two years because my parents were so poor, so I set a goal to become a millionaire in two years or less."

Abell looked at the booming restaurant franchise market and decided that while most of the chains were going after hamburgers or fried chicken, there was much less competition for hot dogs. His initial plan was to begin a chain of Snoopy's Dog House hot dog restaurants, and he approached United Feature Syndicate with his idea. He was a week too late: the *Peanuts* characters had just been licensed to Interstate Brands for food products, so it was back to the old drawing board. His second choice was Snuffy Smith. "I turned to King Features for Snuffy and originally they wanted more money than I had at the time . . . $10,000. After some negotiation, they agreed to my terms: $1,000, because that was all I had."

According to Abell, he opened his first Snuffy's Shanty in 1968, and the next week, he sold the company for one million dollars to the company that already owned the Kentucky Fried Chicken franchise for Florida. Therefore, he had reached his goal of becoming a millionaire, and the Snuffy's Shanty chain was off and running. Actually, so were Snuffy and his family, depicted in a running pose ("Come an' git it!") on the outside walls of each restaurant as well as on the serving trays and other advertising. Since Fred Lasswell was a longtime resident of Tampa, his proximity to the chain's parent company made it a simple matter for him to create the artwork required and to make personal appearances at the grand openings. Because Abell was out of the company by that time, he does not recall just how many locations eventually existed, but apparently they lasted for approximately three years before disappearing back into the Hootin' Holler underbrush.

Actually, King Features seemed to be the leader of all cartoon owners when it came to tapping into the potentially lucrative restaurant franchising market, even if most of the resulting efforts had little success. The 1968 *Editor and Publisher* article claimed that a chain based on King Features' *Little King* pantomime strip had been in operation since the winter of 1967–68 and was up to twenty locations by that point. The article went on,

> Little King International, Inc. is awarding bargain-price "Earldoms" ($7,995 "plus good credit and character") to interested parties who want to venture into the fast-food business. The "Little King" structures resemble mini-English castles, but the bill of fare features moderately priced Italian hero sandwiches.

It is not known what became of the Little King restaurants, but Nebraska still has a chain of sub shops bearing that name, and they may well be a remnant of the project . . . especially since the company's website gives 1969 as the date of its establishment. Its king logo bears no resemblance to the comic strip character, however.

Another property licensed from King Features for restaurants was *The Katzenjammer Kids*. In early 1970, the first of what was intended to be a string of Katzenjammer Haus restaurants opened in Sayville, New York. The ads promoted the chain's ties to the Germanic-accented comic characters by

Quadriplegic entrepreneur Roy Abell founded the Snuffy's Shanty restaurant chain in 1969, hoping that hot dogs would be a novelty among the flood of franchised hamburger and fried chicken brands.

Dinty Moore was originally a character in George McManus's *Bringing Up Father* comic strip, but somehow old Dinty's name also became applied to numerous restaurants, including this one between Gulfport and Biloxi, Mississippi, and a line of canned goods.

claiming it featured "foods out of two worlds"—that is, American and Swiss-Bavarian dishes. "The kids will especially love it here, just as our kids—the Katzenjammer Kids—will especially love having them!" the ads promised. Like most of the other cartoon restaurants, the eventual number of locations is undocumented, but before long the Kids were out of the food business and back to tormenting Der Captain and Herr Inspector.

King Features' archivist Mark Johnson has cryptically hinted that at various times the syndicate licensed restaurants based on or at least named for Betty Boop, Beetle Bailey (serving Army rations?), and Krazy Kat. But before at least one other restaurant chain that traded on one of that firm's trademarks, officially or not. In George McManus's highly popular strip *Bringing Up Father*, Irish millionaire Jiggs was constantly trying to get away from his shrewish wife, Maggie, to have a lowbrow meal of corned beef and cabbage at Dinty Moore's tavern. The Dinty Moore name became associated with a line of grocery products manufactured by Hormel, and numerous diners and restaurants bore the Dinty Moore name, but whether any of them were licensed through King Features cannot be determined. However, the Dinty Moore name lives on in grocery stores nationwide today, probably making it the most successful cartoon/food tie-in ever—if, indeed, it was one.

At least one comic strip had multiple false starts in the restaurant biz. *Li'l Abner* was so popular in the newspapers and then on the Broadway stage and subsequent movie that it seemed quite the franchiser's dream. There were apparently at least two different attempts to bring the Dogpatch denizens to the great American roadside, the first coming to life in Morton Grove, Illinois, in the late 1950s or early 1960s. Typically for that era, if not for the characters, it was a drive-in. The back of the printed menu had a personal greeting from Abner Yokum:

All mah livin' y'ars, ah has dreamed of havin' mah own eatin' parlor—Now it's all come true, in mah own Li'l Abner's Drive-In. An' yuh knows the bes' paht? Ah kin not only feed Daisy Mae, Pappy Yokum, Tiny, Sadie Hawkins an' all the rest of mah kinfolk, but all mah hunreds of friens an' admahrers all ova Chicagoland—all real nice folks, jes' lak in Dogpatch.

The menu also advertised that "Dogpatch characters will serve you right in your car," confirming that there was not much of a stretch from the traditional female carhops to cutoffs-clad Daisy Mae and Moonbeam McSwine. Whether this effort ever expanded outside the Chicago metro area is unknown, but curiously, a Li'l Abner's still in business in Auckland, New Zealand, uses the same artwork that appeared on the Chicago location's menu.

The next Li'l Abner restaurant attempt came out of quite another area of the country. The November 1968 *Editor and Publisher* article revealed that New York–based restaurant company Longchamps had just signed a contract with Al Capp for a new Abner chain, with Capp receiving one million dollars up front.

Longchamps plans the first "Li'l Abner" within 50 miles of New York City and "one or two" in Florida. The restaurant's facade will portray a typical structure in Dogpatch and will have an "endless string of frankfurters coming out of the kitchen." "Hammus Alabammus" barbecued sandwiches and "Mammy Yokum" fried chicken will be featured. Food prices will range from 20 cents to $2.

How many Li'l Abners did Longchamps open? Again, there are no records to answer that question, but a Li'l Abner's Steakhouse is still operating in Tucson, Arizona. It may or may not be a former outpost of the long-forgotten chain. (Incidentally, Abner's and Capp's biggest influence on roadside tourism would also be born in 1968, about which more a little later in this chapter.)

Occasional novelty attempts such as Snuffy's hot dogs and the Katzenjammers' Bavarian food were anomalies in the fast-food world, which continued to thrive under its two original primary components, hamburgers and fried chicken. In January 1968, those two forces combined in a partnership between Hardee's and South Carolina restaurant entrepreneur Eugene Broome to form Yogi Bear's Honey Fried Chicken.

Since Yogi was, at least in part, originally based on Art Carney's portrayal of Ed Norton on *The Honeymooners*, it might seem strange that his fried chicken was promoted with the catchphrase of that show's star, Jackie Gleason,

In 1968, South Carolina restaurateur Ernest Broome joined forces with Hardee's to begin Yogi Bear's Honey Fried Chicken. (Butch Broome collection)

This rare view shows not only the original Yogi Bear's Honey Fried Chicken menu but the various types of decorated boxes and plastic tubs in which food could be taken home or on a pic-a-nic. (Butch Broome collection)

"How sweet it is!" But as Broome's son explains, there was a logical explanation: when the elder Broome first had the idea of using that slogan, he wanted to call his chain Jackie Gleason's Honey Fried Chicken. Ultimately, Gleason declined the honor, fearing that any failure on the part of the franchisees might reflect negatively on him. (He might have been watching what was happening with the similar Minnie Pearl's Fried Chicken chain, which became inextricably mired in state and national politics and accusations of wrongdoing, a lethal combination.) Ed Justin's licensing office had no such objections, so Yogi became an ursine Colonel Sanders.

By the end of 1968, the company was reporting the existence of at least seventy-five franchises. Naturally enough, the carry-out boxes were shaped like Yogi's favorite pic-a-nic baskets, and his face and image were splashed across all the signage. The restaurant property was decorated with statues of the characters, manufactured by International Fiberglass in California. Yogi clutched an enormous chicken drumstick in his right hand, while Boo Boo and Ranger Smith were molded in permanent running poses—Boo Boo with a look of terror on his face and the Ranger with his mouth wide open in mid-yell and a threatening hand raised above his head.

Like so many of the franchised cartoon restaurant chains, Yogi Bear's Honey Fried Chicken had flown the coop by the early 1970s, leaving abandoned buildings in its wake. (Broome remained in the restaurant business, founding the Ponderosa Steakhouse chain and later establishing a license with Universal Studios for a string of hot-dogs-and-beer outlets known, naturally, as Frank 'n' Stein.) At some point, many of the fiberglass Yogi's Fried Chicken statues were collected and displayed at a truck stop along I-95 near Halifax, North Carolina. By the end of the 1990s, these decaying figures were on their way to becoming roadside history legends, as they were unceremoniously dumped in a landfill-type area behind the truck stop. Roadside geeks filed enthusiastic reports and disturbing photos of the corpses, twisted and intertwined "like a cartoon mass-burial Holocaust orgy," as one individual colorfully described the scene. By ten years later, even those remnants had disappeared. The only documented set of the three characters still known to exist mostly intact sits in the yard of a private home in Rocky Mount, North Carolina. In an amazingly similar situation as that of the Little King and Li'l Abner's, a single Yogi Bear's Honey Fried Chicken has managed to survive into the present, located on U.S. 15 in Hartsville, South Carolina. It still features its original neon Yogi sign but not the fiberglass replicas of the characters.

(Other people maintain that at about the same time Yogi was going into the chicken business, a chain of Yogi Bear Burgers locations were operating in the Sacramento, California, area. The outdoor seating areas reportedly featured green umbrellas meant to represent pine trees, and employees were required to take turns dressing in Yogi and Boo Boo costumes and cavorting in the parking lot to attract customers. All traces of Yogi Bear Burgers have seemingly disappeared, but the very idea that there were two different Yogi food franchises, on opposite coasts, at the same time is certainly unusual.)

As it turned out, the cartoon character with the most successful fried chicken concession was one who was usually considered healthier and less gluttonous than the scheming Yogi. In 1972, Al Copeland opened what would eventually be the first in the chain of Popeyes (no apostrophe) Famous Fried Chicken outlets in New Orleans and later began franchising in 1976. Now, if one believes the company's official story as it is told today, Copeland named his restaurants not after Popeye the Sailor but instead after Popeye Doyle

Fiberglass statues of Yogi, Boo Boo, and Ranger Smith were part of the decor at some of the Yogi Bear's Honey Fried Chicken restaurants. This is the only known surviving set, frozen into an eternal chase in front of a private residence in North Carolina. (Debra Jane Seltzer collection)

of the movie *The French Connection*. Be that as it may, it did not stop Popeyes Famous Fried Chicken from licensing the cartoon characters from King Features for the better part of the next three decades.

The Popeye characters could be seen just about everywhere at a 1970s Popeyes location except the signage out front. Some stores used them more extensively than others; for example, the company made available glass panels that could be used as partitions or dividers in the restaurants, decorated with individual artwork of the characters and also a re-creation of one of George Wildman's Charlton Comics versions of the history of Popeye. Others were content to display a painting or two on their walls; the variation in quality and accuracy in these designs indicates that neither the parent company nor King Features spent a lot of time overseeing or approving them. An impressive part of all the stores was its simulated stained-glass light fixtures—actually, plastic—with the faces of Popeye, Olive, Swee'Pea, and Brutus illuminated from behind. (Oddly, Wimpy hardly ever appeared in any of the Popeyes advertising, possibly because he was so closely associated with the *other* major fast-food staple.)

Popeyes issued many, many premiums and other artifacts using the characters over the years. Among these was a combination calendar and coloring book that is notable because it clearly depicts the Popeye cast as residents of New Orleans rather than an eastern whaling village or sunny West Coast locale. For several years, Popeyes offered a different set of drinking glasses annually. One set gave a crash course in comic strip history by depicting the characters as they originally appeared (1929 for Popeye, 1919 for Olive, and 1933 for both Swee'Pea and Brutus) on one side and their present-day look on the other. Another set took the form of miniature comic strips; in one, Popeye offers Olive a ring, and the lovesick female is disappointed to find out he means onion rings. In another, Popeye threatens Brutus, "Unhand me goil and me chicken," but Olive makes peace by pointing out that there is enough food for them all. The story concludes with the bearded bully musing, "I wish this spicy delicious chicken was called Brutus's!"

Although the official company story is that Popeyes Fried Chicken was named for Popeye Doyle rather than Popeye the Sailor, the chain's many premiums and giveaways seem to contradict that idea.

The cast of the Popeye cartoons, comic strip, and comic books apparently were unaware that they were patronizing a restaurant named for a character in *The French Connection*.

Some of the Popeyes Fried Chicken outlets went to great lengths to decorate their interiors with cartoon motifs. The results were uneven, as evidenced by these shots.

In 1979, Popeyes Fried Chicken offered these glasses with miniature comic strips based on the various items on the menu.

Of course, Popeyes Fried Chicken is still a major player in the fast-food world, but around 2001, the use of the licensed characters began to be phased out in North America. They reportedly continued to appear overseas until 2012, when the company made news by officially terminating its King Features license. So far, no one has seen them issuing Popeye Doyle toys or drinking glasses to tie in with the official story of their name.

By the time Popeyes was serving up chicken instead of spinach, most other fast-food restaurants were depending heavily on mascot characters for their advertising. Restaurants that did not already have a character of their own—such as Ronald McDonald, Burger King's cartoon monarch, and Hardee's cowpoke Gilbert Giddyup—went shopping for one. Dairy Queen had depended mostly on the mouthwatering image of its "cone with the curl on top" to sell ice cream but also used the cartoon figure of a cute Dutch girl whose head matched the shape of the DQ logo. She had never made much of an impression on patrons, so Dairy Queen went looking for another character to fill her wooden shoes.

At this point, Dairy Queen approached IMG Marketing about the possibility of using Dennis the Menace and his comic strip cast in its advertising. Arthur LeFave, whom we met several chapters ago handling such matters for Hank Ketcham, says he traveled to DQ's home office in Minneapolis to meet with company president Harris Cooper and arrange the details to put the little brat to work. "We did retain the rights for Dennis to endorse other food products," LeFave recalls, "but for some reason, we never had an occasion to use them."

Dairy Queen built years of promotion around Dennis, using him in posters and premiums and in just about every possible way. The Dennis characters became the embodiment of DQ's new tag line, "Scrumpdillyishus!" According to LeFave, Hank Ketcham stayed busy turning out original artwork for all of DQ's various needs, including a constantly changing stream of designs for the firm's waxed paper cups. LeFave explains that creating a drawing that is to be printed on a cup, which is wider at the top than at the bottom, requires some very tricky work to be sure it does not look distorted when it is formed into that shape. The Dennis premiums from Dairy Queen were always delightful, but the artwork on the intended throwaway items is more often than not just as appealing. When the original twenty-year contract ran out, Dairy Queen chose not to continue with Dennis, turning him loose to menace somewhere else.

As the baby boom generation grew up and another followed behind, tastes in marketing changed. In the late 1970s and especially the early 1980s, the hot trend was restaurants that doubled as arcades, with video games blinking and beeping and frequently entertainment provided by animatronic

The original Superman statue in Metropolis, Illinois, was apparently modeled after how the Man of Steel looked after spending too much time hanging around the Sonic Drive-In. (Donnie Pitchford collection)

In the early 1970s, Dennis the Menace and his comic strip companions became the mascots for Dairy Queen and its "scrumpdillyishus" frozen treats.

Hank Ketcham (and his assistants) were kept busy turning out an endless variety of artworks to be reproduced on Dairy Queen's many different sizes of waxed paper containers. As the deteriorating condition of these examples indicates, they were never intended to survive for forty years.

characters that sang and told jokes while customers ate. The two main purveyors of this form of eatertainment were Chuck E. Cheese and Showbiz Pizza, but in 1983, two different chains attempted to do the same by using long-established cartoon characters.

One bore the lengthy name Bullwinkle's Family Food 'n' Fun, sometimes shortened to simply Bullwinkle's Family Restaurants. Jay Ward chronicler Keith Scott has learned that the restaurant concept originated with veteran Ward voice actor Paul Frees, who joined Bill Scott and June Foray in recording new dialogue for the animatronic versions of their old characters. Because the late 1950s agreement between Ward and Peter Piech was still in effect, Piech insisted on supplementing the Bullwinkle cast with his other properties from the late Total TeleVision Productions. Bullwinkle, Rocky, and Boris therefore performed alongside Underdog and Tennessee Tuxedo. Up-and-coming voice actor Corey Burton helped out by re-creating the voices of some of these characters whose original performers were no longer available (or alive).

Just how long the Bullwinkle's chain lasted is unclear; Keith Scott reports that by the end of the 1990s, most of the locations had already closed, although at least a few of them seem to have managed to hang on by their antlers in Oregon and Washington as late as 2014.

An almost identical concept was licensed by Warner Bros. that same year, but unlike Bullwinkle's, its name gave no hint as to its cartoon connections. Gadgets, as it was to be called, also featured animatronic likenesses of Bugs Bunny and the whole looney gang. Mel Blanc was called back to the recording studio to provide the necessary voices, reportedly performing some fourteen hundred different popular songs that would be incorporated into the programs. By December 1983, there were Gadgets in Springfield, Ohio, and Baltimore, Maryland, with grandiose plans for 150 more. As with nearly anything he worked on, Blanc was full of enthusiasm for the project.

By the middle of the next year, though, it was obvious that Gadgets was going to need more than Blanc's boosterism to make it. *Nation's Restaurant News* reported,

Because of high development costs and demographics, Gadgets has altered its original concept of combining the ambience of an eating place and lounge for young adults with a family restaurant that features robotic cartoon characters on a stage. The new concept, Gadgets Cafe, is smaller and does not have the Looney Tunes show. Even in the full-sized Gadgets, the stage shows have been reduced in frequency to just two to three hours a day.

Yes, times were rapidly changing, and even "modern" innovations began to look old less than five years after their debuts. Simplicity was certainly the theme when a chain of Dagwood's Sandwich Shops were introduced in the 2000s, but despite Mr. Bumstead's long association with that type of meal, they were gone within a decade.

Sometimes restaurants tried to get away with using licensed characters without paying for a license, which usually resulted in an unusually large number of lawyers among their clientele. One nightspot in Miami, Florida, thought it could get away with calling its lounge the Yabba Dabba Doo Room, which did not sit well with Hanna-Barbera. Besides the clear infringement on the studio's trademark, there was the very unwanted association of Fred Flintstone with a not-so-family-friendly environment, and in short order, the Yabba Dabba Doo Room was a page in, rather than right out of, history.

And now we come to probably the largest, and most successful, category of roadside cartoon character licensing, that of amusement parks and other such attractions. Actually, we might say that this story begins with cartoon "unlicensing," because there is plenty of evidence that the characters' initial association with the amusement business was done without the consent of their rightful owners.

Photos of carnival rides from the early 1940s show them decorated with the owners' own renditions of Mickey Mouse, Popeye, Jiggs, and other characters that appear to be moonlighting (and usually not looking their licensed best). But the biggest genre of these familiar personages' appearance at traveling carnivals nationwide was the seemingly endless array of chalkware prizes available to those who knocked over milk bottles or burst multicolored balloons—sometimes in spite of the carnival owners' machinations to prevent such success.

Most popular characters from the 1930s and 1940s   Popeye, Superman, Snow White, the Lone Ranger, Pinocchio, and Porky Pig—found themselves

Unlicensed chalkware versions of famous cartoon characters were staples of traveling carnivals for decades. Even though they were created without their copyright owners' permission, their funky appearance makes them highly desirable to today's collectors.

mutated into chalkware, sometimes slightly disguised to hide their true identities but more often designed just as their legal guardians intended. Ironically, the companies that manufactured such figures and offered them to amusement companies frequently copyrighted their own bootleg copies of already-copyrighted characters, using new appellations: Popeye was registered as "Comical Sailor Man," Jiminy Cricket as "Comical Cricket," and Charlie McCarthy as "Dummy," to name a few. Despite their unlicensed status, these once-cheap doodads now command impressive prices among collectors, their bizarre appearance, gaudy colors, and glued-on glitter only adding to their appeal.

In a world of cartoon characters working as free agents, it should be obvious that the first true amusement park to use them legally was Disneyland. As far back as the late 1930s, Walt Disney had considered building a "Mickey Mouse Park" near his Burbank studio, with simple rides and statues of his most famous characters. As most people know, this idea kept growing until it became the world-renowned theme park in Anaheim in 1955. Experts in Disney collectibles have pointed out that Disneyland was the only park in

The first Disney character costumes were designed for the Ringling Bros./Barnum and Bailey Circus and the 1954 edition of the Ice Capades. The average kid might well have run away from these versions of the Seven Dwarfs instead of embracing them.

the company's history to be merchandised as if it were a character. As we saw earlier, storybooks, coloring books, games, and any number of other items were based on Disneyland, with any ancillary characters just providing atmosphere.

What has been forgotten over the years—even by the Disney company—is that the cartoon characters originally could not be found roaming all over the property; they appeared only in Fantasyland, which was considered their true home. While Walt did not want to risk overusing them, he did realize that they were the most unique part of his park. Their comparative scarcity in Disneyland's early days resulted at least in part from the fact that the Disney studio had no previous experience with turning its pen-and-ink drawings into figures that could walk and shake hands with guests. The earliest Disney character costumes had been made in the early 1950s for the Ringling Bros./Barnum and Bailey Circus (they can be seen in that aggregation's movie, *The Greatest Show on Earth*) and the traveling Ice Capades shows. For Disneyland's earliest years, the park had to borrow the circus/ice show costumes, and judging by photos of them, they were far more likely to frighten kids away than be appealing.

By the 1960s, the Disney costumes had gotten better, although there were still occasional lapses, such as a design for Mickey and Minnie in which their heads took up most of their bodies. Some characters, including Winnie-the-Pooh, the Seven Dwarfs, and the Three Little Pigs, had no operational arms or hands, because the stuffed appendages hung at roughly the waist level of the person inside. (The performer could, however, use his or her hands to operate the character's mouth, eyes, or ears in the style of a giant puppet.) And then, there was the inherent problem that no human was small enough to portray Jiminy Cricket or Chip 'n' Dale as the size they appeared on-screen. Seeing a five-foot-tall insect or rodent was a bit shocking, but sooner or later, kids and their parents seemed to accept things for the way they were, and the characters became one of the most anticipated parts of a Disneyland visit.

To protect their uniqueness, the costumed characters were not often seen outside Disneyland, but in 1969, Disney and NBC joined forces to create *Disney on Parade* as a touring arena show. In retrospect, sending the characters on a junket across the nation could be viewed as part of the giant buildup toward the opening of Walt Disney World in Florida in 1971. The tsunami of that park's looming advent caused tidal waves throughout the licensing world; suddenly, it seemed that every entity owning valuable cartoon properties sought to turn them into theme park material, much as the franchised restaurant craze had eaten them up during the previous few years.

Even in the early 1960s, the costumed characters at Disneyland had a way to go before evolving from creepy to cute.

Like Atlas holding up the world, Superman supported New Jersey's Palisades Amusement Park in comic book ads. (Donnie Pitchford collection)

The Harvey Comics characters moved into Palisades Park around 1970, appearing in their own dark ride, Casper's Ghostland. The park's presence was not enough to stop the gradual deterioration of the neighborhood, and Palisades closed forever in 1971. (Donnie Pitchford collection)

One of the first non-Disney parks to establish a strong cartoon connection was the venerable Palisades Park in New Jersey. At some point in the early 1960s, Palisades enlisted Superman to serve as its official spokessuperman, inviting readers of his comic books to visit Palisades at a discount via coupons printed in the ads. (Just as non–West Coast kids could only dream of ever seeing Disneyland in person, so did those who did not live within driving distance of New York City long for the forbidden fruit of Palisades Park.) It is speculated that Superman's connection with Palisades came about at least in part because the park's principal owner, Irving Rosenthal, was also a heavy National Periodical Publications stockholder. Be that as it may, Rosenthal was not a purist when it came to partnering with comic book companies.

Archie Comics and Harvey Comics also found outlets for their most famous characters at Palisades. Archie's name was pasted onto one of the car rides, but Harvey scared up even more attention when Palisades' former Tunnel of Love was remodeled into a Casper's Ghostland dark ride, with all the famed Harvey characters performing their souls out (providing they still had souls, that is). All of this cartoon fun was not enough to save Palisades from changing times, its changing neighborhood, and changing tastes in the amusement industry. It is a cruel twist of fate that Palisades, one of the most famous traditional amusement parks in the nation, closed in 1971, just as the newer, corporate-owned theme parks were about to hit new heights.

Most theme parks were located in areas with a heavy tourist population, but one of the best-known cartoon conclaves was anywhere but. In 1967, a group of businessmen in the Ozark Mountains town of Harrison, Arkansas, made plans for a hillbilly-themed park and took those plans to Al Capp, whose *Li'l Abner* cast members were the most famous hillbillies in Cartoonland. Although the first *Li'l Abner* strips in 1934 had specifically placed Dogpatch in Kentucky, when presented with a lucrative offer, Capp had no compunction about saying he had always thought of the desolate community as being in Arkansas.

Perhaps it was statements such as that one that made some of Arkansas's leaders less than enthusiastic about playing up the hillbilly theme up in them thar hills, but the folks in Harrison were eager to have such a major tourist draw. Capp, for his part, was happy to travel to Arkansas for pre-opening publicity, the first in October 1967 for the ceremonial groundbreaking ceremony. In anticipation, the Harrison newspaper blared the news on its front page:

> The basic layout of the park will consist of the villages of Dogpatch and Skunk Hollow, including the dwellings of Li'l Abner and Daisy Mae and of Pappy and Mammy Yokum, and the "chapel" of Marryin' Sam.
>
> Construction of Dogpatch is now in the first phase, concerned with initial site preparation, construction of dams and bridges, and theme buildings. Phase two will include building of motels, housekeeping units for tourists, a theater and additional rides.

Although some of the Dogpatch buildings, such as the characters' homes mentioned in that article, were genuine mountain structures carefully moved to the Dogpatch site, most of the park was modeled largely on the sets designed for the hit 1956 *Li'l Abner* Broadway musical and the 1959 Paramount movie based on it. In the center of the town square was a bronze statue of Dogpatch's hero, Confederate general Jubilation T. Cornpone ("First in war, first in peace, first to holler 'I QUIT!'"). The park's costumed characters, at least in the early years, did not have to be concerned with the possible heat stroke facing Disney's heavily disguised employees. Li'l Abner, Daisy Mae, Mammy and Pappy, and the rest required little or no makeup, and at least in the case of the younger female members of the cast, were not even encumbered by much clothing—true to their pen-and-ink counterparts.

Capp was back at Dogpatch for the grand opening on May 18, 1968. "It's every kid's dream to own his own amusement park, and here it is," he told

Dogpatch USA opened near Harrison, Arkansas, in May 1968, much to the horror of the state's progressives, who desperately wanted to get away from its long-standing hillbilly image.

Although the female characters in Li'l Abner traditionally went barefoot, at least the performers who portrayed them at Dogpatch USA got to wear sneakers on the theme park's hot pavement.

For a park located so far from any population center, Dogpatch USA had an amazing variety of rides, shops, and restaurants—even if its attempts to recapture the style of Al Capp's artwork were not totally successful.

the press. Everything looked like an "Oh, happy day," as one of the strip's catchphrases put it, but trouble began almost immediately after the gates had opened.

The most comprehensive history of Dogpatch's troubled past can be found on the website www.arkansasroadstories.com, where the author apparently prefers to remain anonymous, identifying himself only as RTJ. Anonymous or not, he documents how the park was already undergoing ownership and management changes at the beginning of its second year of operation, which did nothing to comfort Capp, who had entrusted his property to the original founders.

However, the park was still doing well in the early 1970s. It had been hoped that Dogpatch USA could work hand in hand with the planned chain of Li'l Abner restaurants and a hoped-for TV series, but neither of those ventures worked out. In fact, at about the time Dogpatch was picking up steam, rural humor began a rapid downward slide in public consciousness. At the end of the 1970–71 TV season, the many rural situation comedies that had dominated the ratings for a decade were summarily canceled in favor of more urban, hip humor. Al Capp finally retired in 1977, and even he admitted that for the previous several years his strip had ceased to be amoozin'. After his death in 1979, the public slowly began to forget the *Li'l Abner* characters, and Dogpatch USA was irrevocably saddled with them. Slowly, standard amusement rides began to take over most of the property. At first, they were at least named to tie in with the strip, such as with Earthquake McGoon's Brain Rattler. Later additions such as a Space Shuttle ride seemed out of place (though Capp's satiric brain might well have come up with an entertaining story line based on the topic).

During the late 1980s, Dogpatch made a halfhearted effort to remind people of its origins. There was talk of establishing a museum of *Li'l Abner* artifacts, but nothing came of it. As part of that effort, the costumed human characters were joined by the gigantic Shmoo, which made the Disney outfits look air-conditioned by comparison. As we saw way back in chapter 1, the Shmoo had been an enormous part of *Li'l Abner* merchandising in the late 1940s and early 1950s, but those who encountered the huge pillow-like figure at Dogpatch likely had no idea what it was.

Dogpatch USA closed in 1993, and the years that followed featured a morass of legal entanglements concerning just who owned what part of the property and how much money they had never been paid for their participation. Interested historians occasionally would manage to circumvent the barriers and explore the ruins of the park, but there seems to be no viable

When these photos of the Dogpatch USA ruins were taken in June 2005, crumbling buildings and faded signage were practically the only remnants of the once-thriving park. In the abandoned Skunk Works (top right), Barney Barnsmell resolutely sat at his post, awaiting tourists who would never arrive. (Janet McMurrin collection)

reason to believe it will ever reopen with a theme built around characters that are remembered only by fans of classic comic strips.

In contrast to the sad Dogpatch saga, a much more successful cartoon business story began in Wisconsin at about the same time Li'l Abner and Daisy Mae were moving into their new Arkansas home. A marketing executive, Doug Haag, became interested in the heretofore largely untapped potential in the camping industry. Just as the chain motel had been born out of a dissatisfaction with the inconsistencies of the typical mom-and-pop roadside motel, so Haag felt there might be a market for a campground that was more than a place to pull in and hook up; he wanted to do something that was more like a miniature theme park.

Haag says that this topic was on his mind one day when he found his kids enjoying the syndicated reruns of *Yogi Bear* on TV, and suddenly it came to him: build a chain of Jellystone Park Campgrounds. He drew up some plans for what such a venture could involve and went to New York to present it to Ed Justin. With an official Hanna-Barbera license in hand, the first of Haag's Jellystone Parks opened near Sturgeon Bay, Wisconsin, in July 1969.

One of the most successful cartoon roadside businesses was the chain of Jellystone Park Campgrounds, founded in 1969. This stunning aerial view shows one of the early locations in the Wisconsin Dells. (Jim Webb collection)

Archival photos show that even though that pilot campground was an amazingly creative undertaking, some refinements were in order. The first Yogi Bear statue to greet visitors was an undeniably crude rendition of the basket snatcher, looking more like papier-mâché than anything else. Fortunately, about the time the chain began growing, the Yogi Bear's Honey Fried Chicken restaurants began shutting down, and Haag made a deal with Hardee's to purchase as much of that chain's Yogi memorabilia as possible. A number of the walking pose fiberglass Yogis were retrofitted with arms minus the giant drumsticks, and after those were used up, a standing Yogi was manufactured for the rest of the campgrounds.

Each Jellystone Park had its own miniature golf course, which varied in complexity depending on the location, as well as an outdoor drive-in-type movie theater where the classic late 1950s–early 1960s Yogi cartoons would be run from 16mm film prints at dusk. Costumed versions of Yogi, Boo Boo, and Cindy Bear roamed the property, surprising campers with their visits and antics. The central feature of each Jellystone campground was the ranger station, which served as a combination snack bar, amusement area, and general store. Huge quantities of Yogi merchandise were needed to stock all of these ranger stations; some items, such as green plastic ranger hats, were produced especially for the campgrounds, while others were overstock of toys and other doodads that had first been produced a decade earlier. The company had its own theme song, which sounded absolutely nothing like the music from the TV cartoons. Accompanied by a twangy country-western guitar, a rustic-sounding singer drove home the chorus: "Yogi Bear, Yogi Bear, the swingin'est swinger anywhere / We know who's in the ranger's hair, little Boo Boo and Yogi Bear!"

Not long after the company started, Jim Webb joined the fun as an executive, and he still serves as a consultant to the Jellystone system today. He

The first attempt at creating a Yogi Bear statue to greet Jellystone Park campers was less than impressive. This early model was soon replaced by a more professional fiberglass rendition. (Jim Webb collection)

Many of the early Jellystone Park Campgrounds had this eye-catching signage to lure tourists off the highway. (Jim Webb collection)

The variety of merchandise available in a Jellystone Park ranger station is enough to make today's Hanna-Barbera collectors' eyes glaze over. (Jim Webb collection)

witnessed firsthand one of the more ambitious ideas that ended up going nowhere. Having vastly improved the situation for those with a love of camping, the company next decided to do something about those travelers who liked the Yogi idea but preferred sleeping in indoor, air-conditioned comfort. In 1975, there was much fanfare surrounding the launch of Yogi Bear's Family Motor Inns, a motel concept that would be built adjoining existing and new campgrounds.

As at the Jellystone Parks, Yogi's face loomed large in all of the signage. One of the motels' big selling features was that the rooms contained "Yogi Bear bunk beds" that folded into the wall. "The kids will all want to sleep in Yogi's bed!" the brochures predicted. And perhaps they would have—but Webb says that the company learned a hard lesson about the motel business: "The biggest chunk of motel business was salesmen, and traveling salesmen on the road just weren't interested in staying at a Yogi Bear motel." We guess they weren't eager to sleep in Yogi's bunk beds, either. Only a Yogi Bear's Family Motor Inn in Bunnell, Florida, made it from the drawing board to reality. The 1975–76 Jellystone Campgrounds directory reported a second motor inn under development at Danville, Virginia, but Webb says it never opened.

Even without adjoining motels, the Jellystone campgrounds were amazingly successful. By the early 1990s, around seventy of them were in operation, and new ones continue to be built nearly twenty-five years later. They certainly represent a rare success in the realm of cartoon-based roadside attractions, standing tall amid the broken bits of ideas that just did not make it.

Yet another chain of licensed Hanna-Barbera attractions brought the rocky world of Bedrock to life. The first Flintstones Bedrock City opened in Custer, South Dakota, in 1966. Its origins were simple: the owner of a local cement plant wanted to build a tourist attraction and somehow figured out that if cement were going to be the major component, the Flintstone world would be easy to replicate. Rather like the construction of Dogpatch USA, the various characters' residences and businesses were built one by one, without much concern for making them match the appearance of their TV counterparts. The same went for the cement statues of the Flintstone cast,

In 1975, the Jellystone Park company attempted to begin a chain of Yogi Bear's Family Motor Inns, but the only one that ever opened was in Bunnell, Florida. The architect's added a rendition of Ranger Smith chasing Yogi across the motel's lawn. (Jim Webb collection)

The Bedrock City theme park in Custer, South Dakota, had some rather disturbing costumes and concrete statues of the inhabitants of the Flintstones' neighborhood.

until increased oversight from the trademark owners resulted in reasonably accurate fiberglass versions. Early photos show that the costumed Fred and Barney were every bit as frightening as any of the early Disney characters.

Although the South Dakota Bedrock City was very successful and produced dozens of souvenirs and tie-in toys, its location in the Black Hills proved a hindrance to year-round operation. It was only open from mid-May through Labor Day, so the same owners decided to build another one in a much less seasonal location. They chose Williams, Arizona, just south of the Grand Canyon, and the second Bedrock City opened in 1972. It was indeed open all year, but it was located in the middle of nowhere and did not employ the "live" characters. It was and remains, primarily an outdoor diorama for tourists to explore on their own. One highlight was a huge dinosaur slide on which kids could re-create the opening of the TV show by skidding down the tail just like Fred.

A second Bedrock City could be found in Williams, Arizona. Since it sat literally in the middle of nowhere, it had no live performers, only statuary representing the prehistoric world of *The Flintstones*. (Debra Jane Seltzer collection)

Alley Oop, the comic strip caveman created by Vincent Hamlin, was not nearly as famous as Fred Flintstone, but he got his own small park in Iraan, Texas. (Debra Jane Seltzer collection)

Cincinnati's Kings Island theme park tried to do with the Hanna-Barbera characters what Disney had done with its own properties. This first costumed Yogi Bear looked a bit hairier than his animated counterpart.

At some point in the tale of two Bedrock Cities, locations opened in Kelowna and Hope, both in Canada's British Columbia. Some difficulties in international copyright law reportedly forced those to close in the late 1990s, although at least the one in Hope managed to survive under the name Dino Town, removing any traces of the cartoon cavemen. The South Dakota and Arizona Bedrock Cities continue to thrive and have been written up in any number of books and articles devoted to quirky roadside attractions.

Another comical prehistorian got his own park but in a much smaller way. The small town of Iraan, Texas, erected Alley Oop Fantasy Land, more or less a glorified playground area with an adjacent museum explaining the strip's history. Oop's creator, Vincent Hamlin, lived in the area for a number of years, giving it that tie to reality. That was good, because as had happened with *Li'l Abner*, the newspaper strip declined in popularity and people forgot who Alley Oop was. By the 1980s, the small park was reported as looking rather dilapidated, but renewed interest in preserving cartoon history led the city to undertake a massive restoration project in the mid-2000s. Alley Oop Fantasy Land is once again welcoming those who are willing to make the exit off I-10 and drive into another time and place—in more ways than one.

By the early 1970s, the amusement park industry was generally a corporate one. The next big cartoon-themed park opened in 1972, and was a direct result of Cincinnati-based Taft Broadcasting's purchase of the Hanna-Barbera Studios a few years earlier. In 1969, Taft also purchased its home city's venerable Coney Island amusement park and set in motion a plan to replace the aging old fun center with a new, modern theme park that would, not incidentally, have the same access to the vast Hanna-Barbera cast that Disneyland and Walt Disney World had to their famed cartoon stars.

As it was finally built, Kings Island used Hanna-Barbera not as its entire theme but more like the equivalent of Disney's Fantasyland. In the section of the park known as the Happy Land of Hanna-Barbera, some standard amusement rides were given some nominal theming toward such past and present Saturday morning stars as Motormouse and Autocat, Squiddly Diddly, the Funky Phantom, and Winsome Witch. But the focal point of the area was the lavish dark ride called the Enchanted Voyage, which immersed its boats and guests in the Hanna-Barbera environment unlike anything else in the park.

As with most dark rides, good photos from the inside of the Enchanted Voyage are scarce. Fortunately, it generated enough fans during its ten-year life span that it lives on in a number of websites, and those give us at least a dim idea of what awaited in its dark interior. The boats entered the building through a giant television screen, while a relentless theme song enumerated the many hit Hanna-Barbera shows and their characters "who live inside your TV." Scenes variously depicted a haunted house (for Scooby-Doo buffs), Gulliver and his Lilliputian friends (from the 1968 Saturday morning series, not the 1939 Max Fleischer feature), and a burning building with the Banana Splits as inept firefighters. At one point, the riders were caught in the crossfire of a mountain country shoot-out starring the Hillbilly Bears. The grand finale was a circus scene in which the entire Hanna-Barbera cast took part.

(By 1984, the 1960s/early 1970s Hanna-Barbera characters were mostly forgotten, and the ride was converted into the home for the studio's most popular contemporary stars, the Smurfs. That lasted until 1992, when the whole water trough system was removed and it became a standard land-based dark ride known as the Phantom Theater. In 2002, it received another makeover that brought back at least part of the Hanna-Barbera theme: Scooby-Doo and the Haunted Castle.)

Outside the Enchanted Voyage's walls, the costumed Hanna-Barbera characters made up a small army that might have even dwarfed Disney's (although Disney had dwarfs and Hanna-Barbera did not). Early photos show that rendering the characters in costume form took a bit of experimentation; the original 1972 Yogi Bear, for example, had fur all over his face rather than the barren muzzle of his animated counterpart. Several of the park's costumed characters could be glimpsed when TV sitcoms *The Brady Bunch* and *The Partridge Family* filmed episodes at Kings Island. Of course, dozens of Kings

This is apparently concept art for Kings Island's Hanna-Barbera–themed dark ride, the Enchanted Voyage. At one point, visitors' boats were caught in the crossfire of this Hillbilly Bears mountain feud.

Some of the Hanna-Barbera souvenirs packaged for sale at Kings Island were also distributed to retail stores throughout the country.

Costumed Hanna-Barbera characters also hung around Kings Island's sister park, Kings Dominion, near Richmond, Virginia.

Warner Bros. first tried to get into the theme park business with Jungle Habitat in West Milford, New Jersey. The wild animals were accompanied by these not-so-wild ones in the Looney Tunes–themed Jungle Junction section.

Island souvenirs bearing the Hanna-Barbera characters were sold at the park and in some instances at variety stores nationwide, identifiable by their Happy Land of Hanna-Barbera logo. One souvenir, a Yogi Bear poster with a hot pink background that was also sold at the Jellystone Park campgrounds, became a pivotal plot point in the *Brady Bunch* episode set at Kings Island.

In 1975, Taft Broadcasting opened Kings Dominion, a virtual clone of Kings Island, near Richmond, Virginia, and acquired another park, Carowinds, near Charlotte, North Carolina. The Hanna-Barbera costumed characters and souvenirs overflowed from Cincinnati into these new ventures as well, although Kings Dominion seems to have made the most use of them. Kings Dominion lacked a dark ride equivalent to the Enchanted Voyage; the closest Virginia parallel was Yogi's Million Dollar Cave, which was certainly dark enough but was a walk-through attraction instead of a ride. Although it featured a few animated dioramas, it made nowhere near the impression on former kids' consciousness left by its more elaborate Ohio cousin.

The only other studio with enough cartoon characters to rival Disney and Hanna-Barbera was Warner Bros., and its initial attempts to bring Bugs Bunny and his friends to the theme park world were a bit clumsier than Elmer

Bugs Bunny and his looney pals were fixtures of Marriott's Great America theme parks beginning in the mid-1970s.

The companies that manufactured fiberglass figures for use as miniature golf course obstacles occasionally could be caught using earlier cartoon character toys as their models. These were "inspired" by Bugs Bunny and Pinocchio.

Fudd. In 1972, Warners put highly off-model costumed versions of its characters into Jungle Habitat, a park in West Milford, New Jersey, that traded heavily on a trend in the amusement industry of having visitors drive through simulated wildlife habitat and view lions, ostriches, and other fauna living free rather than in cages. (The chain of Lion Country Safari parks was the most successful at this; the idea also lives on, after a fashion, at Disney's Animal Kingdom, and elsewhere.)

Jungle Habitat could not survive in the even more fierce tourism jungle, and its former property is now maintained by the city of West Milford as a series of walking trails. Bugs, Daffy, Porky, and company next moved on to the Marriott Corporation's Great America parks, opened in 1976 near Chicago and near Santa Clara, California. Both locations used the Warner Bros. characters in much the same way the Taft Broadcasting enterprises used Hanna-Barbera. Great America souvenirs featuring the Looney Tunes characters are not overabundant but are plentiful enough to indicate that the parks did big business in that regard. As we shall see in the closing chapter of this book, the Bugs Bunny bunch found an additional permanent home at the Six Flags chain of parks during the 1980s.

(Country music superstar Conway Twitty built his own mini–theme park, Twitty City, surrounding his home near Nashville, Tennessee. The ubiquitous logo character was the Twitty Bird, a hardly subtle rendition of Warner Bros.'s Tweety in a cowboy hat. Unlike the story of the Bugs Bunny Motel, apparently this bit of trademark infringement was allowed to chirp away until the attraction closed.)

Over the years, a number of manufacturers of amusement rides have marketed devices with varying degrees of official licensing from the cartoon characters' owners. In the 1970s, inserting a coin into a Flintstones vending machine featuring either Fred or Dino would produce a plastic egg containing a cheap prize. That was an example of the licensed type, but the other kind could take many different forms.

Remember the coin-operated bouncing horses that could be found in front of nearly every dime store? Well, there were cartoon versions of those too; one was shaped like a strangely elongated waterfowl in a blue sailor suit and bore the slogan, "Ride Donald the Duck." (A variation of the same figure was also available to be used as an obstacle in miniature golf courses.) To this day, some traveling carnivals still have rides with cars that resemble bizarrely mutated versions of Donald or Woody Woodpecker, frequently with heads and bodies that do not match. One common roller-coaster-type ride is usually found under the name Go Gator, and through some mind-boggling

arrangement that will likely forever remain unknown, the cars are human-sized reproductions of the Wally Gator Bubble Club bottle made by Purex in the 1960s (with Wally on his stomach, with his hands under his chin).

Many times, cartoon characters could be found along the roadside without having entire theme parks built around them. Probably no single character has been immortalized in statue form more often than that old salt Popeye the Sailor. In 1937, an eight-foot-tall replica of the one-eyed ancient mariner was erected in Crystal City, Texas. Why Crystal City, you ask? Well, Crystal City's main export was spinach, and Popeye's nationwide effect on the sale of that product was enough to cause the Crystal City fathers to publicly thank him with the type of statue normally reserved for statesmen and other real-life heroes. Unlike most of the future Popeye statues, Crystal City's was fashioned with reasonably lifelike human proportions, notwithstanding Popeye's prodigious chin.

A coin-operated "Donald the Duck" ride and an even stranger carnival ride with bizarre mutations of Woody Woodpecker and other characters were among the freaky sights along the American roadside.

Crystal City, Texas, was known as the spinach-growing capital of the world, and in 1937, the town expressed its gratitude to Popeye's creator, Elzie Segar, by erecting this replica of the sailor man.

Today, Elzie Segar's birthplace, Chester, Illinois, is decorated with statues not only of Popeye but also of many of the supporting players from his comics and animated cartoons.

In a sign of changing times, in 2007 the original seventy-year-old Popeye was moved inside the city hall to protect it from vandals. (Spinach might be good for defeating Bluto, but it apparently doesn't work so well against modern-day hoodlums.) The outdoor statue was replaced by a six-foot-tall fiberglass substitute—easier to replicate in the event of damage or destruction.

The town of Chester, Illinois, where Popeye creator Elzie Segar was born, got its own bronze Popeye statue in 1977. It became the centerpiece of Segar Memorial Park, perched on a bluff overlooking the Mississippi River at the spot where a bridge connects Illinois with Missouri. Later, the town expanded its Popeye pride to include other members of the comic strip cast, with granite replicas of Olive Oyl, Wimpy, Bluto, the Sea Hag, Alice the Goon, and others scattered along the streets.

In our previous chapter, we saw how the logical supermarket link between Popeye and spinach resulted in an official brand. In northern Arkansas, where much of the spinach that ends up inside those cans is grown, two different towns decided to memorialize their vegetable's supersalesman. In Lowell, the Allen canning plant put up a Popeye that was modeled after the 1965 drawing on the spinach labels. However, the statue lasted only as long as the company was operating out of that building, and as of 2007, Popeye was reported as having vacated the premises. Meanwhile, over in Alma, another Popeye gained fame because it hardly resembled the beloved character. Built in 1987 from fiberglass and papier-mâché, it was not only ugly but rather insubstantial. It was eventually retired to a local gift shop and replaced with a more accurate bronze Popeye that serves as the centerpiece of a fountain.

Steve Canyon, the comic strip creation of Milt Caniff, bore more realistic proportions than did Popeye. For no good reason except to honor the servicemen and -women of World War II, Colorado's Squirrel Gulch was renamed Steve Canyon in 1947. Two years later, the nearby town of Idaho Springs commissioned a forty-foot-tall statue of Caniff's wartime hero, and from all reports it is still there. According to visitors, the commemorative plaque cites the U.S. Treasury Department's salute to "Steve Canyon, and through him, all American cartoon characters who serve the nation." (Perhaps it is significant that at the time the text on that plaque was composed, the U.S. Army had not yet recruited Beetle Bailey.)

An even more super but equally fictitious American hero took up residence in the small town of Metropolis, Illinois. And who might that be? Let's see . . . which cartoon hero spent most of his time in a place called Metropolis? It couldn't have been Superman, you reply, since his Metropolis was merely a pseudonym for New York City. Ah, but you would be wrong. Even though the Illinois burg more closely resembled Clark Kent's hometown of Smallville, in 1972, Metropolis made a deal with DC Comics and was officially declared the "Hometown of Superman," with grandiose plans for a fifty-million-dollar theme park to be known as the Amazing World of Superman.

The most comprehensive collection of material from this attraction-that-never-was can be found at the Superman website www.fortress-of-solitude. net. There one can see a list of the features this thousand-acre wonder world would have presented, beginning with the two-hundred-foot-tall statue of Superman straddling the entrance gate. It should be obvious by now that the idea of building this sort of amusement park in rural southern Illinois turned out to be as implausible as Superman himself, and for the next decade, all was quiet in Metropolis, even as the town steadfastly maintained its licensing agreement with DC.

In 1986, Metropolis finally took a cue from all those Popeye statues and erected its own Superman (seven feet tall, not the two-hundred-foot one) in the town square. One wit who saw the original statue remarked that the statue of the Big Boy in checkered overalls in front of hundreds of restaurants had a better physique. Finally, Metropolis got a much more super-duper

This Popeye statue once stood guard in front of the Popeye Spinach canning plant in Lowell, Arkansas. (Debra Jane Seltzer collection)

This considerably more accurate rendition of the superest superhero of them all replaced the rather deformed version of Superman that originally graced the town square in Metropolis, Illinois.

Superman in 1993; in one of those photo ops made in heaven, local newspapers carried photos of the statue, chained to a flatbed truck, as it stopped in Chester en route to Metropolis. The mayor's little daughter was pictured offering a can of Popeye Spinach to the imprisoned superguy, helping him fortify for the journey ahead.

It did not always take millions of dollars to create a memorable attraction. In 1956, the Dennis the Menace Playground in Monterey, California, was dedicated. It was designed in part by Hank Ketcham, with able assistance from former Hollywood movie set designer Arch Garner. Its beauty was in its simplicity: as Ketcham later explained, the idea was to replace the old-fashioned (and often hazardous) swings and slides with abstract shapes on which kids could play, using their imaginations to decide what each one should be. Although it has been updated several times, the Dennis the Menace Playground demonstrates that at least in the world of roadside attractions, sometimes less really is more.

Chapter 10

TO INFINITY AND BEYOND

It's been quite a journey so far, hasn't it? But it isn't quite over yet. Just because the last of the baby boomers were graduating from high school (and thus ending their childhood) in the early 1980s, the business of licensing cartoon characters for merchandise was not going away. Instead, it only seems to have increased, although with less variety than was seen from the 1950s to the 1970s. Like seemingly almost everything else in American life, licensing has come down to a few huge corporations rather than the many different companies and individuals who once controlled it.

Since none of these corporations is bigger than Disney, we should spend some time seeing how its approach to licensing changed as the twenty-first century loomed. As we have seen in every chapter, merchandising had been a major income producer for Disney since the earliest days, but by the late 1970s and early 1980s, things were going less well. Most of the merchandise continued to feature the staples: Mickey, Minnie, Donald, Goofy, and Pluto, with occasional appearances by the second tier, including Ludwig Von Drake and Uncle Scrooge. Merchandise based on the animated features tended to run in the same cycles as those films' periodic theatrical re-releases, generally every seven years or so. In other words, besides records (which seem to have been available in perpetuity), it would be difficult to find *Snow White*, *Pinocchio*, or *Jungle Book* merchandise when those films were not playing in theaters. The catalyst for the big change in that regard was the advent of home video in the early 1980s.

At first, Disney's VHS/Beta/laserdisc releases of the animated classics were considered as something of an extension of the theatrical schedule; they would be made available for a while, then withdrawn. While that is still done occasionally in this era of DVDs and Blu-Ray, practically anyone can have access to any Disney animated feature whenever they want it—and the merchandising has responded accordingly. Since Michael Eisner assumed control of the struggling studio in 1984, each animated feature beginning with *The Little Mermaid* (1989) has spawned more merchandise than any of the previous releases ever did. Perhaps for this reason as well as new corporate-brand-based concepts, today's merchandise seems to have a cookie-cutter sameness to it. As we have seen, for most of the history of licensed items, every toy, book, puzzle, game, or whatever had artwork—frequently quite stunning—created especially

Tinker Bell was once the secret crush of thousands of American boys, but since becoming a big star of the "Disney Fairies" merchandise line in the twenty-first century, she no longer has time to pay attention to her old beaus.

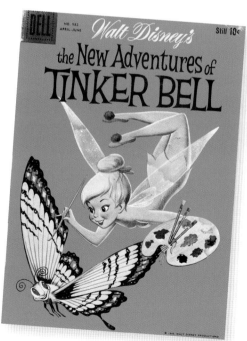

for that item. Today's merchandise has a set of corporate-approved depictions of each character that are used over and over again for multiple types of merchandise.

With the new emphasis on animated features, Disney began coming up with ways to group characters that had originated in varying productions. One of the most successful of these has been the Disney Princesses campaign, which historian Jim Korkis credits to Disney's consumer products chair, Andy Mooney. At the launch of the line in 2000, Mooney was quoted as stating, "The Disney Princess brand is a natural extension of these timeless stories and characters, and enables a girl to become a part of the world of her favorite princess." As Korkis has also rightly pointed out, the brand would not have been feasible prior to the Eisner era; incredible as it sounds, until 1989, Disney had only three princesses: Snow White, Cinderella, and Sleeping Beauty. *The Little Mermaid* was the first of the animated features in the new princess parade, and it shows no sign of abating any time soon.

(More imagination had to be required when introducing the companion "Disney Fairies" brand. Since Tinker Bell had no prior known peers, a cast of similarly shapely companions had to be created to fill the massive needs of the home video, theatrical feature, and merchandising markets. It is interesting that Disney has found its greatest merchandising success with the audience of young girls, especially since for decades, many boys secretly had crushes on Tinker Bell. Sorry . . . she belongs to the world now, guys.)

Not all ran smoothly for the house that Mickey built, though. From many, many pages ago you will remember being introduced to Shirley Slesinger, who cheerfully sold her family's long-held merchandising rights to Winnie-the-Pooh to Walt back in 1964, with a certain percentage of the profits still owed to the Slesingers. Trouble in the Hundred Acre Wood began when Shirley began noticing Pooh items for which she was not receiving any compensation. By 1991, she had enough evidence to file a lawsuit, and in so doing, she managed to keep the Slesinger, Disney, and Pooh names in the media for many more years. Shirley died in 2007, with the lawsuit still unsettled; it finally ended in 2009, with terms undisclosed but apparently satisfactory to all involved, since more Pooh merchandise is now being sold now than even when Sears had its exclusive line.

Those who had followed Disney history for years were stunned by an out-of-the-blue incident in 2006, while the general public likely wondered what all the fuss was about. NBC Universal wanted to buy out the contract of sportscaster Al Michaels, who was at the time gainfully employed by Disney's ABC-TV and ESPN subsidiaries. Disney CEO Bob Iger came back with

The unexpected success of *Who Framed Roger Rabbit* in 1988 produced a flood of tie-in merchandise, but its time on store shelves was relatively brief.

Each time a beloved cartoon series was adapted into a live-action feature film, such as with Universal's *The Flintstones* (1994), the related merchandise was equally likely to depict the original characters or the actors who played them in the new movie.

FLINTSTONES ARE HERE!

Get in on the rock buster product event of 1994!

an offer that made some jaws drop: Disney would release Michaels from his contract if NBC Universal would give back Oswald the Rabbit. "Done, and done," as the saying goes, and almost eighty years after Walt lost his first merchandised character, the lucky rabbit came home. (This only applied to the original Disney version of Oswald; presumably NBC Universal still owns the version used by Walter Lantz and the innumerable artists and writers from Western Printing over the decades.) The Disney company wasted no time in rushing out new merchandise featuring old Oswald and has made him a major character in its highly successful "Epic Mickey" video game series. If anyone had suggested this scenario in 1928, they might have been branded a looney toon.

Speaking of Looney Tunes, that was another of the big success stories of the 1980s and 1990s. Things had certainly changed since the days when Leon Schlesinger handled the licensing for Bugs and his buddies or even when they were controlled by "Warner Bros. Cartoons Inc." Somewhere along the way, Warner Bros. merged with magazine publisher Time to become Time-Warner, and with that international conglomerate behind them, the Looney Tunes characters became more visible than they had been in years. Part of this newfound popularity resulted from the fact that large chunks of the Warner Bros. cartoon library, syndicated to local stations since 1956, were now airing on cable TV, bringing them to a huge nationwide audience. (The Saturday morning *Bugs Bunny Show* remained a fixture, but its selection of cartoons had mysteriously shrunk over the years, and the ones that were still airing were butchered beyond all logic to make them "safe" for 1980s kid viewers.)

In 1985, the Warner Bros. characters became the official mascots for the chain of Six Flags theme parks, at last finding a permanent home. Time-Warner also owned the DC Comics characters, so Superman, Batman, Wonder Woman, et al. also made the scene at Six Flags. In fact, the ever-growing theme park industry provided comfortable accommodations for many cartoon icons of the past. The thinking used to be that no one could run a successful theme park but Disney, but the success of Six Flags and Kings Island had proven that canard to be wrong.

In 1983, the *Peanuts* characters moved into their own Camp Snoopy area in California's fabled Knott's Berry Farm and became a part of the enormous park housed inside Minnesota's Mall of

America. The debut of this new theme park prompted McDonald's to issue yet another set of drinking glasses, and the number of those available on the collectors' market today is certainly second only to Pepsi's 1973 Looney Tunes designs. Although the Minnesota Camp Snoopy was later handed over to the animated characters owned by the Nickelodeon network, the original at Knott's is still full of happy campers. In the spring of 2014, Knott's announced that its train ride would be enlivened with animatronic *Peanuts* characters acting out scenes from their adventurous camping trip in the High Sierras.

In 1987, New England Playworld in New Hampshire defied all logic by licensing the Terrytoons characters as its mascots. By that time, a few nostalgic people might have remembered Mighty Mouse and Heckle and Jeckle, but only the most rabid cartoon fans could have been expected to know who Lariat Sam or Sad Cat were.

California's Ocean World hooked Popeye and his cast in 1994 and made as much use of them as possible. One of the rides had Popeye's head with multiple arms supporting its swings; when in motion, it resembled Popeye after having eaten a can of spinach, whirling around with a multitude of arms and fists. There was also an arcade when kids could fire at various Popeye character targets, a successful hit triggering funny dialogue in close approximations of the established voices.

This was just the forerunner to an announcement during the annual Popeye's Picnic celebration in creator Elzie Segar's home town of Chester, Illinois, held in September 1994. Representatives from King Features Syndicate and Universal Studios Orlando staged an elaborate ceremony to announce that Popeye would be getting his own theme park, Islands of Adventure. Costumed actors representing Popeye, Olive Oyl, and Brutus acted out a skit in which the big bully tried to sign the Universal contract but, thanks to the timely application of a can of spinach, Popeye triumphed and was able to

In 1985, Bugs Bunny and the rest of the Warner Bros. crowd moved into the Six Flags theme parks for a long stay. They were eventually joined by the DC Comics superheroes.

Chester, Illinois, was the setting for Universal's 1994 announcement of its new theme park, at that time promoted as Popeye's Islands of Adventure. Comic book artist George Wildman was on hand to be photographed with Universal's Popeye as well as "one million cans" (give or take a few) of Allen's Popeye Spinach. (Donnie Pitchford collection)

sing, "Let's start the rehearsal / To go to Universal / I'm Popeye the Sailor Man!" (Okay, we know that all of you are mentally adding "toot toot" to the end of that, so we'll just go ahead and do it for you.)

When Islands of Adventure finally opened, Popeye turned out to not be the center of attention. He was one of several King Features properties assigned to the new park's Toon Lagoon section; Universal also got the rights to the Jay Ward characters, so Rocky, Bullwinkle, Dudley Do-Right, and others roamed the property. (Undoubtedly as part of the same deal, Universal released a live-action *Rocky and Bullwinkle* feature film in the summer of 2000.) In addition, Universal had been using Woody Woodpecker and the other Walter Lantz characters—their familiarity to general audiences unfortunately declining—since its opening, so that particular Florida theme park ended up with quite an eclectic mix of characters of various origins.

Speaking of eclectic mixes, that, too, became a factor in the puzzle of determining who controlled which licensed properties. Media mogul Ted Turner, a cartoon fan with more than the average money, busied himself with buying up the rights to various film libraries and their characters to exploit on his various cable television networks, and his largest acquisitions included the MGM cartoons and the Hanna-Barbera studio. Things really got strange when Turner sold his various holdings to Time-Warner; for the first time in history, the Warner Bros. characters, Tom and Jerry and their MGM cohorts, and the vast Hanna-Barbera cast of characters were all under common ownership. Time-Warner wasted no time in producing some of the most unusual merchandise to hit the market, combining Tom and Jerry with Tweety and Sylvester, to give just one example.

Then, in the summer of 2012, another merger created some even stranger bedfellows in Toontown. Dreamworks Animation announced its intention to acquire the properties belonging to Classic Media, which had for years been buying up rights to various characters from many different owners. When the deal went through, suddenly Dreamworks found itself the new home for (among others) the Archie Comics cast, the Total TeleVision shows, the Harvey Comics characters, United Productions of America's properties (most importantly Mister Magoo), Felix the Cat, and the Jay Ward characters. It is too soon to know just how this move will affect any future merchandising, but it does seem more than notable that virtually every famous animated or comic book character is now owned by Disney, Time-Warner, or Dreamworks.

Newspaper comic strips are a different matter, although the steadily dwindling readership for printed newspapers has caused some turmoil in that world, too. Fortunately, the strips also have a strong Internet presence, but merchandise based on them is becoming rare—other than that old standard, the strip reprint book, which seems to be as healthy as ever.

When Taco Bell enlisted the Flintstones for a 1995 promotion, it strangely decided to use versions of the characters based on original rough sketches that never made it onto the air.

The connection between cartoon characters and grocery products was just as strong in the 1990s as it had ever been.

Even though Soaky and Bubble Club were no longer being marketed, other manufacturers have taken up the slack and sold figural bubble bath bottles of many newer cartoon stars.

Back in 1978, Charles Schulz negotiated a new contract with United Feature Syndicate that gave him the right to approve any new potential piece of *Peanuts* merchandise. As he told interviewers at the time, he was not bothered by anything that <u>had</u> happened as much as he was afraid of what <u>might</u> happen if he did not insist on such control. We may never know what suggested items were killed under this new arrangement, but it put to rest the question of having "ghost artists" creating the artwork for such merchandise. From that point on, Schulz's staff became diligent in making sure that only authentic drawings that had first appeared in the strip were used. As Schulz developed a more-than-noticeable tremor in his hand following heart surgery, his drawing style followed a wavy line, and even a casual observer will note that the no-longer-smooth outlines of Charlie Brown, Snoopy, and the others carried over into their merchandising appearances.

While one can no longer go into a store and buy a new Give-A-Show Projector or Rub-Ons or Gloppy (at least not under those names, as old concepts have a way of returning after a new generation comes along), many of the toy types we have seen are still available in one form or another. View-Masters and their reels can still be purchased, although as pointed out earlier, the beautiful dimensional representations of cartoon characters were long ago nixed in favor of flat artwork that conforms to the studios' concern for a consistent image. Neither Soaky nor Bubble Club has made a comeback as a brand, but other companies continue to turn out cartoon bubble bath bottles based on current hit characters. Metal lunch boxes from Aladdin and Thermos ceased production in the mid-1980s, but especially during the Christmas season, manufacturers will often market metal boxes with nostalgic graphics of beloved characters as novelty gift items.

A unique phenomenon to hit the world of merchandising began with the somewhat unexpected success of Pixar Animation Studios' *Toy Story* in November 1995. Even though Disney had signed on to distribute the film, no one was quite certain how audiences would respond to an animated feature created by computer—although, as the Pixar people have been pointing out ever since, real artists still have to work with those computers. The first *Toy Story* produced most of the usual types of merchandise related to a new animated movie, but manufacturers still seemed cautious about this untested type of entertainment. They were caught off guard when the toys in the movie inspired a run on their real-life toy equivalents. The movie's comical and rustic Slinky Dog was no longer even being produced, having been discontinued by James Industries in 1991 (and that item had never resembled the Pixar version very closely). By the time the demand for new Slinky Dogs began, James Industries had to rush a new model into production, missing the prime 1995 holiday buying season.

When *Toy Story 2* was released in 1999, someone had been paying attention to the history of licensed products (even without this book to help them out). The origins of Woody the Cowboy had been left vague in the first film, but now he was revealed to be the centerpiece of an entire merchandising campaign from a 1950s children's TV show that gently parodied *Howdy Doody*. The Pixar artists

Toy Story (1995) and its sequels were unique in that they were movies about character merchandise that generated *more* character merchandise. By the time of this Burger King promotion, an animated film's release on home video produced as much fanfare as the original theatrical debut.

obviously reveled in their assignment to create a visual world of collectors' items from this fictional program, with the on-screen results being more than believable. There was also a funny inside joke relating to the original film. In a store meant to spoof Toys"R"Us and other such big-box retailers, tour guide Barbie points out the Buzz Lightyear aisle and chirps, "In 1995, shortsighted retailers failed to order sufficient quantities."

The *Toy Story* films did something that no other previous animated movies had: in the film, the toys were depicted in their original packaging, as they would be found on store shelves. Then, real kids went to toy stores and saw the toys in the same packages in which they had been seen in the movie. There really had been no precedent for licensed merchandise being featured so prominently in the very cartoons from which it was being licensed, so just trying to imagine the funhouse-mirror-type *Toy Story* effect is enough to make one's head swim. And just to make the view even more confusing, in 2000, Disney premiered an animated TV series, *Buzz Lightyear of Star Command*, intended to represent the cartoon on which the movies' Buzz toy was based. Buzz's famous motto, "To infinity and beyond," had come to represent the entire licensing phenomenon.

So, in keeping with that thought, even though the story of cartoon character merchandising had a definite beginning, there will apparently never be an end. It seems appropriate to close with a story Charles Schulz—who certainly had a few experiences when it came to the topic—told historian Michael Barrier in 1988.

> I was driving along one day, and came to a stop sign, and there was a truck in front of me, and glued to the window of that truck was a little cartoon character of Yosemite Sam. Now, I defy you to tell me what Yosemite Sam has done. . . . He was a funny character, but you can't tell me anything he ever did, really, or that he ever said. And yet, this just showed me that people like cartoon characters. . . . I think this was the foundation of cartoon licensing; people just like cartoons, that's all. . . . If you can come up with a cartoon character that is even more appealing than the others, then it's a real natural, and I think that's where it all starts.

> And that's where this all ends.
> That's all, folks!

BIBLIOGRAPHY

Abbott, Judi. "Boop Boop a Doop!" *Country Accents Collectibles*, Winter 1994.

Abraham, Adam. *When Magoo Flew: The Rise and Fall of Animation Studio UPA*. Middletown, Conn.: Wesleyan University Press, 2012.

Adams, T. R. *The Flintstones: A Modern Stone Age Phenomenon*. Atlanta: Turner, 1994.

Adamson, Joe. *Tex Avery: King of Cartoons*. New York: Popular Library, 1975.

——. *The Walter Lantz Story, with Woody Woodpecker and Friends*. New York: Putnam's, 1985.

Arnold, Mark. *Created and Produced by Total TeleVision Productions*. Albany, Ga.: BearManor, 2009.

——. "Evanier, Spiegle, and a Dog Named Scooby-Doo." *Back Issue*, October 2011.

——. "Hanna-Barbera at Marvel Comics." *Back Issue*, September 2012.

Ault, Donald, ed. *Carl Barks: Conversations*. Jackson: University Press of Mississippi, 2003.

Bang, Derrick. "Jim Sasseville: The Ghost in the (Peanuts) Machine." *Comics Buyer's Guide*, February 8, 2002.

Barrier, Michael. *Hollywood Cartoons: American Animation in Its Golden Age*. New York: Oxford University Press, 1999.

Barrier, Michael, and Martin Williams, eds. *A Smithsonian Book of Comic-Book Comics*. New York: Abrams, 1981.

Beck, Jerry. "Dreamworks to Acquire Classic Media." CartoonBrew.com, July 16, 2012.

——. *The Hanna-Barbera Treasures*. San Rafael, Calif.: Insight, 2007.

——. *Pink Panther: The Ultimate Guide to the Coolest Cat in Town*. New York: DK, 2005.

Bennett, Julie. "What Really Happened to Minnie Pearl Fried Chicken?" *Franchise Times*, June–July 2007.

Bigbee, Nelle. "Buster Brown Living Trademark." *Birmingham (Ala.) News*, October 16, 1972.

Blackwell, Sam. "Memories of Wimpy's." *Cape Girardeau (Mo.) Southeast Missourian*, July 27, 1997.

Blitz, Marcia. *Donald Duck*. New York: Harmony, 1984.

Borgzinner, Jon. "Inept Heroes, Winners at Last." *Look*, March 17, 1967.

Bradley, Eric. "Kings Island Honors Its Roots." *Cincinnati Enquirer*, September 6, 2009.

Brown, David, and Virginia Brown. *Whitman Juvenile Books*. Paducah, Ky.: Collector, 1997.

Brown, Rodger Lyle. "In Arkansas, a Dogpatch Way Past Its Prime." *Atlanta Journal-Constitution*, July 11, 1993.

Bruce, Scott. *The Fifties and Sixties Lunch Box*. San Francisco: Chronicle, 1988.

Bruegman, Bill. *Cartoon Friends of the Baby Boom Era*. Akron, Ohio: Cap'n Penny, 1993.

"Bubblegum Banks." *Country Accents Collectibles*, Winter 1999.

Burke, Timothy, and Kevin Burke. *Saturday Morning Fever: Growing Up with Cartoon Culture*. New York: St. Martin's Griffin, 1999.

Cabarga, Leslie. *The Fleischer Story*. New York: Da Capo, 1987.

Canemaker, John. *Felix: The Twisted Tale of the World's Most Famous Cat*. New York: Pantheon, 1991.

Cawley, John, and Jim Korkis. *The Encyclopedia of Cartoon Superstars*. Las Vegas: Pioneer, 1990.

"Chalkware: Yesterday's Amusement Park Prizes." *Country Accents Collectibles*, Spring 1995.

Chase, Mark E., and Michael Kelly. *Contemporary Fast-Food and Drinking Glass Collectibles*. Radnor, Penn.: Wallace-Homestead, 1988.

Conrad, Barnaby. "Good Ol' Charlie Schulz." *The 1970 World Book Year Book*. Chicago: Field, 1970.

Daniels, Les. *Batman: The Complete History*. San Francisco: Chronicle, 1999.

———. *Superman: The Complete History*. San Francisco: Chronicle, 1998.

———. *Wonder Woman: The Complete History*. San Francisco: Chronicle, 2000.

Davis, Greg, and Bill Morgan. *Collector's Guide to TV Toys and Memorabilia: 1960s and 1970s*. Paducah, Ky.: Collector, 1999.

"Dogpatch Lawsuit Finalized Tuesday; New Owners Named." *Harrison (Ark.) Daily Times*, May 4, 2011.

Ellison, Harlan, ed. *Li'l Abner Meets the Shmoo*. Princeton, Wis.: Kitchen Sink, 1992.

Finch, Christopher. *Winnie-the-Pooh: A Celebration of the Silly Old Bear*. New York: Disney, 2000.

Frey, Tom. *Toy Bop: Kid Classics of the Fifties and Sixties*. Murrysville, Penn.: Fuzzy Dice, 1994.

Garshman, Barbara J. "Bubble Bath Bottles." *Country Accents Collectibles*, Spring 1995.

Gershon, Freddie. "Myrna's Prehistoric Journey to 'Yabba Dabba Doo.'" *Huffington Post*, October 7, 2010.

Giarrusso, Michael A. "Toy Story Co-Star Left in Yule Lurch as Production Falters." Associated Press, December 19, 1995.

Goldschmidt, Rick. *The Enchanted World of Rankin/Bass*. Issaquah, Wash.: Tiger Mountain Press, 1997.

Grandinetti, Fred. *Popeye the Collectible*. Iola, Wis.: Krause, 1990.

Grendahl, Spencer. "The Mickey Mouse Trap." *Crawdaddy*, February 1977.

Hake, Ted. "A Mouse in the House." *Country Accents Collectibles*, Winter 1996.

———. "Yabba Dabba Doo! The Flintstones Hit Forty." *Country Accents Collectibles*, Summer 2000.

Hargrove, Thomas. "Stores Sad to See Comic Go." Scripps Howard News Service, December 18, 1999.

Harmon, Larry, and Thomas Scott McKenzie. *The Man behind the Nose*. New York: HarperCollins, 2010.

Heide, Robert, and John Gilman. *Cartoon Collectibles: 50 Years of Dime-Store Memorabilia*. Garden City, N.Y.: Doubleday, 1983.

———. *Disneyana: Classic Collectibles, 1928–1958*. New York: Hyperion, 1994.

———. *Mickey Mouse: The Evolution, the Legend, the Phenomenon*. New York: Disney, 2001.

Hollis, Tim. *Ain't That a Knee-Slapper: Rural Comedy in the Twentieth Century*. Jackson: University Press of Mississippi, 2008.

———. *Christmas Wishes: A Catalog of Holiday Treats and Treasures*. Mechanicsburg, Penn.: Stackpole, 2010.

———. *Hi There, Boys and Girls! America's Local Children's TV Programs*. Jackson: University Press of Mississippi, 2001.

———. *Part of a Complete Breakfast: Cereal Characters of the Baby Boom Era*. Gainesville: University Press of Florida, 2012.

Hollis, Tim, and Greg Ehrbar. *Mouse Tracks: The Story of Walt Disney Records*. Jackson: University Press of Mississippi, 2006.

"Hot Off the Drawing Board." *TV Guide*, February 2, 1963.

"How a Package Quadrupled a Market." *Business Week*, May 11, 1963.

Janzen, Jack, and Leon Janzen. "Disneyland's Book Store." *The "E" Ticket*, Fall 1999.

Johnson, Rheta Grimsley. *Good Grief: The Story of Charles M. Schulz*. New York: Pharos, 1989.

Johnston, David Cay. "Connie Boucher, Pioneer in Licensing Cartoon Characters." *New York Times*, December 27, 1995.

Kaonis, Donna C. "Mutt and Jeff." *Collectors Showcase*, December 1989.

Kelly, Selby Daley, and Steve Thompson. *Pogo Files for Pogophiles*. Richfield, Minn.: Spring Hollow, 1992.

Ketcham, Hank. *The Merchant of Dennis the Menace*. New York: Abbeville, 1990.

Kidd, Chip. *Peanuts: The Art of Charles M. Schulz*. New York: Pantheon, 2001.

Korkis, Jim. "Evolution of the Disney Princesses." MousePlanet.com, February 13, 2013.

———. "How Disney Fans Found Carl Barks." MousePlanet.com, July 25, 2012.

———. "Super Goof Flies Again." MousePlanet.com, January 16, 2013.

Korkis, Jim, and John Cawley. *Cartoon Confidential*. Westlake Village, Calif.: Malibu Graphics, 1991.

Lawson, Tim, and Alisa Persons. *The Magic behind the Voices: A Who's Who of Cartoon Voice Actors*. Jackson: University Press of Mississippi, 2004.

Lesser, Robert. *A Celebration of Comic Art and Memorabilia*. New York: Hawthorn, 1975.

Lifson, Hal. *Hal Lifson's 1966*. Chicago: Bonus, 2002.

"Li'l Abner Creator Al Capp Arrives at Dogpatch Today." *Harrison (Ark.) Daily Times*, October 2, 1967.

Litt, Jennie. "Jigsaw Puzzles." *Country Accents Collectibles*, Fall 1996.

Longest, David. *Character Toys and Collectibles: Second Series*. Paducah, Ky.: Collector, 1987.

———. *Collecting Disneyana*. Paducah, Ky.: Collector, 2008.

Maley, Don. "Super Roads to Riches Are Paved with Comics." *Editor and Publisher*, November 30, 1968.

Maltin, Leonard. *Of Mice and Magic: A History of American Animated Cartoons*. New York: New American Library, 1980.

Marcus, Leonard S. *Golden Legacy*. New York: Golden Books, 2007.

Margolin, Freddi Karin. *Peanuts: The Home Collection*. Iola, Wis.: Antique Trader, 1999.

———. "Where Collectors Get Snoopy." *Country Accents Collectibles*, Summer 1994.

Markowski, Carol, and Gene Markowski. *Tomart's Price Guide to Character and Promotional Glasses*. Radnor, Penn.: Wallace-Homestead, 1990.

McCracken, Harry. "There He Is to Save the Day." HarryMcCracken.com, August 6, 2007.

McKimson, Robert Jr. *"I Say, I Say . . . Son!" A Tribute to Legendary Animators Bob, Chuck, and Tom McKimson*. Solana Beach, Calif.: Santa Monica, 2012.

Mebane, John. *Collecting Nostalgia: A Guide to the Antiques of the Thirties and Forties*. New York: Arlington House, 1972.

Medrano, Eduardo. "Felix Chevrolet: A Tale of Two Kitties." SoCalAutoNews.com, 2008.

"Mellowed Kickapoo." *Newsweek*, February 22, 1965.

Mendelson, Lee. *Charlie Brown and Charlie Schulz*. Cleveland: World, 1970.

Mingo, Jack, and Erin Barrett. *Lunchbox: Inside and Out*. New York: HarperCollins, 2004.

Mirtle, Jack. *The Capitol Records Children's Series: 1944 to 1956: The Complete Discography*. Victoria, B.C.: First Choice, 2012.

Mittelbach, Margaret. "Colorforms." *Country Accents Collectibles*, Fall 1995.

———. "A PEZ of History." *Country Accents Collectibles*, Winter 1999.

———. "Pop Art." *Country Accents Collectibles*, Summer 1998.

———. "Pull-String Talking Toys." *Country Accents Collectibles*, Spring 1996.

———. "Trick or Treat." *Country Accents Collectibles*, Fall 1995.

Moore, Greg, and Joe Pizzo. *The Collector's Guide to Bubble Bath Containers*. Paducah, Ky.: Collector, 1999.

Muldavin, Peter. *The Complete Guide to Vintage Children's Records*. Paducah, Ky.: Collector, 2007.

Murray, R. Michael. *The Golden Age of Walt Disney Records, 1933–1988*. Dubuque, Iowa: Antique Trader, 1997.

Nesteroff, Kliph. "From Wall of Sound to Huckleberry Hound: The Vinyl Side of Hanna-Barbera." Blog.wfmu.org, August 12, 2007.

Nuhn, Roy. "Small Packages." *American Country Collectibles*, Winter 1997.

Ohmart, Ben. *Mel Blanc: The Man of a Thousand Voices*. Duncan, Okla.: BearManor, 2012.

Polizzi, Rick, and Fred Schafer. *Spin Again: Board Games from the Fifties and Sixties*. San Francisco: Chronicle, 1991.

Reed, Robert. "Quick Draws." *American Country Collectibles*, Fall 1996.

Rich, Mark. *100 Greatest Baby Boomer Toys*. Iola, Wis.: Krause, 2000.

Robinson, Jerry. *The Comics: An Illustrated History of Comic Strip Art*. New York: Putnam's, 1974.

Robison, Joleen, and Kay Sellers. *Advertising Dolls: Identification and Value Guide*. Paducah, Ky.: Collector, 1980.

Roden, Steve, and Dan Goodsell. *Krazy Kids' Food: Vintage Food Graphics*. Cologne, Germany: Taschen, 2003.

Rosenfeld, Megan. "Ed Justin Rules a Lucrative Empire of Names." *Washington Post*, January 31, 1973.

Sagendorf, Bud. *Popeye: The First Fifty Years*. New York: Workman, 1979.

Santi, Steve. *Collecting Little Golden Books*. Iola, Wis.: Krause, 1998.

Scheimer, Lou, and Andy Mangels. *Lou Scheimer: Creating the Filmation Generation*. Raleigh, N.C.: TwoMorrows, 2012.

Schneider, Stuart, and Bruce Zalkin. *Halloween Costumes and Other Treats*. Atglen, Penn.: Schiffer, 2001.

Schumacher, Michael, and Denis Kitchen. *Al Capp: A Life to the Contrary*. New York: Bloomsbury USA, 2012.

Scott, Keith. *The Moose That Roared*. New York: St. Martin's, 2000.

Scott, Vernon. "Restaurants Serve Up Mel Blanc Characters." United Press International, December 4, 1983.

Sell, Mary Ann, Wolfgang Sell, and Charley Van Pelt. *View-Master Memories*. Maineville, Ohio: Sell and Sell, 2007.

Stafford, Leon. "Popeyes Ditches Ex-Spinach-Eating Pitchman." *Atlanta Journal-Constitution*, November 26, 2012.

Sternfeld, Sue. "PEZ: Candy Dispenser Turned Pop Culture Icon." *Baby Boomer Collectibles*, January 1994.

———. "PEZ-Zazz." *Country Accents Collectibles*, Summer 1994.

Tennyson, Jeffrey. *Hamburger Heaven: The Illustrated History of the Hamburger*. New York: Hyperion, 1993.

"Terribly Excited Al Capp on Hand as Dogpatch Becomes a Real Place." *Little Rock Gazette*, May 19, 1968.

Thompson, Steven. "More Kings Island." BookStevesLibrary.blogspot.com, January 28, 2006.

Torcivia, Joe. "Happy Fiftieth Anniversary to Gold Key Comics." Tiahblog.blogspot.com, July 20, 2012.

Tucker, Ed. "Curse You, Red Baron! The True Story of the Royal Guardsmen." CrazedFanBoy.com, 2006.

Tumbusch, Tom. *Tomart's Illustrated Disneyana Catalog and Price Guide*. Dayton, Ohio: Tomart, 1987.

Van Citters, Darrell. *Mister Magoo's Christmas Carol: The Making of the First Animated Christmas Special*. Los Angeles: Oxberry, 2009.

White, James L. "Dogpatch Ownership Questioned." *Boone County (Ark.) Headlight*, June 24, 1999.

———. "Dogpatch Park Cleaned Up." *Harrison (Ark.) Daily Times*, August 25, 2005.

Wilkins, Mike, Ken Smith, and Doug Kirby. *The New Roadside America*. New York: Simon and Schuster, 1992.

Woodall, Allen, and Sean Brickell. *The Illustrated Encyclopedia of Metal Lunch Boxes*. West Chester, Penn.: Schiffer, 1992.

Yakomin, Lisa. "Everyone's Favorite Grey Hare." *Country Accents Collectibles*, Fall 1994.

"Yogi Bear's Chicken Holds Grand Opening." *Spartanburg (S.C.) Herald-Journal*, November 21, 1968.

"You're an Adman's Dream, Charlie Brown." *Business Week*, December 20, 1969.

Zillner, Dian. *Collectible Coloring Books*. West Chester, Penn.: Schiffer, 1992.

PERSONAL INTERVIEWS AND CORRESPONDENCE

Roy Abell, Adam Abraham, Mike Ambrose, Mark Arnold, Michael Barrier, Jerry Beck, Ken Beck, Jim Bennie, Mel Birnkrant, Betty Boyle, Eugene "Butch" Broome Jr., Julie Capp Cairol, Frank Caruso, Stephen DeStefano, Greg Ehrbar, Cathy Sherman Freeman, Myrna Gershon, Rick Goldschmidt, Doug Haag, Marcus Hamilton, Jerry Hooyman, Ernest Hueter Jr., Sid Jacobson, Mary Janaky, Mark Johnson, Raymond Keese,

Al Konetzni, Dick Krown, Arthur Lefave, Larry Leshan, Leonard Marcus, Harry McCracken, Janet McMurrin, Penny Peed, Donnie Pitchford, Christopher Radko, Steve Reisiger, Rita Rubin, Pat Saperstein, Bill Smith, Steve Thompson, Darrell Van Citters, Brian Walker, Tiffany Ward, Jim Webb, Betty Ren Wright, Dana Young

WEBSITES

AntiqueToyCollections.info
Blog.dailyink.com
CartoonBrew.com
CartoonResearch.com
CollectPeanuts.com
Fortress-Of-Solitude.net
Icanbreakaway.blogspot.com
KICentral.com
MelBirnkrant.com
MichaelBarrier.com
MousePlanet.com
MyTVToys.org
POVOnline.com
RoadsideAmerica.com
RoadsideArchitecture.com
YowpYowp.blogspot.com

Special photography by David Pridemore

INDEX

Page numbers in **bold** refer to illustrations.

ABC-TV, 21, 25, 27, 28, 41, 77, 163, 214, 279–80
Abell, Roy, 244–45
Adamson, Joe, 214–15
ADCO Liberty, 233
Air France, 15
Aladdin, 231–37, 285
Alameda, Calif., 210
Alice in Wonderland, 45, 54, 76, 97, 234
Alka-Seltzer, 223
Allen's Canning Co., 213, 274
Alley Oop, 240, 268
Alley Oop Fantasy Land, 268
Allied Chemical, 229, **230**
Alma, Ark., 275
Alvin and the Chipmunks, 89, 113, 114, 116, 145, 164–65, 194, 230, 237
Ambrose, Michael, 62, 64
Anaheim, Calif., 25, 77, 256
Andrews, Julie, 28, 105
Andy Capp, 97, 222, 237
Andy Panda, **16**, 17, 55, 73, 76, 79, 112, **121**, 136, 157, 158, 206, **207**
Apollo 10, 184
Apollo 16, 184, **185**
Aquaman, 86
Archie Comics, 61, **179**, 221, 227, 235, 258, 283
AristoCats, The, 45

Arnold, Mark, 60
Arrowhead, 229
Associated Artists Productions (AAP), 174
Astronut, 89
Atlanta, Ga., 218
Atom Ant, 145, 178, 235
Atomic Mouse, 59
Auburn University, 244
Auckland, N.Z., 247
Augie Doggie, 141
Aurora, **48**
Autry, Gene, 76
Avalon, Frankie, 184
Avery, Tex, **ii**, 214–15

Babes in Toyland, 149
Baby Huey, 19, 67, 89, 186
Backus, Jim, 171–72, 180
Bagdasarian, Ross, **113**, 164–65
Baker, George, 66
Ballard, Kaye, 182
Baltimore, Md., 254
Bambi, 97, 103, 118, 196, 242, **243**
Bambi Motel, 242, **243**
Banana Splits, The, 237, 269
Bang, Derrick, 57
Barbera, Joseph, 16, 20–23, 58
Barbie, 119, **127**, 133, 224, 237, 286
Barks, Carl, 50–51, 52, 57, 66, 84, 202

Barney Bear, 16, 57, **58**, 158

Barney Google (song), 149

Barney Google and Snuffy Smith, **37**, 38, 105, 121, 143, 149, 169, 194, 199, 245

Barrier, Michael, 286

Bartsch, Art, 68

Batman, 41–42, **48**, 49, 86, 105, 125, 128, 186, 187, 201, 224, **225**, 232, 280

Beaky Buzzard, 54, 155

Beals, Dick, 177

Bean, Orson, 182

Beany and Cecil, 115, 119, 123, 237

Beck, Jerry, 16

Bedford, Annie North, 74, 90

Bedrock City, 265–68

Bee Chemical Co., 114

Beetle Bailey, 37–38, 97, 121, 169, 194, 246, 275

Ben Cooper, **190**, **192**, 193–94

Benaderet, Bea, 168

Benny, Jack, 19, 153

Benny Burro, 57

Berman, Shelley, 178

Bestor, Don, 151

Betty Boop, 17–18, 209, 246

Bewitched, 121

Bibo, Irving, **156**, 158

Big Little Books, 54, 71–73, 74, 85–87, 91, 152, 202

Biloxi, Miss., 242, **246**

Birnkrant, Mel, 129–32

Bixby, Bill, 42

Blanc, Mel, 55, 154, 157, 158, 162, **167**, 168, 174, 177–78, 179–80, 188, 254

Blanc, Noel, 55

Blitz, Marcia, 51

Blondie, 35, 36, 38, 66, 69–70, 73, 89, 194, 235

Bloomington, Ind., 244

Bluebird Records, 150, 151, 174

Bogas, Ed, 184

Bonanza, 85

Borden, 217

Bosko, 15

Boston, Mass., 232

Boucher, Connie, 32, 95

Bourne, Saul, 151

Boy Named Charlie Brown, A, 33, 96

Bozo the Clown, 117, 120, 124, 129, 132, 141, 145, 152, 153, 165, 180, **189**, 235

Brach's, 197–98

Brady Bunch, The, 269, 271

Brer Rabbit, 55, 75, 108, 197, 208

Bringing Up Father, 9, 73, 246

Brooklyn, N.Y., 193

Broom Hilda, 40

Broome, Eugene, 247–48

Brown Shoe Company, 9

Bruce, Scott, 232, 237

Brunswick Records, 149

Bryan, Arthur Q., 154, 162

Bubble Club, 115–17, 273, **284**, 285

Buckley, Floyd, 150, 152, 174

Buddy, 15

Buell, Marjorie, 19, 66

Bugs Bunny, ii, **6**, 16, 20, 53, 54, 73, 75, 76, 78–79, 86, 98, 103, 108, **109**, 113, 120, 123, 132, 136, **142**, 145, 146, 154, 155, 162, 174, 180, **181**, 186, 194, 197–98, 214–17, 223, 224, 242, 254–55, 271–72, 280, **281**

Bugs Bunny Follies, The, 188, **189**

Bugs Bunny Motel, 242, 272

Bugs Bunny Vitamins, 224

Buitoni, 213

Bullwinkle, 24–25, 62, **63**, 81–82, 97, 124, 128, 138, 141, 145, 169–70, 193, 194, 223, 228, 230, 237, 254, 282

Bullwinkle's Family Restaurants, 254

Bunnell, Fla., 265

Burger King, 252, **285**

Burton, Corey, 254

Business Week, 33, 34, 38, 113, 220, 239

Buster Brown, 8–9

Buster Brown Textile Company, 9

Butler, Daws, 154, 157, 166, **167**, 176–77, 178

Butternut bread, 218
Buzzy the Crow, 19, 89

C. A. Reed, 205–6
Calvin and Hobbes, 39
Camarata, Tutti, 164
Cameo, 122
Candy Land, 108
Caniff, Milt, 275
Cape Girardeau, Mo., 244
Capitol Records, 152–55, 158, 159, 160, 162, 165, 180, 188, **189**
Caplin, Elliot, 68
Captain America, 222
Captain and the Kids, The, 8
Captain Kangaroo, 123, 146, 237
Captain Paul, 174
Capp, Al, 40, 68, 179, 218, 247, 259–61
Capps, Al, 179
Carlton Cards, 199, **200**
Carney, Art, 247
Carowinds, 271
Carter, Lynda, 42, 186
Casper the Friendly Ghost, 19, 66–67, 89, 108, 117, 120, 123, 125, 133, 138, 145, 160, 161, 172–73, 184–86, 194–95, 208, 218, 221, 222, 258
Cat in the Hat, 123
CBS-TV, 17, 33, 68–69, 161, 162
Change-a-Channel TV Set, **144**, 145
Charlie Brown Christmas, A, 32, 33, 95
Charlie Brown's All-Stars, 32–33, 96
Charlie Chicken, 55, 79, 136, 206
Charlie McCarthy, 256
Charlotte, N.C., 271
Charlton Comics, 59–63, 65, 70, 250
Chatty Cathy, 119, 120
Cherokee, N.C., 243
Chester, Ill., 274–75, 276, 281–82
Chicago, Ill., 71, 272
Chicago Tribune, 71
Child Guidance, 106

Chilly Willy, 112, 136, 206
Chocks, 223
Christensen, Don, 86
Christmas Wishes, 124
Chuck E. Cheese, 254
Cincinnati, Ohio, 268, 271
Cinderella, 15, 45, **80**, 97, 147, 153, 279
Citrus World, 212
Clarabelle Cow, 13, 84
Classic Media, 283
Clyde Crashcup, 89
Coca-Cola, **228**, 229
Colgate-Palmolive, 113–17, 118
Collegeville, Penn., 193
Collegeville Costumes, 193–94
Colorforms, 128–32, 133
Colpix Records, 166, 167, 169, 176, 178, 182, 188
Columbia Pictures, **14**, 15, 20–21, 23, 35, 69, 166
Colvig, Pinto, 152, 153, 160
ConAgra Foods, 222
Conrad, Con, 149
Conrad, William, 24
Cooper, Harris, 252
Copeland, Al, 249–50
Corden, Henry, 178
Costello, William, 150, 151
Crawford, Mel, 82
Cricket Records, **156**, 158, 172, 173, 174, 183, 186
Crockett, Davy, 153, 157
Crosby, Cathy Lee, 42
Crosby, Percy, 210
Crusader Rabbit, 89
Crystal City, Tex., 273–74
Custer, S.D., 265, **266**
Cuti, Nicola, 60, 62

Daffy Duck, 54, 154, 155, 162, 217, 224, 272
Dagwood's Sandwich Shops, 255
Dairy Queen, 252–53, **254**
Daniels, Les, 41, 42

Danville, Va., 265

David McKay, 70

DC Comics, 19, 41–42, **43**, 69, 125, 147, 186–87, **203**, 228, 258, 275, 280, **281**

Decca Records, 154, 157

Dell Publishing, 50–58, 62, 68, 75, 76, 79, 84, 87, 98, 103, 176

Dempster, Al, 75

Dennis the Menace, 8, 36–37, 59, 97, 167, 202, 252–53, **254**, 276

Dennis the Menace Playground, 276

Deputy Dawg, 17, 89, 113, 116, 237

Destefano, Stephen, 213

Determined Productions, 32, 95

Dick Tracy, 23–24, 71, 72, 86, 116, 121, 128, 129, 143, **190**, 235

Dinky Doodle, 10

Dinky Duck, 68, 88, 159

Dino Boy, 105

Dinty Moore's, 246

Dippy Dawg. *See* Goofy

Dirks, Rudolph, 8

Disney, Roy, 11

Disney, Walt, 10–15, 17, 25–30, 38, 45, 51, **54**, 55, 72, 77, 151, 256–57, 279, 280

Disney Fairies, **278**, 279

Disney Magazine, 242

Disney on Parade, 188, 257

Disney Princesses, **80**, 198, 279

Disneykins, 123

Disneyland (park), 25, 77–78, 79–80, 84, 97, 101–3, 108, **109**, 111–12, 201, 233, 256–57, 258, 259, 261, 268

Disneyland (TV show), 25, 77

Disneyland Records, 163–64, 170–71, 172, 176, **177**, 184, 186, 187, 241

Dixon, Ill., 213

Doctor Dolittle, 123

Doctor Seuss, 39, 53

Dodd, Jimmie, 163

Dogpatch USA, 259–62, 265

Dollar, Al, 149

Dolly Madison, 218

Donald, Peter, 161

Donald Duck, **12**, 13, 22, 27, 28, 50–51, 53, 57, 66, 74, 76, 77, 78, 79–80, 84, 86, 98, 101, 103, 113, 116, 123, **124**, 129, 130, 138, 153, 160, 196, 197, 202, 211–12, 224, 225, 229, 230, 237, 241, 272, **273**, 277

Dora the Explorer, 224

Double-View Movie Viewer, 147

Dreamworks Animation, 283

Droopy, 57, **58**, 158

Dudley Do-Right, 62, **63**, 228, 282

Duenewald Printing, 98

Duncan, Herb, 169

Eagle, 230

Easy-Bake Oven, 133

Easy-Show Projector, 143–45, 147

Editor and Publisher, 244, 245, 247

Edwards, Sam, 164

Ehrbar, Greg, 163

Eisman, Hy, 8

Eisner, Michael, 46, 277, 279

Elias, Horace J., 90–91, 179

Elmer Fudd, 16, 54, 75, 78–79, 115, 134, 154, 155, 162, 217, 224

Etch-a-Sketch, 133

Evanier, Mark, 60–61

Fairbanks, Douglas, Jr., 159

Fallberg, Carl, 86

Family Circus, The, 97

Famous Studios, 19–20

Fantasia, 28

Fantastic Four, 86, 187

Farmer Al Falfa, 10, 17, 89, 162

Fat Albert, 235

Fawcett, John, 129

Fawcett Publishing, **93**, 95, 97

Felix, Winslow, 239

Felix Chevrolet, **238**, 239, 243

Felix the Cat, 10, 67–68, 69, 73, 88, 149, 173, 194, **238**, 239, 283

Ferrigno, Lou, 42

Filmation, 41, 227

Fisher-Price, **146**, 147

Flash Gordon, 59

Fleischer, Dave, 18–19

Fleischer, Max, 17–20, 150, 151, 269

Flintstones, The, 21, **22**, 23, 62, 82, 86, 91, 107–8, 109, 124, 141, 145, 167–68, 169, 177–78, 179, 188, 196, 198, 205–6, 217, 223–24, 226–27, 230, 235, 255, 265–68, 272, **280**, **283**

Flintstones Fun Bath, 117

Flintstones Vitamins, 223–24

Flipper, 85

Fontaine, Frank, 178

Foray, June, 153, 154, 155, 157, 169, 177, 254

Ford Motor Co., 239

Foster, Hal, 89, 159

Foster, Warren, 155

Fox, Philip, 167

Fox and Crow, 69

Frank 'n' Stein, 248

Frankenstein Jr., 86

Freberg, Stan, 153, 154, 157

Frees, Paul, 28, 84, 169, **170**, 171, 177, 179, 254

French Connection, The, 250

Frey, Tom, 128

Fun and Fancy Free, 153

Fung, Paul, Jr., 70

Funicello, Annette, 27, **80**, 210

Funky Phantom, 269

Funny Company, The, 84, 123

Futura, 205–6

G. I. Joe, 133

Gable, Clark, 179

Gadgets restaurants, 254–55

Gandy Goose, 17, 68, 89

Garfield, 40, 198

Garner, Arch, 276

General Aniline and Film (GAF), 145–46

General Electric, 27, 146

General Foods, 214–17

General Mills, 24–25, 214

Gerald McBoing Boing, 23

Gernhard, Phil, 182

Gesner, Clark, 182, 184

Gibson Greetings, 203

Gill, Joe, 60

Gilman, John, 11, 13, 191, 211

Giordano, Dick, 60

Girl Phantom, **59**

Give-a-Show Projector, 125, 139–43, 284

Gladstone Gander, 53

Gleason, Jackie, 247–48

Glendale, Ariz., 222

Gloppy, 125–26, 284

Gold, Ed, 244

Gold Key Comics, 58, 60, 62, **64**, 65, 69, 70, 85, 90, 176

Golden Legacy, 71–72

Golden Shape Books, 97–98

Goober and the Ghost Chasers, 235

Good Humor, 223

Goodie the Gremlin, 67

Goodmark Foods, 222

Goofy, 13, 28, 74, 77, 78, 84, 86, 98, 103, 113, 115, 130, 152, 153, 154, 160, 196, 197, 234, 277

Gould, Chester, 24

Goyette, Desiree, 184

Grandma Duck, 53

Great America, **271**, 272

Great Depression, 6, 11, 71, 129, 130, 210

Great Grape Ape, 93

Greatest Show on Earth, The, 257

Grendahl, Spencer, 46

Grosset and Dunlap, 87

Guaraldi, Vince, 182

Gulf Oil Co., **240**, 241–42

Gulliver's Travels, 18–19, 269

Gumby, 85

Gund, 121–22

Gyro Gearloose, 53

Haag, Doug, 262–63

Halco Costumes, 193–94

Hale, Dale, 57

Halifax, N.C., 248

Hall Brothers. *See* Hallmark Cards

Hallmark Cards, 195, 199, **200**, 203, 207–8

Hamlin, V. T., 240, 268

Hanna, William, 16, 20–23, 58

Hanna-Barbera Parade, **62**

Hanna-Barbera Productions, 20–23, 27, 35, 41, 42, **43**, 58, 60–62, **65**, 82–83, 86, 90–93, 98, 109, 115–17, 121, 123, 125–26, 128, 129, 137, **140**, 141, 145, 165–67, 176–79, 180, 188, **192**, 193, 196, 202, 213–14, 222, 230, 235, 236, 255, 262, 265, 268–70, 282–83

Hanna-Barbera Records, 176–79, 188

Hannah, Jack, 50

Happy Hooligan, 9

Happy Time Records, 187

Hardee's, 247, 252, 262

Harmon, Larry, 180

Harrison, Ark., 259

Hart's bread, 218

Hartsville, S.C., 249

Harvey Comics, 19, 66–67, 68, 70, 89, **90**, 115, 125, 138, 172–73, 184–86, 194, 221, 228, 258, 283

Harvey Records, 184–86

Hasbro, **2**, 120, 123–24, 125, 132, 215

Hearst, William Randolph, 7, 34

Heckle and Jeckle, 17, 68–69, 89, 141, 281

Hector Heathcote, 89

Heide, Robert, 11, 13, 191, 211

Help! It's the Hair Bear Bunch, 235

Hennessy, Jim, 33

Henry, 40, 89

Here Comes the Parade, 76

Herman, Woody, 152

Herman and Katnip, 19, 67, 89

Herriman, George, 38

He's Your Dog, Charlie Brown, 96

Hi-C, 218

Hicklin, Ron, 179

Hillbilly Bears, 269

Hillbilly Brew, 217

Hinnant, Bill, 182

Hogan's Alley, 7

Hokey Wolf, 82, 167, 196

Holt, Rinehart and Winston, **93**, 94–96

Homer Pigeon, 55, 79, 157, 206

Honey Halfwitch, 67

Honeymooners, The, 247

Hong Kong Phooey, 93, **142**, **190**

Hopalong Cassidy, 76, 209, 231

Hope, B.C., 268

Hoppity Hooper, 85

Horace Horsecollar, 13, 77, 84

Hormel, 246

Hostess, 221–22

Hot Stuff, 67, 186, 221

Howdy Doody, 76, 159, 199, 226, 227, 285

Huckleberry Hound, **2**, 3, 21, 22–23, 58, 82, 91, 105, 115, 121, 137, 140, 141, 145, 166–67, 177, 179, 202, **204**, 205, 206, 213, 230, 235

Hueter, Ernest, 220

Hungerford, 31

Hutton, Dan, 176, 179

Ice Capades, **256**, 257

Idaho Springs, Co., 275

Ideal Toys, 21, 106, 121, **122**

Iger, Bob, 279–80

Imco Container Co., 114

IMG Marketing, 36–37, 252–53

Inch High Private Eye, 235

Incredible Hulk, The, 42, 87, 187

Ingersoll-Waterbury Clock Company, 11

International Fiberglass, 248

Interstate Brands, 218–21, 245

Iraan, Tex., 268

Irving Berlin, Inc., 151

It's the Great Pumpkin, Charlie Brown, 32, 96

J. Chein & Co., 33

Jabberjaw, 93

Jacobson, Sid, 66–67, 184–86

James, Judy, 158

James Industries, 285

Janzen, Jack and Leon, 25

Jaymar, 101–5

Jellystone Park Campgrounds, 230, 262–65, 271

Jetsons, The, 21, 82, 91, 105, 109, 126, 169, 235

Jiminy Cricket, 103, 113, 115, 118, 234, 256, 257

Joe Palooka, 40, 209, 231

Johnson, Lyle, 33

Johnson, Mark, 246

Jones, Chuck, 39

Judge, Diane, **143**

Jun, Rose Marie, 169

Jungle Book, The, 97, 228, **229**, 230, 277

Jungle Habitat, **270**, 272

Justin, Ed, **20**, 21–23, **192**, 248, 262

Kamen, Kay, 11, 13, 15, 27, 71, 195, 211, 225

Kansas City, Mo., 10, 195

Karin, Fia, 171

Kartoon Disko, 187

Katzenjammer Haus, 245–46, 247

Katzenjammer Kids, The, 8, 245–46

Kaufman, Andy, 162

Kaye, Danny, 154

Kayo, 210

Kellogg's, 21, 24, 213–14

Kelly, Selby, 39

Kelly, Walt, 38–39, **92**, 93, 171, 193

Kelowna, B.C., 268

Ken Films, 148

Kenner, **34**, 125–26, 128, 139–45

Kentucky Fried Chicken, 245

Ketcham, Hank, 36–37, 252–53, **254**, 276

Kickapoo Joy Juice, 217–18

King Comics, 59, 60, 70, 176

King Features Syndicate, 18–20, 34–38, 58–59, 62, **65**, 66, 70, 89, **90**, 104, 121, 169, 175, 194, **203**, 213, 244, 245–46, 250–52, 281, 282

King Leonardo, 24

Kings Dominion, **270**, 271

Kings Island, 268–71, 280

Kipling, Rudyard, 97

Kislevitz, Harry, 128–29, 130

Knickerbocker Toys, 22–23, 121

Knott's Berry Farm, 280–81

Kojak, 187

Koko the Clown, 17

Konetzni, Al, 27, 101, 130, 131, 233–34

Kool-Aid, **6**, 214–17

Korkis, Jim, 53, 279

Krazy Kat, 38, 169, 246

Krondes, Jimmy, 184

Lady and the Tramp, 196

Lake Wales, Fla., 212

Lakewood, Colo., 242

LaMoy, Olive, 150

Lantz, Walter, 10, **16**, 17, **52**, 55, 58, 75, 76, 112, **121**, 152, **156**, 157, 159, 173, 206, **207**, 280, 282

Lariat Sam, 281

Lassie, 23

Lasswell, Fred, 38, 245

Laurie Records, 182

Lefave, Arthur, 37, 252–53

Lenox Ware, 229

Lerner, Sammy, 150

Lesser, Robert, 129

Lester, Robie, 164

Lewis, Bill, 244

Liberty Records, 165

Li'l Abner, 40, 68, 73, 108, 149, 179, 192, 194, 217–18, 246–47, 259–62, 268

Li'l Abner's Drive-In, 246–47

Li'l Abner's Steakhouse, 247, 249, 261

Li'l Genius, 59

Linus the Lionhearted, 85, 120, 143, 194, 237

Lion Country Safari, 272

Lionel trains, 11

Lippy the Lion, 82, 109, 117
Liptak, Joe, 137, 138
Lispi, Lou, 27
Lite-Brite, 132
Little Audrey, 19, 67, 89, 186
Little Dot, 67
Little Golden Books, 54, 58, 74–78, 80–84, 87, 90, 108, 159, 202
Little Golden Records, 158, 159–62, 163, 166–68, 169–71, 172, 173, 175, 176, 186, 188
Little King Restaurants, 245, 248
Little Lotta, 67
Little Lulu, 19, 66
Little Mermaid, The, 201, 277, 279
Little Nemo in Slumberland, 149
Little Orphan Annie, 71, 72, 149, **190**, 192, 199
Little Roquefort, 68
Livingston, Alan, 152, 153
Lloyd, Anne, 160
LoBianco, Nick, 33–34, 95, 132, 232
Lois and Clark, 41
Lombard, Carol, 179
Lone Ranger, The, 23, 255
Longchamps, 247
Looney Tunes, **14**, 15–16, 53–54, **103**, 151, 154, 157, 162, 201, **216**, 217, 272, 280, 281
Los Angeles, Calif., 74, 223, 239
Lowe, Samuel, 71–72
Lowell, 112
Lowell, Ark., 274
Lowell, Gene, 169
Ludwig Von Drake, 28, 53, 84, **102**, 103, 109, **170**, 171, 233, 241, 277
Luks, George, 7–8
Luno, the Soaring Stallion, 89

Macdonald, Jim, 153, 160
Mack, Gilbert, 166, **167**, 188
Macy's Thanksgiving Day Parade, 76, 122, 202
Magic Slate, 132–33
Magilla Gorilla, 83, 91, 105, 121, 126, 177, 205, **206**, 230

Mall of America, 280–81
Maltin, Leonard, 172
Man From U.N.C.L.E., The, 85
Mandrake the Magician, 59
Marcus, Leonard, 71–72
Markowski, Carol and Gene, 225
Marmaduke, 97
Marriott Corp., **271**, 272
Marvel Comics, 42, 49, 61, 68, 147, 187, 221, 222
Marx Toys, 123
Mary Poppins, 28, **44**, 105, 173, 230
Masour, Myrna, 21
Mattel, 119–20, 122–23, **127**
Mattel-O-Phone, 120
Matty Mattel, 119
McCay, Winsor, 149
McDonald's, 281
McGovern, Ann, 81
McKennon, Dallas, 164
McKimson, Tom, 75
McManus, George, 246
Meader, Vaughn, 182
Meet Me in St. Louis, 8
Melendez, Bill, 96, 220
Melmac, 229–30
Melvin, Allan, 177
Memphis, Tenn., **244**
Mendelson, Lee, 184
Mercer, Jack, 150, 160, 166, **167**, 175–76
Merrie Melodies, 15–16, 53–54, 154, 162, 188
Messick, Don, 166, 176–77
Messmer, Otto, 67–68
Metro-Goldwyn-Mayer (MGM), 16–17, 20, 57–58, 59, 75, 76, 158, 159, 182, 228, 282–83
Metropolis, Ill., **253**, 275–76
Miami, Fla., 255
Michaels, Al, 279–80
Mickey Mouse, 10–15, 27, 28, 45–47, 72, 73, 74, 76, 77, 78, 86, 98, 103, 113, 117, 123, 124, 129–31, 138, 153, 160–61, 173, 187,

191, 194, 195–96, 197, 199, 201, 202, 203, 207, **208**, 209–10, 224, 225, 228, 233, 239, 241, 255, 257, 277, 280

Mickey Mouse Club, The, **26**, 27, 45–47, 51, 163, 229–30, 233

Mickey Mouse Club Records, 27, 163

Mickey Mouse Magazine, 49

Mighty Hercules, The, 105

Mighty Mouse, 17, 41, 68–69, 88–89, 105, 113, 128, **138**, 141, 159, 161–62, 172, 202, 281

Mighty Mouse Playhouse, 161

Milano, Frank, 166, **167**, 188

Miles Laboratories, 223–24

Millbrook bread, 218

Milne, A. A., 28–29, 108

Milne, Daphne, 28–29

Milton Bradley, **100**, 106–8, 109, 111–12

Minkus, Barbara, 182

Minneapolis, Minn., 252

Minnie Pearl's Fried Chicken, 248

Mister Bug Goes to Town, 19

Mister Ed, 120

Mister I. Magination, 206

Mister Magoo, 23–24, 89, 112, 124, 128, 145, 171–72, 180, 194, 283

Mitchell, Walt, 154

Mittelbach, Margaret, 117–18

Modern Promotions, 90–93

Moe Hare, 19

Monath, Norman, 171

Monterrey, Calif., 276

Moon Mullins, 9, 210

Mooney, Andy, 279

Morrison, Bret, 158

Morton Grove, Ill., 246–47

Motormouse and Autocat, 269

Motorola, **190**

Mountain Dew, 217, 218

Mouse Tracks, 163–64

Movie-Wheels, 166, **167**

Moxie, 218

Mrs. Karl's bread, 218

Murray, Billy, 149

Murray, R. Michael, 151

Mushmouse and Punkin Puss, 83, 117, 205, **206**

Nabisco, **216**, 217

Nash, Clarence, 153, 160

Nashville, Tenn., 193, 231, 232, 272

National NuGrape Co., 218

National Periodical Publications. *See* DC Comics

Nation's Restaurant News, 254–55

Navajo Marketing, 222

NBC-TV, 28, 39, 81, 193, 257, 279–80

Nesteroff, Kliph, 179

New England Playworld, 281

New Funnies, **54**, 55

New Orleans, La., 249, 250

New York, N.Y., 10, 11, 21, 24, 27, 33, 129, 130, 135, 159, 166, 169, 173, 174, 232, 233, 247, 258, 262, 275

New York Journal, 7

New York Times, 32, 201

New York World, 7, 8, 94

Newgarden, Mark, 243

Newhart, Bob, 182

Newman, Paul S., 86

Newsweek, 218

NHP, 229

Nickelodeon, 281

NOMA Corporation, 199

North, Jay, 36, 167

Ocala, Fla., 182

Ocean World, 281

O'Hanlon, George, 169

101 Dalmatians, 109, **110**

One-a-Day Vitamins, 223

Oriolo, Joe, 68

Orlando, Fla., 111

Oscar Pig, 68

Oswald the Rabbit, 10, 11, 13, **16**, 17, **54**, 55, 73, 79, 112, **121**, 140–41, 157, 158, 206, 209, 243, 280

Oswald's Restaurant, 243
Ottenheimer Publishing. *See* Modern Promotions
Our Gang, 11
Out of the Inkwell, 17
Outcault, Richard, 7–9

Paas Dye Company, 197
Pac-Man Vitamins, 224
Palisades Park, 258
Palmer, Arnold, 36–37
Pan-Am gasoline, 240, 242
Paramount Studios, 17–20, 35, 57, 66–67, 89, 104, 161, 259
Parents magazine, 115
Parker, Fess, 157
Parker Brothers, 108, **109**, 111–12
Part of a Complete Breakfast, 214
Partridge Family, The, 269
Peanuts, 30–34, 35, 38, 39, 40, 57, 93–97, 109, 111, 112, **119**, 120, 123, **127**, 131–32, 138, 147, 149, 180, 182–84, 196, 199, 203, 207–8, 210, 218–20, 232, 234, 239, 244–45, 280–81, 284
Pearson, Bill, 62
Pearson, Lelia, 137–38
Pebbles cereal, 217
Peed, George, 28, **29**, 105, 109, **110**, 180, **181**
Peet, Bill, 28
Pepsi-Cola, 217, 227–28, 229, 281
Perry, Fla., 242, **243**
Peter Pan Records, 28, **43**, 172–73, 174–75, 179–80, **181**, 183, 186–87
Peter Potamus, 83, 121, 126
Pete's Dragon, 233
PEZ, 27, 117–18
Phantom, The, 59, 194
Piech, Peter, 24–25, 62, **63**, 228, 254
Pierce, Tedd, 155
Pines Comics, 68
Pink Motel, 243
Pink Panther, **64**, 87, 124
Pinocchio, 28, 97, 103, 225, **226**, 230, 233, 234, 241, 255, **272**, 277
Pitchford, Donnie, 67–69

Pixar Animation Studios, 285–86
Play-Doh, 125
Pluto, 13, 77, 78, 113, 130, 160–61, 197, 241, 277
Plymouth, 240–41
Pogo, 38–39, **92**, 93, 171, 193, 208
Ponderosa Steakhouse, 248
Popeye, 18–20, 34–35, 55–57, 58–60, 61, 62, **64**, 65, 66, 73, 82, 86, 87–88, 98, 103–4, 116, 117, 120, 121, 122, 123, 124, 125, 128, 129, 138, **139**, 140, 141, 145, 146, 149–51, 160, 166, 173–76, 179, 180, 187, 188, **190**, 191, 192, 194, 199, 206–7, 209, 212–13, 224, **228**, 229, 235–36, 239, 243, 249–52, 255, 256, 273–75, 276, 281–82
Popeye Spinach, 213, 274, **282**
Popeye Vitamins, 224
Popeyes Famous Fried Chicken, 249–52
Pop-Ice, **212**, 213
Porky Pig, **14**, 15, 53, 54, 75, 79, 116, 123, 145, 155, 162, **181**, 224, 255, 272
Portland, Ore., 135, 137
Post cereals, 85, 209–10, 214, 217
Poynter Products, 38–39
Precious Pupp, 145
Presto-Paints, 126, 128
Prince Valiant, 40, 89, 159
Procter and Gamble, 39, 242
Producers Associates of Television, 24–25
Producers Dairy, 218
Pudgy Pig, 59
Pulitzer, Joseph, 7
Purex, 115–17, 118, 273
Purity Mills, 213

Questel, Mae, 174, 175
Quick Draw McGraw, 21, 23, 82, 115, 121, 137, 140, 166, 213, 230, 235

Racine, Wisc., 49, 71
Radio City Music Hall, 33
Radko, Christopher, **200**, 201
Rand McNally, **92**, 93

Random House, 96–97, 98

RCA Victor, 150, 151, 159, 160, 162, 172, 241

Reed, Alan, 167, 177–78

Reeve, Christopher, 41

Reeves, George, 41

Reisiger, Harry, **143**

Reisiger, Steve, **143**

Remco, 120

Rescuers, The, 45, 228, 233

Richie Rich, 67, 184, **185**, 186, 221

Richmond, Va., 242, **243, 270**, 271

Ricochet Rabbit, 83, 205, **206**

Ringling Bros., **256**, 257

Roach, Hal, 11

Road Runner, 53–54, 57, **64**, **85**, 86, 138, 194, 240–41

Roalex slide puzzles, 105

Robin Hood, 45

Rock Island, Ill., 135

Rocky and His Friends, 24–25, 62, 81–82, 128, 141, 145, **168**, 169–70, 188, 237, 254, 282

Rocky Mount, N.C., 248

Roclar, 117

Rodgers, Jimmie, 184

Rogers, Roy, 76, 231

Romper Room, 158

Ronald McDonald, 252

Rootie Kazootie, 209

Rose, Billy, 149

Rosefield Packing Co., 210

Rosenthal, Irving, 258

Royal Guardsmen, 182–83

Rub-Ons, 125, 132, 215, 284

Rudolph the Red-Nosed Reindeer, 118, 209

Ruff and Reddy, 21, 58, 109, 141

Russell, Todd, 159

Ruttenberg, Dudley C., 218

Saalfield, 112

Sacramento, Calif., 249

Sad Cat, 281

Sad Sack, 66

Sagendorf, Bud, 20, 57, 58, 60, 87–88, 98, 104, 138, **244**

San Francisco, Calif., 32

San Jose, Calif., 243

Santa Clara, Calif., 272

Saperstein, Henry, 23–24

Sasseville, Jim, 57

Saturday Evening Post, 19

Sawyer's, 135, 136, 137, 145

Sayville, N.Y., 245

Schlesinger, Leon, 15–16, 280

Schulz, Charles, 31–34, 35, 57, 131–32, 138, 182–83, 207, 218, 232, 239, 284, 286

Scooby-Doo, 93, 117, 124, 224, 269

Scott, Bill, 24, 151, 169, 254

Scott, Keith, 24, 169–70, 254

Scrappy, **14**, 15

Screen Gems, **20**, 21, 23, 121

Screen-a-Show Projector, **142**, 143

Sears, Roebuck & Co., **13**, **15**, 29–30, 32, **33**, **35**, 37, 113, 122, 191–92, 199, 279

Secret Squirrel, **105**, 126, 145, 178–79, 235, 236

See-a-Show Viewer, 142–43

Segar, Elzie, 18, 20, 244, 275, 281

Selby, John, 94

Sell, Mary Ann and Wolfgang, 137

Sesame Street, 224

Seville, David. *See* Bagdasarian, Ross

Shadow, The, 158

Shaw, Artie, 152

Shazzan, 86

Shepard, Ernest, 29, 108

Show 'n' Tell, 146

Showbiz Pizza, 254

Siegel, Arthur, 182

Silly Putty, 125

Simon and Schuster, 74, 78, 80, 93, 159, 171

Sinclair Oil Co., 240

Six Flags, 272, 280, **281**

Six Million Dollar Man, The, 187

Skippy peanut butter, 210
Sleeping Beauty, **80**, 279
Slesinger, Shirley, 29, 38, 108, 279
Slesinger, Stephen, 29, **108**
Slinky Dog, 285
Smith, Jack, 27, 130
Smith, Kate, 152
Smitty, 9
Smokey Bear, 113
Smurf Vitamins, 224
Smurfs, 224, 269
Smythe, Reg, 97, 222
Snagglepuss, 109, 141, 178
Sniffles the Mouse, 54, 55
Snooper and Blabber, 141
Snoopy Come Home, 96, **207**
Snow White and the Seven Dwarfs, **2**, **12**, 13, 18, 45, **80**, 97,
    103, 118, 120, 147, 151, **190**, 201, 210, 225, **226**, 230, 233, 241,
    242–43, 255, **256**, 257, 277, 279
Snow White Motel, 242, **243**
Snuffy's Shanty, 245, 247
Soaky, 113–17, **284**, 285
Song of the South, 153, 197
Sourpuss, 17
Space Ghost, 86, 105, 126
Space Mouse, 55, 112
Sparkle-Paints, 126, 128
Speed Buggy, 93
Spider-Man, 42, 87, 117, 187, 222, 224
Spider-Man Vitamins, 224
Springdale, Ark., 213
Springfield, Ohio, 254
Squiddly Diddly, **105**, 236, 269
St. John, Arthur, 68
St. John Publishing, 57, 66, 68
Stafford, Grace, 157, 158
Standard Toykraft, 112
Star Trek, 187
Steck, Gene, 169
Steele Canning Co., 213

Steve Canyon, 235, 275
Stewart, Jimmy, 178
Stewart, Mike, 160, 171
Sticker Fun Books, 99, 125
Stone Mountain Park, Ga., **208**
Strobl, Tony, 84
Stumbo the Giant, 67
Sturgeon Bay, Wisc., 262
Sullivan, Pat, 10, 67, 239
Sun Valley, 229
Super Friends, 42, **43**
Super Goof, 53
Super Show Projector, 141–42
Superman, 19, 40–41, **48**, 49, 105, 116, 125, 143, 149, 186, 201,
    218, **219**, **225**, 229, 235, **253**, 255, 258, 275–76, 280
Swift, Allen, 174, 179
Swifty and Shorty, 67
Sword in the Stone, The, 146, **170**, 171, 241

Taco Bell, **283**
Taft Broadcasting, 60, 179, 268, 271, 272
Talking View-Master, 145–46
Tampa, Fla., 182, 245
Tanaka, Jim, 27
Ted Bates & Co., 113
Teenage Mutant Ninja Turtles, 198
Tell-a-Tale Books, 54, 78–80
Tennessee Tuxedo, 24, 116, 254
Tennyson, Jeffrey, 244
Terry, Paul, 10, 17
Terry Bears, 89
Terrytoons, 17, 68–69, 88–89, 148, 159, 161–62, 172, 281
Tetley, Walter, 169
There's No Time for Love, Charlie Brown, 96
Thermos, 33, 231–37, 285
Thomas, Ann, 169
Thomas, Florence, 137
Thomas the Tank Engine, 224
Thompson, Bill, 178
Three Dog Night, 176

Three J's Packing Co., 223

Three Little Pigs, 77, 151, 153, 175, 196, 199, 257

Three Stooges, 128, 139

Timberg, Sammy, 150

Timely Comics, 68

Time-Warner. *See* Warner Bros.

Timmy the Timid Ghost, 59

Tinker Bell, 77, 97, 103, 118, 123, 241, 243, **278**, 279

Toby Press, 68

Tom and Jerry, 16–17, 19, 21, 57–58, **64**, 76, 78, 86, 89, 120, 123, 136, 158, 202, 228, 282, 283

Tom Corbett, 137

Tom Terrific, 17, 89

Tommy Tortoise, 19

Toonerville Trolley, 9

Top Carrot, 222

Top Cat, 21, 82, 91, 115, 178, 222

Torcivia, Joe, 58

Total TeleVision Productions, 24–25, 62, 228, 254, 283

Touché Turtle, **62**, 82, 109, **110**, 115, 126, 178

Toy Story, 285–86

Toys and Novelties, 15

Transogram, 106, 109, **110**

Treasure Books. *See* Wonder Books

Tripp, Paul, 206–7

Trova, Ernest, 129

Tru-Vue, **134**, 135, 136, 137–38, 142

Tubby the Tuba, 207

Tucker, Ed, 182

Tucson, Ariz., 247

Turner, Ted, 282–83

TV Guide, 21

TV Tinykins, 123

Tweety and Sylvester, 53, 87, 154, 155, 157, 162, 180, **181**, 217, 272, 283

20th Century Fox, 17

Twitty, Conway, 272

Twitty City, 272

Tyer, Jim, 68

Tyler, Ginny, 164

Tyson, **216**, 217

Uncle Remus, 55, 141, 152

Uncle Scrooge McDuck, 51, 53, 55, 66, 84, **202**, 277

Uncle Wiggily, 159

Underdog, 24, 25, 62, **63**, 84–85, **100**, 133, 194, 208, 228, 254

UNICEF, 194–95

United Artists, 17

United Feature Syndicate, 33, 40, 57, 182, 218, 244–45, 284

United Productions of America, 23–24, 121, 128, 283

Universal Pictures, 10, 11, 17, **54**, 187, 248, 279–80

Universal Studios Orlando, 281–82

Van Dyke, Dick, 105

VanderPyl, Jean, 168

View-Master, **134**, 135–39, 142, 145–46, 147, 285

Vocalion Records, 176

Wadewitz, Edward, 71

Waldo, Janet, 178

Walker, Mort, 37–38

Wally Gator, 82, 115, 126, 273

Walt Disney Productions, 11–15, 18, 25–30, 42–47, 49–53, 65, 71–75, 82, 84, 86, 97–98, 101–3, 105, 108, 109, 116, 117, **119**, 121, 123, 125, 129, 136–37, 146, 147, 148, 151–52, 153–54, 157, 159, 160–61, 162–64, 170–71, 173, 175, 179, 180, 187, **189**, 191, 193, 195–96, 197, 199, 201, 202, 203, **204**, 207, 209–12, 222, 225, **226**, 228, 231–34, 241–42, 277–80, 283, 285–86

Walt Disney World, 45, **46**, 97–98, 103, 111–12, 212, 233, 257, 268

Walt Disney's Comics and Stories, 50–53, 58, **62**, 222

Walt Disney's Magazine, 242

Ward, Jay, 24–25, 27, 62, 81–82, 85, **168**, 169–70, 214, 228, 241, 254, 282, 283

Ward, Tiffany, 25

Warner Bros., 15–16, 17, 20, 39, **52**, 53–55, 65, 75, 86, 103, **110**, 116, 125, 147, 148, 151, 152, 154–55, 157, 159, 162, 166, 174, 179–80, 188, **189**, 194, 201, 214–17, 223, 227–28, 235, 240–41, 242, 254–55, **270**, 271–72, 280, 282–83

Warren, 112

Watterson, Bill, 39

Webb, Jim, 263–65

Weber's bread, 218

Welch, Harry Foster, 175

Welch's, 226–27

Wendy the Good Little Witch, 67, 89, 115, 186, 221, 222

Werner, Jane, 74

West Milford, N.J., **270**, 272

Western Printing and Lithographing, 17, **25**, 49–59, 60, 61, 62, **64**, 65–66, 68, 70, 71–87, 90, 97, 99, 101, 104–5, 106, 109, 112, 125, 133, 136, 158, 160, 241, 280

What a Nightmare, Charlie Brown, 97

Wheatena, 212

White Lightnin', 217

Whiteman, Paul, 149

Whitman Publishing, 54, **64**, 65, 71, **75**, 78–87, 91, 98–99, **100**, 101, 104–5, 106, 109, 112, 133, 152, 176, 202

Who Framed Roger Rabbit, 76, 116, **279**

Wildman, George, 20, 60, 62, 250, **282**

Williams, Ariz., 267

Williams, Robin, 35, 235

Williamsport, Penn., 205

Wilson, Don, 153

Wilton, **224**, 225

Wimpy Grills, 243–44

Winnie-the-Pooh, 28–30, 37, 38, **44**, 108, 159, 199, 201, 224, 230, 241, 257, 279

Winslow, Barry, 182

Winsome Witch, **105**, 179, 269

Wizard of Id, The, 40, 97

Wizard of Oz, The, 76, 149, 178, 201

Wonder Books, 87–90, 91, 202, **244**

Wonder Woman, 42, **43**, **48**, 49, 186–87, 195, 224, **225**, **231**, 280

Wonderful World of Color, 28, 103, 109, **240**, 241

Wonderful World of Disney magazine, **240**, 241–42

Wood, Wally, **92**

Woody Woodpecker, **16**, 17, 22, **54**, 55, 76, 79, 86, 106, 112, 113, 114, 115, **121**, 124, 136, 140, 141, 152, 157–58, 160, 187, 188, **189**, 206, **207**, 228, 235, 272, **273**, 282

World Publishing, 95–96

World War II, 3, 9, 20, 50, 66, 175, 193–94, 230, 275

Wynn, Ed, 105, 178

Yabba Dabba Dew, 217

Yakky Doodle, 82, 83, 196, 205

Yellow Kid, 7–8, 149

Yogi Bear, **2**, 3, 21, 58, **61**, 62, 82, 83, 91–92, 106–7, 109, 115, 124, 126, **133**, 137, 140, 141, 145, 146, 166–67, 169, 177, 178, 179, 186, 194, 196, 202, **204**, 205, 213, 230, 235, 236, 239, 262–65, 269, 271

Yogi Bear Burgers, 249

Yogi Bear's Family Motor Inns, 264–65

Yogi Bear's Honey Fried Chicken, 247–49, 263

Yosemite Sam, 154, 162, 180, 217, 224, 286

Young, Chic, 35, 66

Young, Robert W., 113

You're a Good Man, Charlie Brown, 33, 182, 183, 184

You're in Love, Charlie Brown, 96

You're Not Elected, Charlie Brown, 96

Zaboly, Bill, 20, 104, 138, **212**

Zorro, 230